TOM KIELY

ERIN'S CHAMPION

KEVIN McCARTHY

MERCIER PRESS

MERCIER PRESS

Cork

www.mercierpress.ie

© Kevin McCarthy, 2020

ISBN: 978 1 78117 711 2

A CIP record for this title is available from the British Library.

Printed and bound in the EU.

CONTENTS

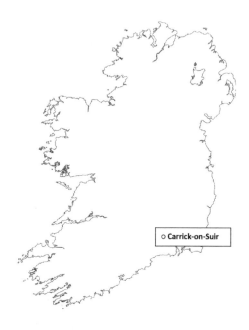

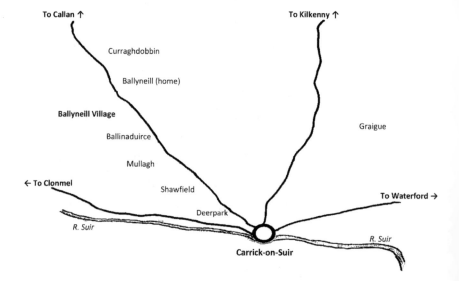

Maps showing the location of Carrick-on-Suir within Ireland and places relevant to Tom Kiely around Carrick-on-Suir.
(*Author's collection*)

INTRODUCTION

'He was, in his day, the world's best athlete. Everyone knew it. Period.'[1]

So wrote American historian Frank Zarnowski, of Tom Kiely from Ballyneill, sometimes spelled Ballyneal, in Co. Tipperary. Zarnowski is the author of several books about the great all-round athletes of sports history, those athletes who refused to specialise in one or two events, but instead sought to master up to ten. These included a number of weight-throwing and jumping events, plus hurdling, running and sometimes walking races. In modern times, these men would generally be known as decathletes. In the late nineteenth century, however, they were called 'all-round' or, in American terminology, 'all-around' athletes.[2]

Kiely was indeed a remarkable sportsman, considered by others to be 'the greatest athlete of Ireland's greatest athletic period', that period spanning the last decade of the nineteenth century and the beginning of the twentieth.[3] Yet, there is much more to any sporting figure than his or her sport. This book was undertaken as much in search of the story of Tom Kiely the man as it was to discover why he achieved such fame as a sportsman. To that end, it has been very important to tap into as much primary source material as possible. There are very few surviving documents that Kiely himself wrote, but his scrapbooks, with his own notes and glosses, show an intense personal ambition behind his strong, silent veneer. It was also wonderful to access his school records and occasional interviews to get an insight into the man behind the legend, so to speak. It has been particularly important to get the input of family members, too; in this instance three of Kiely's grandchildren, who remember him as an older man and a grandfather.

Kiely lived through many challenging times and exciting adventures. He was driven by great self-belief, balanced with a desire to enjoy himself and see the world, yet he always carried himself with a quiet dignity that endeared him to all. He was very much his own man while at the same time being an 'everyman' for the Irish people, coming to be known in sporting terms as 'the Champion' or 'Erin's Champion'.

Much of Kiely's story is rooted in south Tipperary, where his family were among the new type of lease-holding and landowning farmers – in their case, commercial cattle dealers – that came to prominence in post-Famine Ireland. This background played a significant role in his sporting career. The rich farmland of the Golden Vale across Tipperary, north Cork and Limerick produced dozens of great jumpers and weight throwers, world record breakers and Olympic champions. This was especially true before the First World War, most spectacularly in hammer throwing. Amazingly, only one of the eight Olympic hammer titles on offer between 1900 and 1932 was won by an athlete from outside of those three Munster counties.[4] These Olympic hammer champions were John Flanagan (three times), Matt McGrath, Paddy Ryan and Pat O'Callaghan (twice). All of them came from within forty miles of Croom, Co. Limerick.

Kiely came from a household where the Catholic Church played a huge role and where the expectations of a 'good' marriage, dowries and family inheritance were very strong. The Kielys worked hard, made good money and valued that money, while never being overwhelmed by the need to acquire it. Yet, as we will see, Tom Kiely always displayed a stubborn refusal to conform to either religious or societal expectations.

Kiely's career also spanned a period of political turmoil in a country lacking political leadership following the decline and death of Charles Stewart Parnell, the former Irish Parliamentary Party leader who had looked to bring about Home Rule – a form of self-governance – for Ireland. This turmoil and division made its way into sport too, and Irish sporting bodies were at times more interested in political matters than sporting ones. It is one of Kiely's great achievements that he often ignored or just rose above such political divisions, and, in so doing, basically became a national hero without ever seeking such a title.

The years of Kiely's active career in sport saw the initiation of international athletics competitions, including the Olympic Games, the standardisation of many rules and regulations, and a huge emphasis on technical improvements. The big events in Kiely's repertoire were weight throwing and jumping, i.e. field events. Throughout his career, he was one of the great exponents of traditional athletics and never really embraced new ideas about diet and training routines. Yet, he was a groundbreaker in the way he influenced technique and embraced new equipment.

It is absolutely no exaggeration to suggest that, of all the sportsmen in Ireland, Kiely was the one most capable of attracting crowds by the mere presence of his name on a sports programme. He became a talisman to the Irish abroad too, and his visits to the USA were to play an important part in enhancing the sporting and social status of the Irish there.

Amateurism was the dominant force in athletics in the British Isles during Kiely's career, imposed for snobbish reasons as much as for any sporting or altruistic ones. Yet Kiely, when he made his way to the USA in the twilight of his career, was more than a match for those he faced in all-around competitions and did not suffer financially from those trips either, as far as can be gauged. He competed for sport's sake but was nobody's fool either.

The issue of the modernisation of sport creates a headache for the Kiely story: that of records. The contemporary identification of Kiely's best performances, across at least six different athletic events, as Irish, British or even world records is staggering. Many of the claims are accompanied by certification and other detailed evidence verifying them as records. Unfortunately, these were often achieved in events that were declining as recognised events outside Ireland. Matters are further complicated by technological changes in some of his favoured events, and by the fact that standardisation of international record-keeping was still in the future by the time Kiely's career ended. Taking the hammer throw as an example, there were potentially a dozen different versions of this event during Kiely's athletics career. The 16lb hammer could have a wooden or a wire handle, an iron hammer head or a leaden one, and the handle could be three-and-a-half or four feet long. It could be thrown with a run or from a standing position, sometimes with one hand, but more often with two, and from inside a square or inside a circle. The circle, if used, could be of nine feet in diameter, or seven. Each variation could give rise to 'record' claims before everything was standardised by 1912.

Even in events that did not have so many variations, things were very different in Kiely's day. There was no such thing as a running track as is meant by the term today. Long jumping was done following a run-up and take-off from grass, for example, while high jumpers (or pole vaulters) had no soft mattresses to land on. In hurdles races, there was no 'give' if an athlete hit a hurdle. These were solid wooden fences, and striking one invariably meant that the athlete fell or risked injury. As a consequence of these and other differences, it would be impossible to compare an athletic performance of 1900 with one in 2020. The only way of gauging an athlete's greatness when dealing with someone like Kiely is by looking at how his achievements were viewed in his own day.[5]

Still, it is hugely frustrating that very few genuine Kiely records have survived – he had seven records attributed to him in 1893 alone.[6] In many years, contemporary newspaper accounts suggest similar numbers of Irish or occasionally 'world' records were broken. But the Amateur Athletic Association (AAA) in England, known as UK Athletics today, has just one record of his on its lists, for a Kiely hammer throw at Cahir in 1898.[7] Athletics Ireland holds one Kiely record, for throwing the 56lb weight in 1895.[8] Even though we will see several contemporary claims for Kiely world records, the International Association of Athletic Federations (IAAF) has no account of such records, not least because it was only established in 1912, four years after Kiely had retired. One historian has suggested that Kiely was, in fact, not only 'a recurrent record breaker' before the IAAF began its work, but also the last athlete in history to hold a world's best in both a jumping event (hop, step and jump) and a throwing event at the same time.[9]

Without ratified records, the task of proving Kiely's athletic greatness is challenging, though not impossible. What is undeniable is that he was the winner of fifty-three Irish athletic titles.[10] He won five AAA titles and two American Amateur Athletic Union (AAU) all-around titles, the first of which, in 1904, is classed both as a 'world championship' and an Olympic title. What the record tables lack, the contemporary accounts make up for, demonstrating the impact of Kiely in his day, regardless of how posterity has recorded his achievements.

Now let's turn to the story of an extraordinary sportsman and an extraordinary man: Tom Kiely, 'Erin's Champion' or, if preferred, 'Ireland's Champion'.[11] It is the story of a man who was a supreme athlete in his day, of course, but also of a man who had a love of life, a commitment to his parish and his siblings, a keen head for business and an independent streak which made him very much his own man through all the ups and downs of his long life. While this book could never hope to track every sporting achievement, or indeed every record by Kiely, he was a fascinating man in many ways, and his story tells us a lot about life, a lot about sport and quite a deal about Irish society over a century ago.

CHAPTER I

GROWING UP
IN BALLYNEILL

If any single sportsman epitomised the quality of Irish rural athletics at the end of the nineteenth and beginning of the twentieth century, it is the subject of this book. Tom Kiely grew up near the village of Ballyneill in south Co. Tipperary, which lies between the large towns of Clonmel and Carrick-on-Suir, bounded by Slievenamon to the north and a combination of the River Suir and the Comeragh mountains to the south. In Kiely's time, the townland of Ballyneill consisted of just nineteen households.[1]

There have been Kielys around south Tipperary almost as long as there have been people. There is a faded inscription on a small stone near the south door of Kilcash church, barely readable today, where the name of the family is given as *O Cadla*. Geoffrey Keating informs us that a certain Niall Caille, 'Monarch of Ireland' and believed to be of the same clan, was drowned in the King's River at Callan, in the neighbouring county of Kilkenny, in AD 851, his burial place being close to the round tower of Kilree.[2]

Tom Kiely's direct ancestors came down from nearby Kilcash to Ballyneill, in the Kilmurry district in south Tipperary, possibly in Elizabethan times. Certainly, local headstones indicate that Kielys have been buried in Ballyneill since 1611. It is even recorded that a great military and sporting champion called Daithi Ó Cadhla lived around Deerpark in the seventeenth century.[3] Deerpark lay between Ballyneill village and nearby Carrick-on-Suir, and is a place which recurs time and again in our story.

One local historian recounts that:

> *Thomas F. Kiely was born on the 25 August 1869 in Ballyneill, Carrick-on-Suir. He was the eldest son of William J. Kiely. He was a farmer of seventy-seven acres prime land. His family was well established by this time in the district. They were hard working farmers; for example, Thomas F. Kiely's grandfather, also Thomas, cultivated twenty-two acres of potatoes and twenty acres of wheat in 1833, at a time when this represented a hard, back-breaking burden of relentless work.*[4]

This account of the Kielys is broadly accurate, particularly of pre-Famine times.[5] One commentator wrote of Tom himself, that he was 'a tremendous worker on the land and built up a prosperous career as progressive farmer, cattle breeder and fruit-grower'.[6]

However, such sources don't necessarily give the full story. Certainly, at different times there were small herds of dairy cows, or even some acres of fruit and cereal crops, the latter when necessary only. However, the core business of the Kiely family was the buying and selling of animals.[7] William Kiely, and then his son Tom, were farmers in name, but the Kielys have always described themselves as cattle dealers, first and foremost. This helps to explain the high degree of mobility that the future champion athlete was to demonstrate. He was much less 'rooted' in the land than many farmers would have been. At different stages, he lived on or owned a total of eight different farms across three counties, though mainly around Ballyneill.

Kiely was certainly not spoon-fed as a farmer's son. His father, William, constantly reminded him that their friend Maurice Davin had followed sporting pursuits with such passion that he neglected his farm and business. The Davin farm at Deerpark was located just a few fields away from the Kielys' Ballyneill farm. William discouraged Tom and the two brothers who came after him from wasting their time on sport. It is alleged that he never once attended a sports meeting to see them perform, and contributed to the sort of 'deep tensions between fathers and sons' which were found in many Irish farm families of the time and could include disagreements around everyday decision-making and, as would occur in Tom's case, around inheritance too.[8] As the young Tom rose to athletic fame in the early 1890s, a local newspaper mentioned that:

> He comes from a good family, and his father, a splendid specimen of a stalwart Tipperary farmer, was a renowned athlete in his day, and was well described as one of the finest men going into Carrick, and that's saying a good deal.[9]

The idea that Tom's father was a good athlete is one that later Kiely family members have some difficulty believing, not least because of old William's dislike of his son's 'timewasting' with athletics. Certainly, there are no family stories about William's

William and Mary
Kiely, Tom's parents,
pictured *c.* 1865.
(*Kiely Collection,
Tipperary Museum of
Hidden History*)

athletic achievements. Nor are there any trophies that were won by William, so the *Nationalist*'s story can only be taken at face value. One thing is certain though: looking at the above photograph of Tom's parents, it is evident that he inherited his height and physique from both.

William Kiely was born in 1829 and married Mary Downey in the mid-1860s. Mary was thirteen years younger than her husband.[10] As far as can be ascertained, all of Mary's sisters married and her only brother, Patsy, also married but had no family. Accordingly, when Patsy and his wife died, the Downey holding near Ballyneill went to William and Mary Kiely, Mary being the eldest of the Downey sisters. Subsequently, William would buy the lease on a second farm nearby at Curraghdobbin. When added to the land at

Ballyneill, this brought the Kiely farming interests to over 180 acres, a substantial holding by any standards but especially in the nineteenth century.

Within two generations, the Kielys had moved a long way from potato growing and tillage farming. The family farms held by William were typical of the newer type of cattle farm, and of the change from tillage to pasture farming that had accelerated since Famine times. This wealth ensured that the Kiely children had good diets and opportunities for schooling and, despite their father's objections, for athletic training which would have been impossible for others.

In the eighteenth and nineteenth centuries, a lot of Kiely relatives from Ballyneill went to America. When they arrived at the customs in the USA and Canada, their name was often spelled 'Keily' by officials there. A Laurence Kiely, for example, went from the Curraghdobbin area around 1812 to Nova Scotia in Canada, aged just seventeen. He was involved in fishing there and eventually married and had three daughters.

Another story attached to the Kielys of Ballyneill relates how one of the family, John, was involved in an altercation with a bailiff in Famine times or later.[11] John was married to Johanna Hickey of Carrick-on-Suir and they resided at Mullagh, south of Ballyneill. One day, John and Johanna were being evicted by bailiffs and a row took place which resulted in John drowning one of the bailiffs in a pond. John fled to America soon afterwards, having been hidden away in a jaunting car. He is believed to have been assisted by the monks of Mount Melleray, who had a monastery called 'New Melleray' at Dubuque, Iowa.[12]

These American connections are mentioned at this point

to highlight the fact that Tom Kiely, like most other Irish people in the late nineteenth century, already had many relatives and friends in the USA when he was growing up. One branch of the Kielys settled in Brooklyn, New York, and became prominent in business there, including in furniture retail. Other Kielys became very successful in legal fields and lived in considerable luxury on Long Island, very near Theodore Roosevelt's home at Oyster Bay. Still more settled in Boston and along areas of the eastern seaboard. There was communication between these relatives and the Kielys of Ballyneill occasionally, fuelling the young Tom's interest in crossing the Atlantic at some point.

William and Mary Kiely had a large family of nine children who reached adulthood. Quite remarkably, five of the six Kiely daughters became nuns. The eldest child was Mary, born in 1867, who became Sister Camillus in the Mercy Convent, Dungarvan, Co. Waterford. She was diminutive in stature but certainly not in personality. Then came Thomas Francis Kiely, known as Tom, their first-born son in 1869, followed by another daughter, Nell, who joined the Order of Jesus and Mary in Willesden, London as Sister Benignus. Nell was also based at the Jesus and Mary Gortnor Abbey in Crossmolina for a considerable time, but died back in Willesden in the late 1950s. Of all the Kiely sisters, Nell is said to have most resembled her elder brother in looks and personality. The next daughter was Joan, who became Sister Ita in the Presentation Convent, Lismore, where she died in the 1940s. The only Kiely daughter who married, Margaret, was born in 1872. She eventually became Mrs Slattery and lived in Dungarvan, a town that her brother Tom would compete gloriously in on many occasions. After Margaret came Katie, who died in a Belgian convent while still only in her twenties. The youngest Kiely sister was Nancy, born in 1878. She too joined the Jesus and Mary Order, just as Nell had done, but did not feel cut out for religious life and eventually returned to live at home. William and Mary welcomed another son, Laurence (known as Larry), in 1880, so he was eleven years Tom's junior. The ninth child and youngest son was William, known as Willie, born in 1884.[13]

As a prosperous farmer, William almost certainly longed for sons to help him on the land. He was in his fifties by the time Larry and Willie were born, so he must have expected that his eldest son, Tom, would take on a lot of responsibility once he reached adulthood. This helps explain William's discouragement of Tom's sporting activities, but also why he purchased the farm at Curraghdobbin when Tom was twenty-seven. Having five of their six daughters opting for religious lives, the Kiely family acreage was not threatened unduly by a need to provide dowries. Family tradition has it that each daughter was accompanied by a donation of £1,000 to each convent, on condition that they would be educated and not used as servants. As a result, most of the sisters became teachers in their respective convent schools.[14]

It is not likely that Tom's schooldays were particularly wonderful or enjoyable. At the time of his birth, a body known as the Powis Commission was in the process of changing the curriculum. Just before Tom entered Ballyneill National School, this resulted in the introduction of the infamous 'payment by results' system. A considerable portion of a teacher's income depended on how many pupils passed annual examinations, so everything that went on in school tended to be geared towards these examinations. This caused an almost total concentration on reading, writing and arithmetic (the '3Rs'), to the detriment of more imaginative, creative or enjoyable pursuits like sport, singing or music:

> *In a climate of concern about low standards and teacher accountability, the 3Rs being obligatory subjects for examination, constituted the main elements of curriculum content. Detailed programmes were laid down for each grade in each subject, and no allowance was made for local factors or children's interests. The dominant teaching styles were mechanical in nature and were characterised by routine and repetition. Throughout this era, the system was rigid, harsh and educationally crude. It ignored teaching skills and encouraged cramming and rote learning.*[15]

According to a local historian:

> *Thomas F. Kiely attended the local national school in Ballyneill. His record here was quite unique. In these days, compulsory attendance was not in force and farmers' sons were needed so much at home that their school attendance was appallingly bad by today's standards. Yet the young Tom Kiely had a record for attendance which could bear comparison with the best nowadays …*[16]

The roll books for Ballyneill National School certainly testify that the young Tom had a good attendance record. Starting school in June 1874, his annual attendances are recorded as 188 days in first class, 181 days in second class, 207 days in third class and 201 days in fourth class. The primary school year nowadays runs for 183 days, but in the nineteenth century the total per annum was 220 days. At the time Tom started his schooling, the average daily attendance of pupils in primary school was not much over thirty-seven per cent, whereas he had an attendance record of eighty-five to ninety per cent during most of his school years.[17]

There were no infant classes in schools in Tom's time. From first class, he studied just four subjects: reading, spelling, writing and arithmetic. He got a top grade, known as a 'creditable pass', in three of the four, and a pass in writing. For these four passes, the teacher was paid a bonus of the princely sum of four shillings. As things got progressively harder, Tom's writing skills improved, but he did not get a pass in arithmetic in second class. In third class, two new subjects were added, grammar and geography. In third class, Tom achieved a pass or creditable pass in everything except grammar, and his teacher got a bonus payment of ten shillings that year. In fourth class, the number of creditable passes outweighed the passes, but grammar was again a stumbling block. No Irish was taught in the national schools. However, later family memories recall Tom and his brother Larry having some Irish because the language was still quite strong around the Ballyneill area in the late nineteenth century.

Primary education was as far as the vast majority of rural children went in those days, if they attended at all. Accordingly, the fifth and sixth class curriculum became very challenging, and it was customary for fifth class to be split into two distinct stages, each lasting a full year, and likewise with sixth class. Thus, it would take at least eight years to complete schooling from first to the end of sixth class.

Tom finished fourth class at the end of May 1879, when

he was not yet ten years old. He continued to be a diligent scholar, attending for 203, 183 and 185 days in the three years after fourth class. However, in common with many pupils in those days, because arithmetic was a challenge to him again in the second stage of fifth class, he seems to have had to repeat the year. In the parlance of the time, if you failed a key subject you would not be 'promoted'.

Tom never seems to have enjoyed arithmetic, though he was well able in later life to buy and sell cattle, and trade in stocks and shares. The greater irony is that the child who struggled to pass his arithmetic examinations in primary school would display, as an athlete, a greater grasp of measurements, physics, aerodynamics and the laws of leverage and propulsion than any primary schooling could have given him.

As late as 1883, as Tom was approaching his fourteenth birthday, no more than thirty-four per cent of all primary teachers had received proper training. Therefore, it is very likely that his difficulties with the technicalities of arithmetic or formal grammar may not all have been down to himself.[18] When agriculture was added to the curriculum from fourth class, Tom was able to pass in both stages of fifth class, while his writing and spelling at the end of fifth class were both awarded the highest grade, a creditable pass.

After that, his attendance at school went fairly sharply downhill. In two years of sixth class, he attended for 145 days, and then for 106 days, until finally his official departure from Ballyneill school was confirmed mid-year, on 28 February 1885.[19] He was needed on the farm.

By 1885, his elder sister Mary had gone to the convent in Dungarvan, but Tom's five other sisters were still at school in Ballyneill. Neither of Tom's brothers had even started primary school by the time he finished, and he had become quite a father figure among his siblings even by the time he was fifteen.

Tom was more than equipped to look after himself in the adult world, as evidenced by the few examples of his handwriting which have survived. As the eldest male child in the Kiely household, once he hit what today would be called his teenage years, work on the family farm became the priority. The months from spring onwards were taken up by going with his father to learn about cattle buying, helping with droving and, eventually, hay making, when late June arrived each year.

There are very few other solid details to be gleaned from the available evidence of Tom's schooldays. According to local sources, he learned to play both the fiddle and the fife, apparently rather well.[20] It is difficult to imagine that these were skills acquired in school time, where the grind of the '3Rs' and little else was relentless. Nevertheless, these were skills that remained with him and were occasionally commented upon throughout Tom's life.[21] For instance, at the age of twenty-four, it was reported of him:

> Socially T.F. Kiely is most popular. He can take the floor and dance an Irish jig, with a grace and expertness that a professional might envy, and what is more, can tune the fife to discourse most excellent music, and has done so it may be said at many meetings, where dancing competitions formed part of the programme.[22]

It may well have been around this time that Tom was first introduced to the literary figure of 'Mat the Thresher'. Charles Kickham's *Knocknagow*, set in the very heart of south Tipperary and subtitled *The Homes of Tipperary*, was published in 1879. It had gone through seven editions by the year 1887, being so popular that it needed to be reprinted almost annually.[23] This novel captured much of rural Irish life in the late nineteenth century, including agrarian change, depopulation, dying villages, friction with landlords and rural sports. This was also the novel that introduced the heroic figure of manliness, hurling, hammer throwing and, dare it be said, 'Tipperaryism', known as 'Mat the Thresher'. Throughout his sporting life, Tom would frequently be compared to Kickham's hero, for example:

> *Born in Ballyneill, under the shadow of Slievenamon and in the neighbourhood where Kickham found the man he immortalized in 'Matt [sic] the Thresher', Tom Kiely … was the blood relative of the protagonists of the Gael – the Davins of Deerpark. With such connections he could not have been otherwise than an athlete, and adding to them his own splendid bodily inheritance, he could not have been otherwise than a champion.[24]*

This idea that Tom was introduced to athletics in his teens by the Davin family of Carrick-on-Suir is rarely if ever in dispute. Maurice and Pat Davin were, respectively, the finest exponents of weight throwing and jumping in Ireland and had reputations far beyond the island. Both had been multiple Irish and English champions. Maurice's ten Irish titles were split between hammer and shot put, and he actually specialised in throwing the 16lb hammer one-handed! His brother Pat amassed five

Irish high jump titles, plus five in the 120 yards hurdles, four in the long jump and one title each in the shot put and 100 yards flat.[25] Although this and other sources suggest that Tom was a relative of the Davins, this is incorrect.[26]

The Kielys and the Davins were not quite 'neighbours'. Travelling by the main road north of the River Suir, there are several miles between Ballyneill and Deerpark. However, the distance over the fields is much shorter. Later in life, when they really were neighbours, Tom used to walk regularly down to the Davin farm from his farms in Mullagh and Shawfield on the Carrick-on-Suir side of Ballyneill. Accepting that the Kielys and the Davins lived in the same neighbourhood, to the west of Carrick-on-Suir, it is much more important to look at the impact of their meeting, probably at some point after Tom had left primary school in Ballyneill:

> As a young boy Tom Kiely must have followed the victories of Maurice, Tom and Pat [Davin] at the Irish and English championships with awe and wonder. At their home in Deerpark, Carrick-on-Suir, the equipment and facilities they used for training were available to local boys. The three brothers found time on summer evenings to help and encourage any who were interested, both in athletics and the revived Gaelic games that Maurice was busy codifying and promoting.[27]

The Davins' farm at Deerpark was a very fine one, just on the outskirts of Carrick-on-Suir. One brother, Tom, was a solicitor, while Maurice and Pat had another laborious, but lucrative, source of income from their barge business. A couple of fields to the south of Deerpark flowed the great River Suir. Barely thirteen miles to the west was the largest town in Tipperary,

Clonmel. Carrick-on-Suir itself was on the tidal portion of the Suir and was quite reachable by good-sized cargo ships coming up from Waterford. Getting the goods from there to Clonmel, upstream against a strong current, required the use of horse-drawn, flat-bottomed barges. It was back-breaking work but helped to make the Davins incredibly strong and fit.

The Davins, for all their hard work, never let it get in the way of their sport. Maurice Davin, founding president of the Gaelic Athletic Association (GAA) in 1884, loved Gaelic games, athletics and rowing, and was a cricketer when that sport was popular in Tipperary too. The rowing boat which he and others used, having lain for years in a barn at Deerpark, now forms part of a dramatic display at Tipperary Museum of Hidden History in Clonmel. The enthusiasm of the Davins for sport also saw them create one of the first enclosed sportsfields in Ireland, at Deerpark. The venue was a mecca for athletes, and a vitally important one for hurling and football matches for many years.

Despite William Kiely's discouragement, the young Tom was surrounded by sport. To this day, Ballyneill proudly displays a plaque directly across the road from its national school, claiming that: 'In November 1884 the first Gaelic football match was played in this field, between the former Ballinamona cricket team and a Callan team. There were twenty-one a side and Pat Davin refereed the game …'. Other places make similar claims, but this plaque is still testimony to the importance of football in Kiely's home parish from the very start of the GAA.

Sport played a huge part in this rural society, making it almost inevitable that Kiely would be sucked in. One account, written when Tom was barely twenty-three, indicated that:

He is the athlete all over and is a noticeable figure wherever he goes. When stripped for 'action' he is an object of universal admiration. He lives at home with his people at Ballyneill and is a temperate and hard-working farmer's son. He takes a deep interest in football, cricket, hurling, coursing, and indeed in every branch of local sport and pastime.[28]

Regarding Kiely's initial meeting with the Davins, a newspaper account in 1904 recalled:

Thomas F. Kiely was born ... half a mile across the fields from the home of the Davins – Maurice, Patrick and Tom, who made Ireland famous in the world of athletics in the seventies and early eighties by their record performances in weight throwing, jumping and running. As a boy, Kiely was attracted to the training grounds of the Davins and in the course of some schoolboy competitions, Maurice Davin noticed the extraordinary ability of the young Kiely, and there and then set to train him to his style in the different weights. In this he was successful, and Kiely made his first appearance at sports in 1887, at the age of 17 years ...[29]

While the Davins were leading figures in Gaelic football, hurling and indeed rowing circles, their first love was really athletics. Maurice Davin literally 'wrote the book' for athletics in Ireland:

[The] rules for athletics under the auspices of the GAA were published by Maurice Davin, initially appearing in United Ireland *on 7 February 1885, and in early May they were reprinted and sold in pamphlet form at the cost of 6d.*[30]

Pat Davin (left) and Kiely at Davin's home in 1944, reminiscing with some of the old throwing weights from the Davin collection.
(*Kiely Collection, Tipperary Museum of Hidden History*)

Of all people, Maurice and Pat Davin must have known that the youngster, close to 6 foot 2 inches in height, incredibly strong but agile enough to beat all others in jumping and running too, was what might today be called 'something special'. The Davins realised in 1887 that they were about to unleash on an unsuspecting public one of the greatest all-round athletes that Ireland and indeed the sporting world had yet seen.

CHAPTER 2

MOULDING THE CHAMPION

In the space of four years, Tom Kiely would go from a beginner athlete to Ireland's best – even considered by some to be the world's best – all-round athlete. This would happen through a triumphant combination of natural talent and training, and was all set against a backdrop of commitments at home, learning a lot about life and, curiously, dealing in his own way with the fact that many people just could not spell his name correctly.

Kiely could not have had better trainers than the Davins. They gave him their enthusiasm, their technical expertise and the belief that a young fellow from south Tipperary could be as great an athlete as anyone, anywhere. Maurice Davin was particularly meticulous when it came to athletic preparations, diet and training in their family gymnasium, down to details like monitoring an athlete's height and weight.[1] One writer summed the Davins up as:

Tipperary's brightest ornaments of athletics who have made for us a chapter of history greater than that of any other family for any other county in ancient or modern times … 'I think,' said a sports writer, 'that it can be safely stated that there is not another house in the world, under whose roof there are sheltered so many championship medals, and other athletic trophies, won in Ireland, England and America as in the home of the Davins of Deerpark.'[2]

Kiely made his first appearance at an adult athletics event in 1888, at the nearby sports in Clonmel. That day, the almost nineteen-year-old Kiely took two second placings in weights events and won a heat of the hurdles. Hurdles races in Kiely's time were always over heavy, rigid wooden fences. The *Clonmel Chronicle*'s correspondent described him as 'a very promising young athlete'. A clue to future greatness came when Kiely lost the 28lb shot event to the already legendary James Mitchel by just 1½ inches that day.[3] Mitchel had set a world record in the 16lb hammer event at Limerick just the day before and would become the most famous weight thrower in America for a decade after that.

Later that year, Kiely went on to win further prizes at Piltown, Carrick-on-Suir and Dungarvan. Dungarvan was easily the most 'exotic' of these trips for the young man, and he probably went there at the suggestion of a very good friend of the Davins, Dan Fraher. Even getting to Dungarvan was no small matter for a youngster from Ballyneill, as it was over twenty-five miles away, with no train connection over the Comeragh mountains. All the Kielys learned to ride horses from a young age, and this was Tom's customary means of transport to more distant places when trains were not available. One can only imagine what William thought of his eldest son and farm worker heading off to the seaside town for a sports event.

Dungarvan was an eye opener for Kiely: a busy port with all the associated attractions, and the town *en fête* for the sports. There were street performers, singers and acrobats thronging the town, and even a barrel organist with a monkey entertaining the townsfolk. There was also violence, drunkenness and a stabbing on the evening of the sports.[4] Dungarvan would have been an 'education' for the innocent youngster, possibly even offering him his first glimpse of the sea.

It was at Carrick-on-Suir Sports in 1888 that the all-round potential of the young Kiely was first in evidence – he won a heat of the 100 yards in 10 seconds, was beaten for second place in the 28lb shot by half an inch, was second in the 220 yards and the running long jump and could have won the hurdles had he not fallen.[5] Betting men, of which there were many at these meetings, would have anticipated much greater things from Kiely in 1889, for certain. He was doing what many young athletes of his day did – having a go at everything. He had no fear of failure.

Kiely's athletics debut occurred a month before the departure of what was to be called the 'Gaelic Invasion', as a large party of GAA athletes and administrators left for a tour of the USA. Tom was too young and not sufficiently established as an athlete to join the party, though his friend William Prendergast was going as secretary of the GAA. In the end, the tour turned out to be a financial disaster for the association, and deprived Irish athletics of several of its brightest stars, including James Mitchel, who stayed in the USA for good.

Records show that Kiely competed in just a handful of athletics meetings in 1889, the main one being his first appearance at the GAA's All-Ireland championships. In these, held at Duke's Meadow, Kilkenny, on Tuesday 27 August, Tom took second place in four weights events and was third in three more, two jumping and a hurdles event. He failed to place only in the 16lb shot put.[6] Tom listed the winning of only four prizes at Kilkenny in his scrapbook, suggesting that there were no medals or otherwise for third placings, or perhaps that the ambitious young Kiely did not much value coming third.[7] Yet, the omens of greatness were there: seven top three placings in the national championships, two days after his twentieth birthday. This was unheard of for an athlete so young, and Irish athletic standards were as high as anywhere at that time.

***

Kiely putting a weight, pictured in James Mitchel's book on weight throwing. (*Spalding Company, 1916*)

For Kiely, the challenges and difficulties of following this sporting life were now emerging, including the cost. For example, the expense of getting to Kilkenny by train, i.e. from Carrick-on-Suir via Waterford, and back. Historian Tom Hunt has clearly established the importance of the railways in helping the growth of organised spectator sports in Ireland. It is logical that such transport was even more important for the competitors who, in the case of athletics certainly, came from remote parts of rural Ireland.[8]

Then there was the cost of taking part in his favoured events. Entering a total of eight competitions could have cost the massive sum of £1, as the entry fee for each event was half a crown (2 shillings and 6 pence). Moreover, the day of the GAA championships (a Tuesday) should have been a normal working day on the farm for Tom. William must have been apoplectic about the lost time and the cost of his son's hobby. Perhaps the marble clock that Tom won at Clonmel Sports a few weeks before Kilkenny was of some compensation, but wealth factors certainly contributed to the shaping of rural Irish sport. Inevitably, it was often the sons of well-off landowners who had the money and time to compete in sports events. In the 1890s, only nine per cent of farms in Tipperary were larger than 100 acres.[9] The Kiely family was farming substantial holdings of high-quality land that placed them in the top five per cent of Irish farm families in terms of wealth by the middle of that decade.

Tom made his way to Dublin later in 1889 for *The Freeman's Journal* Sports on 7 September and the Kickhams Sports (held in Clonturk, north Dublin) the next day. At the *Freeman's* Sports, Kiely's one reported entry was in the quarter-mile handicap, where he was unplaced in the final. The day was not a complete loss, however, as it gave him a chance to see world-class athletes at close quarters and maybe to dream a little when he saw what the likes of Dan Bulger in the sprints and William 'Jumbo' Barry in weights could do.

This point in the narrative brings us to the matter of there being two athletics bodies in Ireland. The GAA was founded in 1884, largely in response to an increasing anglicisation of Irish athletics. Throughout Kiely's career, however, there was a rival athletic organisation in existence: the Irish Amateur Athletic Association (IAAA), founded in early 1885. The *Freeman's* Sports were held under the auspices of the IAAA, while the Kickhams on the following day were under those of the GAA. The IAAA was a more urban and anglophile body than the GAA, and yet Kiely never shirked from attending its meetings, nor representing the IAAA when called upon. The GAA favoured weight-throwing and jumping events somewhat more than the IAAA did, while the IAAA refused to hold meetings on Sundays, which was often the only 'day of rest' available for sport among many rural people. However, there were plenty of competitive opportunities at the sports of both organisations. Kiely cared little that the GAA was more nationalistic or that some of the competitors at IAAA events came from unionist, police or army backgrounds. He just wanted to compete. He was already a determined competitor, innocent enough not to concern himself with politics but shrewd enough to know when prizes were there for the winning.

At the Kickhams Sports, listed as 'T. Keily', he won the 120 yards hurdles in 18 seconds.[10] He was, of course, also broadening his horizons geographically. What must the young man from Ballyneill have made of the second city of the United Kingdom! What must he have made of the young ladies who frequented sports events in their hundreds, dressed in their weekend finery! His exposure to Dublin must have contributed to the personal fashion sense that he developed and retained all his life, as several photographs demonstrate.

***

By this time, Kiely was also playing several team sports, and was very good at Gaelic football. The earliest record located of him on a football team, around 1890, comes from a penned note in his scrapbook, copied from an unattributed newspaper account. It refers to how:

At Carrick-on-Suir on Sunday, the Ballyneill men succeeded in defeating the Waterford Commercials in an interesting football match played at the Deerpark grounds ... Ballyneill scored a goal and a point; the Commercials 3 points. For Ballyneill, T Kiely and J Strapp played best ...[11]

The J. Strapp who starred along with Kiely was to be a lifelong friend. Indeed, when the same Jack Strapp had a cottage built in the early twentieth century, it was Kiely who built it for him. That house still stands on the Carrick-on-Suir side of Ballyneill village. In terms of the scoreline, with a goal then worth five points, the game's result meant a three-point win for Kiely's team.

The GAA in Tipperary, as in many counties, was in chaos in the early 1890s, partly due to the financial difficulties caused by the 'Gaelic Invasion' of the USA, which saw its patron Michael Davitt have to bail it out to the tune of several hundred pounds. There were also club disputes about costs and refereeing decisions, among other issues. *The Freeman's Journal's* specialist newspaper, *Sport*, pleaded in 1890 for clubs to hold tournaments in order to get the national association out of its financial dilemma.[12]

National politics played a part in the problems as well. There were tensions and often open disputes within the GAA between moderate nationalists like the Davins and those who supported the small but militant Irish Republican Brotherhood (IRB). This was further complicated by the Parnellite split in the Irish Parliamentary Party and Charles Stewart Parnell's death in 1891. Parnell, often called in his prime 'The Uncrowned King of Ireland', had been a patron of the GAA as well as leader of the Home Rule movement. The GAA's support for Parnell, after his party dismissed him as leader because of an affair with a married woman, caused a lot of division within the association, and lost it the support of many influential clergymen in rural Ireland too.[13] By the time of the 1892 GAA convention, the secretary's report showed that although the finances had been stabilised, the number of affiliated clubs nationally had fallen from over 1,000 to 220.[14]

The difficulties in Tipperary were demonstrated when not one delegate represented the county at the GAA conventions of 1891 and 1892.[15]

It was 1893 before Kiely was recorded again on the Gaelic football field, starring with Grangemockler, as the parish team was known, but even in that year the GAA's national secretary, Patrick Tobin, expressed deep concern about the 'germs of decay' in the organisation.[16]

The poor state of Gaelic team games in the early 1890s had another effect on Kiely's career. While football and hurling struggled, Tipperary and Irish athletics were in a very healthy state and, in many respects, it was athletics that kept the GAA, and the rival IAAA, going:

> These first-class athletes in the traditional Irish field events and others who competed against them attracted huge crowds of spectators whenever they appeared at sports meetings. On the other hand, the breakdown of the GAA organisation in many counties resulted in a marked falling off in the number of attractive hurling and football matches being played and enthusiasm for the games waned. For example, in the three years from 1891 to 1893, no GAA organisation existed in Tipperary and the county like many others was almost completely deprived of hurling and football activity.[17]

The American historian Frank Zarnowski has commented on the quality of Irish athletics during Kiely's career:

> [With] the possible exception of America, Ireland was the world's premier athletic track and field power in the 1890s. Irishmen held many of the world's best jumping and throwing marks and many of their top athletes immigrated to America. The British may argue this point, but the facts are plain enough ... For example, between 1890 and 1910 Irish-born athletes held world amateur records in the high jump, broad jump, hop-step-jump, hammer, 120-yd hurdles, shot put, and discus.[18]

Other athletes might have departed for the USA, but the exploits of Irish weight throwers like Jumbo Barry or jumpers like Dan Shanahan were proving that the remaining Irish athletes were as good as in any country. Kiely, at twenty, came to realise that he was already good, and could be better yet.

The competitiveness of Irish athletes was demonstrated not merely by records, but also by arguments about the finer points. In 1889, for instance, an IAAA sports meeting witnessed a controversy over Jumbo Barry using a hammer with a lead head, rather than an iron one. The complaints came on the basis that lead was heavier than iron, so the hammer head was smaller and more aerodynamic, and allegedly travelled farther.[19] Irish commentators also wrote frequently, and negatively, about American athletic developments and 'advances' to weights, including grips and handles.[20] These issues would continue on well into the next decade, all while Kiely came into his prime.

***

In 1890, Kiely again competed mainly in local athletics meetings, at Cahir, Clonmel and Carrick-on-Suir, and in Dublin on two occasions. Entering both GAA and IAAA meetings was made easier by an agreement made between the two associations in January 1890, putting an end (for a time, at least) to much of the enmity between the two bodies. In the capital, in late July, Kiely must have been disappointed to win nothing at *The Freeman's Journal* Sports, placing third in the open 16lb shot put and sixth in a 400 yards open handicap. Yet even defeats were of value, as these results showed the twenty-one-year-old that running events were not his forté. Apart from when he competed in ten-event all-round contests, no record of Kiely ever running an individual 400 or 440 yards race again has been found.

In the same week, also in Dublin, at the United Trades Sports, Kiely won 28lb and 56lb weight events, as well as coming third in the high jump and in a heat of the 120 yards hurdles.[21] A modern athlete or coach would find it inconceivable to have an athlete throw weights of half a hundredweight (*c.* 25kg), and then compete in high jump and hurdles on the same afternoon. Kiely would not have batted an eyelid at such a prospect, even at the age of twenty-one. Up to his mid-thirties, he never weighed over thirteen stone (*c.* 82kg).

Entries that year cost two shillings per event at *The Freeman's Journal* Sports, not to mention the cost of getting to and staying in Dublin. Putting this in context, there were twenty shillings in £1 and it has been suggested that the real value of two shillings in 1890 equates to over £12 or €13 today.[22] Therefore, competing in multiple events, one day after another as he sometimes did, was a serious financial investment by Kiely.

A key moment in Kiely's early career occurred shortly after this, at Cahir Sports in 1890, when the prizes on offer were substantial, practical items. The meeting itself was a very lively occasion, with the crowd pushing in on the weight throwers, and several runners being accused of cutting corners. Kiely won five events. Among the prizes he brought home were a suit of tweed for the 56lb weight throw, a dressing case for the hurdles, salad servers and a bowl for the 100 yards, and a photograph album for finishing second in the 220 yards flat race. Undoubtedly, the suit of tweed was a welcome prize for the sartorially aware Kiely. Some of the less perishable items remained Kiely family possessions for many years. The album won for second place became particularly important, as when the young athlete went home that evening, he began to use this album as a scrapbook, filling it with newspaper cuttings of his exploits from then onwards.[23]

One of the remarkable features of Irish sport in the 1890s was that while Gaelic games often struggled, the annual athletics meetings held in small places all over rural Ireland attracted huge crowds and saw performances in field events that were as good as anywhere in Britain or the USA. Kiely mainly competed locally in his early years, not wanting to be away for too long from his farming duties. He won four events at Clonmel Sports in early August 1890, but his most dramatic achievements that summer came at his more or less 'home' meeting at Carrick-on-Suir. In a week when Pat Davin confirmed his retirement from athletics, a new all-rounder emerged on the very field owned by the Davins at Deerpark.

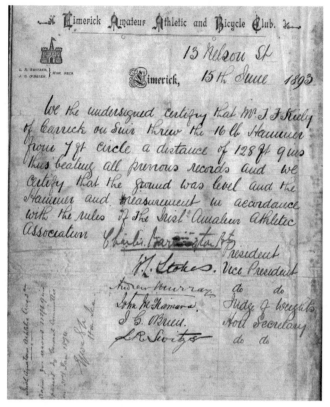

The certificate of Kiely's record at Limerick Sports in 1893.
(*Kiely Collection, Tipperary Museum of Hidden History*)

Here Kiely won nine prizes in total, and even found time to be on the organising committee, along with Maurice and Pat Davin and others.[24]

After both the Carrick results and the United Trades Sports, the relevant cuttings in Kiely's scrapbook indicate that someone has gone over some of the distances given, in pen, making a correction to what the papers had recorded. This can only have been done by Kiely himself, and it suggests that his competitive instincts were fine-tuned even at the age of twenty-one. He was collecting records of his exploits, like many a young man would do, and making sure that the correct performances were being recorded. This kind of editing of newspaper accounts occurred again and again in his scrapbook cuttings and saw him often making corrections to the misspellings of his name in press accounts.

Now established as a serious athlete, Kiely was almost certainly receiving official expenses payments from some meeting organisers. The GAA was a little less strict than the IAAA in this regard and offered modest money prizes for some competitions to help defray competitors' expenses. With that, it is a little surprising that Kiely competed in neither the GAA nor the IAAA national championships in 1890. More than likely, he had enough on his plate, between farming, football and athletics.

One development that must have caught his attention, however, was the proposal that a national all-round athletics championship be held that year. This competition had ceased in 1888, when it was organised by *The Freeman's Journal.* Now, *Sport* carried letters from J. P. O'Sullivan, Killorglin, John Ryan of Tipperary and an athlete who signed as 'Intending Competitor', arguing the need for it to be restored. J. P. O'Sullivan put the case for a GAA-organised all-round championship, but the idea was backed by IAAA members too.[25] In America, the Manhattan Athletic Club of New York was organising all-around competitions, though with slightly different events to the normal suite in Ireland.[26] While most of the subsequent letters argued about what events to include or exclude, they were all very supportive of the general idea. Then, in early August 1890, came the announcement that:

Through the generosity of Messrs West, the eminent goldsmiths, of College Green, a magnificent trophy, taking the form of a silver belt, has been placed at the disposal of Mr D.D. Bulger, for the coming All-Round Athletic Championship of Ireland. The belt consists of four pieces, two already suitably inscribed, while the others remain blank for the names of the winners. The buckle will be composed of the original gold medal, value seven sovereigns, which is fashioned to represent a four-leaf shamrock, with the respective arms of Ulster, Munster, Leinster and Connaught on the leaves. It is a truly magnificent trophy and redounds greatly to the credit of its generous donors.[27]

Mr Bulger was Dan Bulger, an IAAA athlete of great renown and later an Irish representative at the Sorbonne Congress of 1894, at which the modern Olympic Games were founded. In the end, it was the IAAA which resurrected the all-round championship and staged it at Ballsbridge on 30 August. Even in newspapers not normally associated with 'sweaty' human sporting activities, it was advertised that 'all leading athletes and cyclists will compete' and that 'the Finchley Harriers (London) [were] coming over'.[28] However, Kiely was not there in 1890 and the event was won by Tom Donovan. No obvious problems of form or injury have been found to explain why Kiely missed the new all-round championship, though his absence was lamented in the press.[29]

***

In 1891, Kiely extended his competitive season to an extent, competing in eight meetings altogether, with the now customary success, and won a total of thirty-three prizes. Five were won at nearby Bansha and Kilmoyler Athletic Sports, with his scrapbook again containing his corrections to the *Nationalist*'s errors.[30] He was basically keeping this scrapbook as his own record of achievements and he could not abide being short-changed in any reporting. For example, he was reported as coming first in the 56lb weight event in Bansha but was given the wrong distance, so he corrected the distance, in pen, to read 25 feet 8 inches. In the 28lb event, he was listed in the paper in second place to J. R. Dalton, but Kiely overwrote the type, putting himself first and Dalton second, and inserting the measurement of '32–3' in the margin.

In just these events, Kiely's improvement on 1890 was staggering. His 56lb distance was almost 3 feet better than he had done the year before in Dublin, and the 28lb distance was over 5½ feet better than on that occasion. Kiely was also second in the 100 yards open, in the high jump and in the long jump behind Dan Shanahan, showing his all-round pedigree.

Among other successes that year, the inside of the back cover of Kiely's scrapbook shows that there were multiple wins in Waterford, Clonmel, Golden and Cahir. He ventured further, to Mallow and Kilkenny, and won a spectacular haul of nine prizes at Dungarvan, where Dan Fraher's field would go on to be one of his favourite venues throughout his career.

Again, however, he failed to compete at either the GAA championships or the IAAA all-round championships, both held in August. The GAA championships in Tralee were a disaster and even the national officials did not get there. Perhaps this was indicative of the poor state of the association overall.[31] Kiely was among the entries listed for the IAAA all-round event in Dublin but did not compete. Yet his feats were attracting serious attention and he was being seen as the great new hope of Irish athletics. People even began to work a little harder at spelling his name correctly:

> *Noting Tom Kiely's name amongst the entries for the all-round championship, I was reminded of a mistake which occurs very often in the printing of his name in athletic contests. It is that he generally appears as J.F. Kiely. Whoever has invented the spelling of Tom with 'J' is to be envied, but up to this Tom himself, I believe, spells it with the old-fashioned 'T'.*[32]

The spelling of 'Kiely' continued to addle some, with *Sport* recounting how at Clonmel Sports in August 1891, 'TF Kiley [*sic*] won the 120 hurdles and the long jump.'[33] Even the newspaper of Clonmel struggled and Kiely found himself, with his pen, going over the *Nationalist*'s account of his wins there in 1891. His scrapbook cutting noted:

> *T.F. Keilly [sic] of Carrick, won several events. The very worst order was observed by the by-standers, who crowded in on the competitors. The band of the 15th Hussars contributed a pleasing selection of music …*

When a similar cutting referring to Golden Sports informed readers that 'J.F. Kiely of Carrick-on-Suir, got well amongst the pots, winning the 56lb and 120 yards hurdles, and getting seconds in the hammer, long and high jumps …', one finds Kiely's black pen is again at work, changing the 'J.F' to 'T.F.'[34] There is a lovely irony in the fact that Kiely always competed as 'Thomas F. Kiely', at a time when many athletes competed under assumed names, not wanting to either fall foul of one or other athletic body's regulations, or offend their employers or landlords by competing on a Sunday (God's day of rest) in the case of IAAA meetings.[35]

***

The year 1892, without any doubt, catapulted Kiely to the attention of the wider athletics world. His prize haul that year grew to forty-one and he was now competing further afield. He was found in Cork at Queen's College Sports for the first time, in Durrow, Co. Laois (where he won eight, if not nine, prizes), Thomastown, Co. Kilkenny (six prizes) and at a couple of high-profile events in Dublin. Deerpark field at Carrick-on-Suir hosted summer and autumn meetings that year, with Kiely winning a total of eleven prizes between the two days.

His competitive streak again fuelled his concern to get his records straight when newspapers sometimes did not. When he won nine prizes at Carrick-on-Suir, *Sport* reported:

> *Mr T.F. Kiely, the celebrated all-round athlete from Ballyneill was the lion of the Suirside sports on Sunday last. He won the hammer, 56lb shot, long jump, high jump, and tied with the Gaelic champion, M. Ryan, at the hurdles. Thanks to the excellent management of Messrs M. and P. Davin and the old-time champion and the local men, the sports were very successful. We hope an autumn meeting will be held.*

On this occasion, in the relevant scrapbook cutting, the eagle-eyed Kiely inserted a comma in black ink, to show that the 56lb and shot were two separate events, thus '56lb, shot'.[36]

A somewhat more curious thing happened on 18 June that

same year. Kiely was at the IAAA championships that day but competed only in the 56lb event, finishing fourth. Although a GAA man at core, it seems quite strange that he would travel all the way to Dublin to compete in just one IAAA event, and one that was not his favourite.[37] Perhaps he made the trip just to get a feel for the RDS venue at Ballsbridge, but opted not to show his hand too much to others. Why? Because he planned, at last, to enter the all-round championship held there in August.

There was a clue that Kiely was getting ready for a tilt at becoming all-round champion from the previously mentioned meeting at Carrick-on-Suir. The *Nationalist* reported, less than two weeks before the all-round championship, that: 'Mr T F Kiely, the popular secretary of the meeting, was in fresh form and won several events. Mr Kiely is still very young and gives promise of being a first-class all-round athlete.'[38] He won the long jump, 16lb put, 16lb hammer, the high jump and tied first in the 56lb throw and hurdles. In the hurdles, the normally ambitious Kiely 'decided upon giving the Cashel man [Michael Ryan] first prize, despite the judges calling it a dead heat'. Undoubtedly, the Davins in attendance that day must have felt that their protégé was ready for the national championship. Young Larry Kiely went to the meeting with his older brother that day, and finished second in a boys' under–15 race, though barely eleven years of age: a portent of things to come there too.

A few days later, at Durrow, Tom broke his first world record, in the triple jump – almost! *Sport*'s account of Durrow Athletic and Cycling Sports 1892 said that 'T.F. Kiely of Carrick-on-Suir, was in great form in the jumping and weight throwing events. He jumped 22 feet 9ins and 50 feet 9ins in the long jump and hop, step [*sic*] respectively.' In Kiely's scrapbook, in the margin beside where the text first appears, he inserted in red 'world's record 50–2'. Also in the margin he wrote '7 in 50–9', which seems to be shorthand to show that he had increased the world record by 7 inches, from 50 feet 2 inches to 50 feet 9 inches. Unfortunately, the record was not ratified because there was a slope in the ground, making Kiely's distance (at his very first jump) uncertifiable.[39]

Those same Durrow Sports saw Kiely win six events and place second in three more. An unprovenanced cutting in his scrapbook predicted that 'Kiely's grand all-round performances in the Durrow Sports has put a decidedly open complexion on the [all-round] contest'.[40] *Sport* wrote of 'T.F. Keily [*sic*] Carrick-on-Suir (a far better man than most people imagine, and considered by many as a likely winner)'.[41]

With the 1892 all-round championship under IAAA rules to be held on Monday 1 August, Kiely made his way to Dublin by train from Clonmel on the previous Friday.[42] He had to miss the famous Clonmel Sports in order to compete at Ballsbridge on the same day. However, he was anxious for a warm-up contest of some sort before the Monday, so made his way to the Grocers' Sports at Clonturk. Kiely had by this stage become a firm favourite with the ladies and there is no doubt that his presence contributed to the large attendance that day:

From ten o'clock to three all along Drumcondra Road and its branches were crowded with people going to the sports, some hundreds of cars being in use. The crowd was largest about one o'clock, and at that hour

*there must have been fully 5,000 people on the ground. The ladies,
as well as the members of the more stern sex, seemed to take a keen
interest in the contests …*[43]

Kiely won three prizes at the Grocers', all in jumping events
because he did not want to strain any muscles with weight
throwing that day. He made for Ballsbridge the following
morning. The all-round championship turned out to be a very
easy win for him. *Sport*'s athletics columnist 'Cuchulinn' wrote
of 'A worthy pupil of a worthy master':

*Pat Davin's novice surprised everyone on the ground, and the longer
he competed the better he seemed to get … This [referring to Kiely's
decisive victory in the hurdles] was a splendid performance on the
part of Kiely, but it was completely eclipsed by his magnificent victory
in the quarter [mile], which everyone regarded as a 'dead snip' for
Donovan, who, it will be remembered, won the championship in this
event two years ago …*[44]

In the all-round event, a 'standard' was set for each of the
nine events, based on what a good athlete of national standard ought to be able to do, and an athlete could only count
his score if he reached that standard. With five competitors,
the winner of each event got five points, second place got
four and so on. This scoring system was peculiar to Ireland
and made it virtually impossible to compare one set of results
with another, as the number of points scored depended on
the number of competitors. This means that in order to ap-
preciate the quality of athletic performance, the actual results
need to be known. While American all-around competitions

were standardised at ten events, in Ireland the number of events could vary from eight to ten, again making comparisons very difficult.

That day in 1892, Kiely won the high jump (5 feet 5 inches), long jump (20 feet 9 inches), shot put (35 feet 8 inches), hurdles (18 seconds), 440 yards (58 seconds) and hammer (105 feet). He was third in the 56lb weight throw, did not reach the qualifying time of 11¼ seconds in the 100 yards, and, because he was so far ahead coming to the last event, did not bother to run the mile at all. He was never fond of what would nowadays be called 'middle-distance' running, and it was permitted to skip an event if desired, though failure to reach the standard in three events meant disqualification. With thirty-one points, Kiely was champion, well ahead of A. M. Forrest of Blarney (who competed as 'Tom Wood' on other days) on eighteen points, and the previous year's runner-up Tom Donovan, of Queen's College Cork and Edinburgh University, on fifteen. 'Cuchulinn' concluded of Kiely:

This is a splendid athlete and will be better in time with careful training ... In more senses of the word than one he has jumped to the front ranks of Irish athletics, and is a man whom even a country like this, renowned for rearing men of his stamp, might be proud to put forward on any occasion as her representative ... [45]

Kiely may not have gone home at all with his new belt as all-round champion, for the very next evening he was at Bansha, near Tipperary town, competing under GAA rules and the watchful eye of Frank Dinneen.[46] That meeting saw him winning a 56lb event and the hop, step and jump, as well as earning a couple of placings in hammer events behind an up-and-coming rival from Kilfinnane, John Flanagan.

The year 1892 had yet another great day in store. On 10 September Kiely made his way to Jones' Road for the first ever GAA athletics championships to be held at the venue which would later become Croke Park. There, he entered and won seven different events and 'a new star from Davin country, soared into orbit' and became 'far and away the outstanding athlete of the year'.[47] Each of these events saw him compete against event specialists, and the achievement of seven individual Irish titles in one day has never been surpassed since. Statistically, the wins were as follows: hurdles (16⅘ seconds), long jump (21 feet 7½ inches), triple jump (49 feet 7 inches), shot put (38 feet), putting 28lb (31 feet 10½ inches), hammer throw (unlimited run and follow – 123 feet) and throwing 7lb weight (84 feet 4½ inches).[48] These performances were, each and every one, good enough to win many national titles in many nations. Yet again Kiely, the weight thrower, came close to a world record in the hop, step and jump:

> [The] tussle between Shanahan and Kiely in the running hop, step and jump was worth travelling any distance to see. Had the ground been in good condition, Shanahan's record (50ft 0½in) would certainly have gone, and Kiely's winning try of 49ft 7in was precious near it, in fact, the actual distance was 50 feet 1in, as the Carrick-on-Suir man stood six inches behind the trig [i.e. the take-off mark].[49]

While the crowd was small until the evening part of the meeting, the same writer commented that almost every athlete of note was there, competing against Kiely, suggesting that:

Ireland can now challenge the world to an all-round championship. Kiely's brilliant performances demonstrate that he has reached the highest degree of perfection at everything (racing, jumping and weight-throwing) since Pat Davin retired from the arena. It has not altogether been unnoticed that both men were trained in the same stable. Kiely is yet very young, and it is not improbable that next year will mark a startling development in his form as a weight thrower and jumper ...'

Kiely, cutting out newspaper accounts of the GAA championships for his scrapbook, must have been pleased to read:

Rarely in the history of athletics has such splendid performances as those of Keily [sic] been seen. Perhaps Keily's victory in the hurdles was the most meritorious of all. In this event, he left such 'clinkers' Pedlow and Ryan behind him, and finished the last three hurdles as fast as any man did ...[50]

Towards the end of 1892, one review of the athletics season concluded: 'On a fair all-round programme Kiely should be able to defeat any man at present figuring in the athletic world.'[51]

This was no wild notion. Across the Atlantic, Alexander Jordan of New York Athletic Club won his third Amateur Athletic Union (AAU) all-around title in 1891. The AAU champion for 1892, the year of Kiely's triumphs, was Mike O'Sullivan. It has not been possible to trace the statistical records of O'Sullivan's 1892 performances, but a comparison between Kiely's 1892 performances and Jordan's in 1891 makes for very interesting reading.

The American events differed from the Irish to some

extent, with only seven bearing direct comparison with Kiely's GAA performances. Yet conditions, track surfaces and levels of technology and sporting equipment were better in the USA. The table below compares Alexander Jordan's AAU and Kiely's GAA championship performances. Because Kiely did not enter the GAA high jump or 56lb events, the statistics for these come from the IAAA all-round championship, but the comparison is still fairly telling:

Results of the American AAU champion of 1891, Alexander Jordan, and those of Kiely in 1892[52]

Event	Jordan (USA) 1891	Kiely (Ireland) 1892
Long Jump	20 feet 7 inches	21 feet 7½ inches
Shot Put	32 feet 6 inches	35 feet 8 inches
Hammer	97 feet 9 inches	123 feet
120 Yards Hurdles	16⅘ seconds	16⅘ seconds
High Jump	5 feet 2 inches	5 feet 5 inches (IAAA)
56lb	18 feet 9 inches	21 feet (IAAA)
100 Yards	10⅘ seconds	over 11¼ seconds

In the seven comparable events, Kiely was vastly superior to Jordan in five, level with him in one and only slower in the 100 yards. Even though Jordan performed better overall the year before when winning the AAU, he was still only ahead of Kiely in one of the seven events then.

Looking at the British AAA results for 1891–92, Kiely's performances in 1892 would have won him medals in at least four individual events there, not counting the fact that two of his best events were the triple jump and 56lb weight, neither of which was on the AAA programme in those days.[53] There was no doubt that Kiely was the new star of all-round athletics, even if only proven in competition within Ireland thus far.

While fully acknowledging the impossibility of comparing sports performances from one generation to the next, it is nonetheless interesting to note that Kiely's 1892 performances would have stood up very well to Irish championship-winning performances up to the latter half of the twentieth century. Technical changes to weights make it impossible to compare some of Kiely's real specialisms with later performances, but his 1892 GAA championship performances in the 120 yards hurdles and long jump would have been good enough to win five Irish senior titles each in the 1950s. Even more remarkably, Kiely's hop, step and jump distance was not surpassed at an Irish championship until 1970.[54]

As he sat with his scrapbook at the end of 1892, Kiely must have been planning for the years to come. As he did so, his black pen carefully corrected the spelling of 'Keily' to 'Kiely'. One paper had even spelled his name 'Keely' at one point in its coverage, though Tom seems to have missed that. Over the next few years, whatever the spelling, it was a name that would dominate the headlines in many, many newspapers, both in Ireland and abroad.

CHAPTER 3

GLORY YEARS OF 1893-95

As 1893 dawned, Tom Kiely knew that he was now quite famous, what might be termed a 'star' in sporting terms. Between then and the end of 1895, his position as the pre-eminent all-round athlete was established beyond question and was accepted even in the great emerging capital of world athletics, the USA. There were already stories in the Irish press that he was to be approached by the Manhattan Athletic Club to represent it at the sports of the Chicago World Fair in 1893:

> Now we learn that the manager of the Manhattan Athletic Club – the greatest institution of its kind in the world – has sailed to these countries for the purpose of engaging some of the representatives of Irish and British athletic talent to give exhibitions at the World's Fair, and that he hopes to secure the services of our all-round champion, T.F. Kiely, of Carrick-on-Suir, among others.[1]

That club went bankrupt in 1893, so perhaps it was just as well that the plan mentioned here did not come to fruition. Yet, the twenty-three-year-old Kiely cut out and kept this account in his scrapbook. America would happen, but not yet.

There were more pressing matters closer to home. As the only adult son in the house, an increasing amount of responsibility was falling on Tom. By 1893 his father was nearing his mid-sixties and had begun to drink more than was good for him, according to family accounts.[2] This may help to explain why Tom himself rarely drank, beyond a small bottle of Guinness in later life every Friday at lunchtime.

Pressing sporting matters at home came via a major effort to revive hurling and football in Tipperary and nationally. The *Cork Herald* columnist quoted above expressed the concerns of many when it looked as though Kiely might be lost to the USA: 'though I should be delighted to see the Gaelic Athletic Association represented at the World's Fair Sports, I cannot keep from my mind the terrible injury the departure of Kiely would be to this country'.[3] This again points to the pivotal role that Irish athletic accomplishments were playing in creating and nurturing a sense of national pride, in both urban areas where the IAAA was strongest, and in rural Ireland where the GAA was predominant, especially in Munster and in particular when Gaelic team games were going through difficult times.

It is no exaggeration to say that were it not for the great athletic achievements of Kiely, the Ryans and a few others, there would have been little competitive GAA activity in Tipperary at all in 1893:

> [Down] south, Tom Kiely had the Slievenamon heather quivering with cheers from the 'Hollow Field'. Gaeldom still waited for Tipp to return to the national game, and looked to Thurles for another rally like that of '86 ...[4]

Pressed by Maurice Davin to help revive the GAA's team games in 1893, Kiely was one of the attendees at a vital meeting in Dobbyn's Hotel, Tipperary town. Out of this meeting, clubs reformed and competitions were begun. Inevitably, Kiely was drawn back to the football field too, and captained his club against arch-rivals, Arravale Rovers. Unfortunately, that day, like many others, ended in chaos. A dispute over a free saw Arravale refuse to play on, with twenty minutes left. When the match was re-fixed for Cashel, to play just twenty minutes in order to complete the hour, Grangemockler refused to travel and accordingly lost the match.[5]

Tipperary returned to inter-county 'action' in two tournament games which:

> ... came off in a thoroughly satisfactory manner on the grounds of the Kerry Athletic Club at Tralee ... The teams were met at the railway station by several bands, and the town was thronged by the local folk, who gathered to greet the gallant Tips ...[6]

Tipperary won both matches narrowly: the football by one goal and two points to six points, and the hurling by one goal and one point to three points. On the Tipperary football team, in yet another cutting in Kiely's scrapbook, the name J. J. Reilly is listed fifth, and has been corrected to read T. F. Kiely, in Tom's handwriting.

Saving the GAA was all very well, but Kiely wanted to build on his athletics career in 1893. This saw him compete more often. He was at Queen's College Cork Sports in May, where he won seven prizes, including the running hop, step and jump and the IAAA national championship in the long jump with a very good 21 feet 5¾ inches.[7] At the time, the world long jump record was just over 23 feet.

Details of the great meeting under GAA rules at Banteer in Cork show that Kiely won another seven prizes, including first place in the running hop, step and jump (with 47 feet 1 inch, for the championship of Munster) and in another three events. Kiely was listed as second in the 56lb weight championship of Munster at Banteer, but another cutting shows that he wrote to the commentator subsequently, clarifying that his published distance was incorrect: The newspaper explained:

T.F. Kiely writes me as follows: 'In your athletic notes re Banteer Sports my throw with the 56lb was given as 30ft 4½ in. I beg to state that the distance of my longest throw was 32ft 8in; my first and shortest measuring 30ft 4in. I may remark that I had been travelling from seven o'clock that morning till I got to the ground at 2 pm and, without a moment's rest, had to run my heat and the final of the 100 yds, and then, without intermission, contest the 56lbs. Hoping you will correct the mistake I refer to, &c.'[8]

Here again was the competitive Kiely, wanting every detail of his performances recorded correctly. The challenges he faced in just getting to events were also evident. Banteer was and is on the railway line between Mallow and Killarney. In order to get there, it required a twenty-five-mile journey on horseback to Dungarvan, and then a train trip from Dungarvan to Banteer (roughly sixty miles). Alternatively, if train timetables were suitable, Kiely might have gone by train from Clonmel to Limerick Junction, from there to Mallow, and then from Mallow to Banteer. Getting home, using the latter route, would have taken six train journeys, and up to fourteen hours of travel! It is well to remember that as Kiely became a star, expected to break records every day, he generally brought his own 16lb hammer with him too, whether on the train or on horseback.

Of Banteer, the *Cork Herald* reported that 'Kiely's performances throughout the day were most creditable, carrying off as he did, five prizes, including one championship. Good old Kiely! More power to your elbow, and your legs, too.'[9] Seeing Kiely referred to as 'Good old Kiely' at the age of twenty-three was a portent of things to come in terms of his national status.

Despite his commitments to the farm at home, the evidence from 1893 is that Kiely was competing further afield than ever before, and earlier in the season than previously. As a cattle dealer, May, the month when the grass, literally, started to grow again after the winter, was normally when a lot of the buying was done. Generally, cattle were bought as young calves in western counties and reared on the better grass of the south and east throughout the summer months. This may help explain why Tom competed in Banteer, i.e. perhaps he was able to tie the trip in with some cattle dealing in Castleisland, Newmarket or some other venue. Meetings in June were less likely to coincide with cattle dealing but must have been very important to him, as late June could mean missing valuable days of grass mowing and making hay.

One meeting that Kiely skipped in June 1893 was the IAAA national championships at Ballsbridge. He was entered in several events but did not show. According to contemporary sources, the weather was atrocious that day in Dublin.[10] Kiely may have remained in Tipperary to get the hay saved if the weather was any way acceptable there – the great Tipperary adage of mid-summer has long been: 'The hay is saved [referring to the prominence of farming in so many people's lives] and Cork are bet [referring to the great Munster hurling championship rivalry].' People in Kiely's day would have been no different, given that inter-county rivalry had resurfaced.

***

Another major development in Kiely's career from 1893 was the breaking of records. It has to be stressed that records in the 1890s were nothing like as reliable as in more recent times (allowing for modern drug cheats, of course). Weight-throwing events were particularly fraught with difficulty, as the 1890s saw a period of technical improvements and design changes to hammers and even to 56lb weights. A technical coaching book by Irish expert James Mitchel, published in 1916, demonstrated at least five changes to the design of the hammer, and seven changes to the design of the heavier weight, between 1868 and 1910.[11] As a result of such variation, it was very hard for one record to stand against another, particularly when comparing Irish and US performances. Sadly, this also meant that when records were modernised and standardised in the twentieth century, Kiely's were omitted from the official lists:

Around the turn of the century the weight of the hammer became standard at 16 pounds, but the length of the handle (usually 3 ½ to 4 feet) and its composition (from wooden to wire) varied. As well, the size (7 to 9 feet) and shape of the throwing area (circle to square) differed from nation to nation, even meet to meet. Many different hammer records existed simultaneously. The same can be said for the 56lb weight throw, an event where not only did the shape of the instrument and throwing areas differ, but records were kept for various throwing styles (one-handed, two-handed, from side, with and without follow-through).

The number of permutations for just these two events boggles the mind. When the IAAF produced a progression of world bests and records a few years back, all of Kiely's marks for this myriad of combinations were discarded. The same fate befell his records for the Irish version of the hop-step-jump. But make no mistake. In his day Kiely legitimately was considered a recurrent record breaker.[12]

While not directly relevant to Kiely, a fascinating story associated with the American Mike O'Sullivan's hammer throwing illustrates the 'lengths' that athletes could go to in order to gain distance. O'Sullivan, abandoning both wooden and wire handles, once attached his hammer to a grape vine. The vine measured the regulation 4 feet when it was lying on the ground, but when swung with a 16lb ball at the end of it, it unfurled like a rope, increasing in length significantly, helping the thrower develop more power and enabling the 'hammer' to travel much further when released.[13]

All this being said, Irish records and recording procedures were scrupulously observed in Kiely's time. The GAA and IAAA, for all their differences, held common ground on record requirements. Furthermore, these were generally aligned with English Amateur Athletic Association (AAA) records. At this time, before the International Amateur Athletic Federation (IAAF) had come into existence, the AAA was seen by many as the authority over international athletics on the eastern side of the Atlantic.

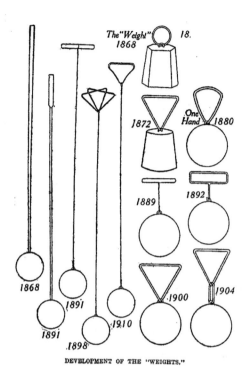

DEVELOPMENT OF THE "WEIGHTS."

A page from James Mitchel's book on weight throwing, showing the variations and developments in 56lb weights and hammers between 1868 and 1910. (*Spalding Company, 1916*)

On 15 June 1893 Kiely won five more prizes at the meeting of Limerick Amateur Athletic and Bicycle Club, breaking what was regarded as a world record in the 16lb hammer (from a seven-foot circle). This required the organising committee to verify that the weight, the circle and the level nature of the ground were all compliant with AAA regulations:

We the undersigned certify that Mr T.F. Kiely of Carrick on Suir threw the 16lb Hammer from 7ft circle a distance of 128ft 9ins this breaking all previous records and we certify that the ground was level and the Hammer and measurement in accordance with the rules of the Irish Amateur Athletic Association.[14]

This was signed by several notable Limerick dignitaries, including Charles Barrington (president of the Limerick club), a Mr Stokes and Andrew Murray (vice president), John McMorrow (judge of weights), J. G. O'Brien and L. R. Switzer (secretaries). On the lower left corner, the IAAA notes: 'claim for record 128ft 9ins passed by General Committee on 31st January 1894', signed by E. J. Walsh, honorary secretary of the IAAA. The Irish certification then went to the AAA in London. There is no record of what happened to the application subsequently.

At Mitchelstown in mid-July 1893, where Kiely won seven prizes, it was announced: 'A world's record is claimed for slinging the 56lbs with unlimited run and follow, which Kiely, of Carrick-on-Suir, threw 34ft 11½ in, at Mitchelstown sports yesterday.'[15]

After Mitchelstown, there were five more prizes won at Durrow Sports and seven at Nenagh on the day when the 56lb record (one-handed) was broken.[16] There:

A lot of people were very sceptical as to the genuineness of the throw, but Kiely set the matter to rest on the 3rd of August, when under the fairest possible conditions, without the shadow of suspicion as to measurement, levelness of ground, or correctness of weight, he pitched the bulky lump of iron the record distance of 35ft 5ins.[17]

Now a real star, Kiely's mere presence or even possible presence at a sports meeting was used to attract crowds. *Sport* then predicted of the upcoming Clonmel Sports:

> *T.F. Kiely is going to try for a record in the weights, and there is little doubt that he will succeed, as he is at present in grand form. The day will be observed as a general holiday in Clonmel. We hope we will be blessed with good weather, and that all will enjoy themselves thoroughly.*[18]

At Clonmel, Kiely almost increased the 56lb record distance by 8 inches, but, unfortunately, the weight when tested was found to be a couple of ounces light. Annoyed at a mere 2 ounces leaving his Clonmel record unrecognised, Kiely still recorded the distance as a 'World's record' in his scrapbook.

Feeling in such form, he headed for Kilkenny, intent on setting the records straight. He managed that, throwing just less than an inch farther than at Nenagh; he also broke a record in the hammer with 131 feet 6 inches on that same day.

To no one's surprise, Kiely repeated his triumph in the 1893 all-round championship, again under IAAA rules, at Ballsbridge on 13 August. Perhaps the biggest surprise was that he had only one opponent, a plucky young Belfast competitor named Farrelly. The challenger ran Kiely close for a long time, and it came down to the last event, a half-mile race, an event which Kiely had rarely been known to run. Then, of course, the competitive streak in the Tipperary man came to the fore:

> *Kiely, making the pace a cracker, literally ran the Northern [sic] off his legs, and breasted the tape in the good time, considering all he had*

previously gone through, of 2 min 14 sec. Farrelly did not finish. This left Kiely the winner by 29 points to 27 …[19]

The newspaper also drew attention to Kiely's physique in an explanation as to why the Belfast man came so close to besting him:

Kiely looked fit enough, but he seemed wanting in elasticity, and ran and jumped very stiffly. His devotion to the 56lbs lately has certainly had a prejudicial effect on his jumping. If Kiely is determined to devote his principal energies to heavy weights, he may be prepared for serious deterioration as an all-round athlete. A feature of the contest was the friendliness and good fellowship displayed by both competitors, who in turn came in for warm applause from the spectators …

The stiffness and lack of 'elasticity' in some of Kiely's running and jumping may have been due to a thigh injury received while playing football. In fact, before Kiely was twenty-four, he was also to pull the muscles of his left thigh and strain his arms throwing the 56lb weight. One commentator suggested that all these injuries did was to 'whittle him down to ordinary world beating size'.[20]

After his second all-round title, the ever-competitive Kiely stayed in Dublin long enough to win two more prizes at sports in Naul the following day, and then won three more at Thomastown in Co. Kilkenny in early September. The 1893 GAA championships weren't quite as successful, with Kiely 'only' winning four gold and three silver medals that day.

Kiely was now being compared, more than favourably, to the best that America had to offer. 'Cuchulinn' commented on

Kiely's unique style of throwing the 56lb, swinging it around in a circle at shoulder height rather than over his head – a modern physicist might explain that Kiely's lower but wider arc made for a better fulcrum and hence more power.

A few weeks back the American papers announced that Mitchell [sic] slung the 56lbs, 35ft 9½ ins, but in America the powers that be allow the weight to be 15 or 16 inches long, and the head to be of any shape whatever. The handle is usually triangular, and the long leverage gives a person an immense advantage, so that, everything considered, Kiely's Kilkenny throw must be regarded as the best recognised performance of its kind.[21]

Of course, Mitchel, the 'American' champion, was originally from Emly, Co. Tipperary. The same 'Cuchulinn' sounded a warning to Kiely too, however, advising that he needed to concentrate on fewer events. Kiely must have been tempted to stick at the 56lb, having broken world records, provisionally or otherwise, five times in 1893 alone. The truth was that Kiely detested that event, saying: 'that's a weight no man should ever be allowed to throw'.[22] He was an all-rounder and would remain so.

In late 1893, while winning five prizes at Kilmallock, Kiely also threw the 16lb hammer a distance of 138 feet 11 inches, but this was not later ratified as a record. Even then, Kiely noted it in his scrapbook, along with his 35 feet 5½ inches in the 56lb event, and a victory in the dancing competition![23] The competitive streak was as insatiable as ever.

***

1894 was almost as successful as 1893 in terms of record breaking, though with a significant difference. Whether the footballing injury to his thigh was partially responsible, Kiely was more of a hammer thrower and less of a 56lb weights man that year. He was credited with a total of eight record throws, all of them with the hammer. Three of these were done with a three-and-a-half-foot handle, the others with a four-foot one. (Normally, a four-foot hammer would travel farther than a shorter one, even though both weighed 16lb. This was owing to the greater momentum that can be generated when swinging the weight at the end of a longer handle.) The large number of 'records' was because some sports meetings traditionally used a seven-foot throwing circle, others a nine-foot one, others had a square, or allowed an unlimited run and follow-through, and each variation was deemed a different hammer record, especially by local organisers anxious to improve the status of their event through Kiely's accomplishment.

The Nenagh Sports of 1894 gave a fine insight into the rising stardom of Tom Kiely. Not alone was he the first named athlete in the local paper when it came to previewing the day, but on the day of the sports, a Wednesday, special trains were laid on from Limerick, Thurles, Templemore and as far away as Birr in Co. Offaly (King's County). The boost to local trade was obvious too:

> *In an advertisement this evening, we publish an announcement that the principal drapers of the town have agreed to close their respective establishments on Wednesday next, the day of the institute sports. The decision is a most commendable one, and we are sure the matter has only to be properly put before the grocers and other shopkeepers to induce*

them to follow the example of the drapers. In the meantime, it is to be hoped those ladies who intend to grace the meeting with their presence will make the most of Monday and Tuesday to do their shopping. As to the gentlemen, well, shopping is either a forgotten or an unknown art to them. At least, we never yet heard one admit he knew anything about it.[24]

Newspapers like *The Nenagh Guardian* provided little if any coverage most weeks of any sporting meetings. To have a star of Kiely's ilk in Nenagh year after year had a big impact on changing the level of sports coverage it and other local papers provided as the 1890s progressed. Of his 1894 visit, the *Guardian* reported:

Amongst the most notable features connected with the day's sport were the splendid performances of the world-renowned Irish all-round athlete, T.F. Kiely, the principal one being his extraordinary throw of the 16lb hammer, by which he broke the world's record by 14 inches. On Monday previous, at the championship meeting in Dublin, with the same weighted hammer and a four foot handle he excelled himself and every other competitor by a throw of 131 feet 7 inches, but at Nenagh the handle was only a 3ft 6in one, and he made a throw of 122ft 9in, which beat all previous records.[25]

Kiely, in his scrapbook, recorded all of his 1894 achievements inside the back cover, as before. The list is written in the identical black pen, so it is likely that it was done at one time, perhaps at the end of the year. The figures tally precisely with newspaper accounts of each meeting. In the margin, Kiely recorded that he had won forty-six prizes in 1894, well down from the sixty-seven recorded in 1893. There are a few

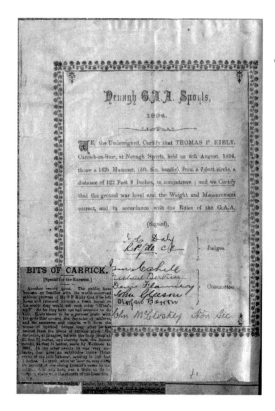

The Nenagh GAA Sports committee certifies Kiely's 1894 record there. (*Kiely Collection, Tipperary Museum of Hidden History*)

explanations. He attended fewer sports meetings in 1894, twelve as opposed to fourteen in 1893. Furthermore, only at Kilmallock, where he won seven prizes, did Kiely win any more than five, suggesting that he had curtailed his entries to a degree. This might be down to his injury, or to not wanting to do too many heavy weights events, or indeed to organisers' concerns that merely mortal athletes would not enter events if they saw people like Kiely competing in and winning everything.[26]

One telling omission from Kiely's own record-keeping comes from Wexford Carnival Sports in July 1894. He may have gone there in part to check out a new mower for the farm, as Wexford was the home of Pierce's and Hearne's works. In his scrapbook, he simply recorded winning three prizes there, with no mention of records. Yet, newspaper accounts show that the prizes included those for winning the high jump (an ebony clock), the 16lb hammer from a seven-foot circle (an aneroid barometer) and the 56lb with unlimited run and follow (a silver biscuit barrel). Another account of the same day tells that:

> Kiely, the all-round champion, was in great form on Tuesday, at Wexford, when he broke two records in the American style of hammer throwing. The hammer weighs 10lbs, with a wire handle, and is thrown with one hand. The record without run or follow previously stood in the name of Condon at 112ft 7in but Kiely did 10ft 4in better than that. From a seven-foot circle Kiely sent the missile 144ft 4in, which is also 9ft 8in better than Condon's previous record for the event ...[27]

That Kiely did not note these 'American style' experiments with wire-handled hammers speaks volumes. As the 1890s progressed, however, wire-handled hammers became increasingly common, especially in America but eventually in Ireland too. The American version also had triangular handles, helping to give maximum rotation when the 'hammer' was swung prior to throwing. Kiely would ultimately give wire-handled hammers their place in his repertoire. However, their introduction and development in America, alongside improvements in diet, training methods and increasing specialisation in one event by US-based throwers, explained why hammer records after the late 1890s went far beyond what Kiely recorded in his heyday.

Among other triumphs in 1894, Kiely won his third all-round championship of Ireland at Ballsbridge that August, being so comfortably ahead that he did not bother to run the final event, the half-mile race. He had won another three prizes just the day before, at the Dublin United Trades Sports. As for Ballsbridge, *Sport* announced the first ever winner of three titles in a row:

> *The All-round championship [IAAA] which was decided on Monday was again won by T. F. Kiely, whose repetition of last year's performance was accomplished in the face of the strongest opposition that has hitherto done battle for the proud title. But the Carrick-on-Suir man was more than a match for their all, and is to be heartily congratulated on his success … This certainly is a great day's work for an athlete even of Kiely's calibre, and was rendered all the harder by the very strong character of those opposed to him, who made him fight for every event as if upon it depended his ultimate success.*[28]

In winning the title, Kiely's hammer reached 131 feet 7 inches from a seven-foot circle, which was deemed a world record. There were only seven events in all on the programme.[29] The long jump, which Kiely also won, saw the use of a take-off board for one of the first times in Irish athletics. Kiely adapted to the board with ease, while other athletes were very cautious about the board, fearing that their spikes would get stuck in it.[30] Kiely always claimed that he did no intensive physical training, but his mastery of technical events was quite remarkable. Many years later, Peter O'Connor wrote of how his own series of breaking world long jump records in 1900–01 was inspired in no small measure by advice from Kiely:

> *Mr Walsh [Edward J. Walsh of the IAAA] ... published an article in* Sport, *describing my jumping ability and predicting that with proper training from a 'board take off', barring accidents, I would someday make a World's Record. He wrote me specially and got Mr Tom Kiely, one of the world's finest all-round athletes, then unknown to me, to also write giving me dimensions of 'board take-off', how to train in order to secure more speed and accuracy ...*[31]

Kiely was neither light nor lithesome enough to be a long jumper of Peter O'Connor's twenty-four-foot class ultimately, but his advice on technique was invaluable. Funnily enough, Kiely also advised O'Connor to give up other forms of jumping and to concentrate on the long jump alone when he wrote to him; a case of pots calling kettles names, it seems, for Kiely was constantly criticised for not specialising in fewer events.

Back in south Tipperary, the Carrick-on-Suir notes in the *Nationalist* recorded Kiely's victory in the all-round with: 'Bravo, good old Tom. Carrick is proud of you, and justly so. On his arrival [in Carrick-on-Suir] he was the recipient of hearty congratulations from all sides and well he deserved them.'[32] The epithet 'good old Tom' is attached to a twenty-four-year-old on this occasion. The first time, noted during the research for this book, when Kiely was referred to as 'Ireland's champion' or the equivalent was in the Carrick-on-Suir notes in the *Nationalist* in late 1893. By the end of 1894, the phrase 'Erin's Champion' was being attributed to 'good old

Tom' more and more. Indeed, often he was known simply as 'the Champion'.

Kiely missed the GAA championships on 21 October 1894. This is difficult to explain, as he competed elsewhere both before and after the GAA championships, so injury can hardly have been the reason. He broke yet another hammer record at Kildorrery, Co. Cork on 8 October, throwing just under 124 feet with a three-and-a-half-foot handle. He threw a four-foot hammer 139 feet 1 inch at Shanballymore, also in Cork, on 12 November, even 'whilst in very bad form as after travelling over 90 miles he had no time to put on his athletic costume, so he only let his braces drop and accomplished this feet'.[33] The fact that six inches of difference in the handle length contributed to 15 feet in throw distance is unsurprising, as any modern hammer thrower will testify. Modern throwers hold the hammer handle literally with their fingertips in order to gain maximum handle length and hence power.[34]

***

By 1895, there was a little less coverage of Kiely in the national and local newspaper headlines. One reason is that he became an international competitor this year, going to his first AAA championship in England and also captaining the first Irish international athletics team in its match against Scotland. These departures will be discussed in coming chapters. Kiely also suffered a bout of illness at the height of the athletics season in 1895 – he was reported in late August to have 'not been feeling well for some time past' and was still 'decidedly off colour' three weeks later.[35] On the latter occasion, he still won five events at the sports in Deerpark.

With Grangemockler football team now well and truly revived, Kiely was again 'distracted', so to speak, from athletics by his commitments to the parish team. Several of the team's matches occurred when he wasn't too busy with farming, at least. Even after his injury in 1893, Kiely was again starring in February 1894, with one newspaper account suggesting that he was easily the most dominant player on the field against De La Salle (Waterford) in a friendly match at Carrick-on-Suir.[36]

Commitment to his GAA club led Kiely to more involvement than his health would have warranted in 1895. In the height of August, even though unwell, he played championship football to great acclaim against nearby rivals Kilcash: 'The reappearance of T.F. Kiely and M. Lyons in the Grangemockler ranks goes to prove that this once famous team mean business this season ... Lyons, Walsh and Kiely repeatedly sent the leather through the posts ...'.[37]

On another occasion, Kiely used his influence with the Tipperary GAA board:

> [A] letter was read from Mr T.F. Keily [sic], Carrick-on-Suir, suggesting that some of the championship matches should be played on Mr Davin's ground at Carrick, and adding that they could derive a revenue from such a course, as the ground in question was properly enclosed, and in every [way] adapted for sporting purposes. The council very much approved of Mr Keily's suggestion, and it was agreed that some of the matches should be played on Mr Davin's enclosure ...[38]

This suggested a solution to a difficulty that many GAA venues had. Without proper fencing around them, it was impossible to charge spectators for entry, and often very difficult to prevent side-line encroachments, or fights. Kiely's letter would bring more games to the Davins' venue, but his aim was also a genuine concern to see the GAA grow and flourish. The association had been good to him and he was eager to give back to it. He refereed matches at Deerpark quite regularly, for example, including a hurling match between Pilltown and Mooncoin when 'Mr Kiely, the all-round champion, threw in the ball at three o'clock, and the slashing began '.[39]

On another occasion, Kiely delayed the start of a match at Deerpark, between Clonmel and Waterford, for an hour and a half because of a continuous downpour.[40] As testimony to the quality of the Deerpark venue, there was also a Co. Waterford football final played there, when: 'Mr T.F. Kiely discharged the duties of referee to everybody's satisfaction, whilst the order maintained during the match was very fair.'[41] Perhaps modern refereeing could do with a few more world-class weight throwers acting in that capacity.

The degree to which the work of Kiely and others had helped to revive the GAA is shown in the report of the association's honorary secretary to the Central Council. Mr Blake referred to the number of clubs in Tipperary specifically being up from twelve in 1894 to thirty-two in 1895. There were new financial pressures as a result, but these were welcome ones. He spoke too of how:

> 70 athletic meetings had been held ... Your Council ... successfully carried out every athletic championship of the Gaelic programme viz. 24, as against 12 in 1894 – a thing unprecedented since 1888 ... No less than 91 gold and 62 silver medals had been awarded

during the year, the sum of £155 19s 5d being expended on medals and prizes, as against £88 2s 6d in 1894 … while in athletic line no less than fourteen world's records fell to the share of the Gaelic athletes (applause).[42]

In 1895, Kiely broke 'only' half a dozen records, according to newspaper accounts. His six prizes at Queen's College Sports included the hammer championship of Ireland, while his five prizes at the IAAA championships included a new hammer record of 133 feet 7 inches. By the end of the year, Kiely's hammer mark had reached 140 feet 7½ inches, thanks to a mighty throw at Dungarvan. Once again, the level of probity and scrutiny required to have this record ratified by the GAA Council was impressive:

An application for a record with the 16lb hammer (4 feet overall), unlimited run and follow, of 140 feet 7 ½ inches at Dungarvan sports, was made by Mr T.F. Kiely. Certificates were handed in by Mr Beary, borough surveyor, Dungarvan; Mr Fraher, hon sec; Mr Barry, judge; Mr Power, Ballywalter, handicapper, testifying to the correctness of the measurements, the size and exact weight of the hammer, and to the fact that the throw was against a rise of 12 inches in the ground. The testimony being deemed in every way satisfactory by the Committee unanimously granted the record, which is a world's record for 16lb hammer, iron head, wood handle, 4 feet overall, with unlimited run and follow.[43]

Kiely also travelled to sports at Thomastown (winning three prizes), Lismore (four) and Nenagh (six). He received a handwritten note of thanks from the Nenagh organisers in 1895:

*Proposed by Mr Joseph Gleeson, Seconded by Mr Michl. [sic] Delany.
'That the Committee of the Nenagh Literary Institute Athletic Sports
beg to return their sincere thanks to Mr T.F. Kiely the Champion
All-round Athlete of Ireland for his kindness in attending at their
Sports year after year and for the deep interest he has always taken in
promoting the welfare and working of the meetings.*[44]

Kiely also made it to Tipperary Sports in 1895, and almost
broke another record: 'The most notable performance of the day
was T.F. Kiely's throw of the 56lbs [unlimited run and follow],
which would have been a world's record if it were not for the
fact that the weight, when tested, was found to be an ounce or
so light'. This did not deter Kiely, who still recorded the 36 feet
7 inches achieved with the dreaded weight as a record in his
own annotated scrapbook.[45]

Perhaps the one big gap in Kiely's athletic exploits during
1895 was his failure to defend his all-round title. The GAA and
IAAA were at this stage collaborating very positively on record-
keeping and general rules, and it was the GAA that organised
the 1895 championships – the IAAA abandoned it due to poor
attendance at the previous year's event. The 1895 championship
was even staged in Clonmel, and it was anticipated the week
before that Kiely would be there.[46] However, as mentioned
earlier, he was suffering from injury or illness when the day
came and was only a spectator in the company of Maurice and
Pat Davin. He had also been unable to compete at the GAA
national championships the previous month.[47] An interesting
outcome of the IAAA abandoning the all-round championship
was the fact that Kiely never had to return the belt he had held
from 1892. He never even bothered to get his third victory

engraved on it, as can be seen at Tipperary Museum of Hidden History, with his name inscribed only for 1892 and 1893.

According to contemporary newspaper accounts, Kiely had broken over twenty national or world records in hammer or 56lb throwing between 1893 and 1895. As will be shown in the coming chapters, his fame and success also spread far beyond Ireland from 1895 onwards, particularly to England and Scotland. Exploits in those lands would only enhance Kiely as a national hero and, indeed, as 'Erin's Champion'.

Kiely at an unidentified championship, probably in Britain, around 1900, throwing the wire-handled hammer. Note that his rotation is so rapid that the camera picked out only his standing foot with clarity.
(*From the collection of Tom Hunt, original source unidentified*)

CHAPTER 4

THE HAMMER OF
THE SCOTS

The world's first international athletics match took place at Lansdowne Road, Dublin in 1875, when Tom Kiely was just coming up to his sixth birthday. Ireland took on England that day, with Maurice Davin taking a starring role, not only in winning the shot put for Ireland, but also in some of the more unusual moments from the day. At one point, he single-handedly carried three of the heaviest members of the English team down the field, in response to a challenge.[1] The same day, he also supposedly sawed two and a half feet off an Englishman's wooden hammer handle to make it comply with Irish 'standards'.[2] There was a return match the following year, at Stamford Bridge, London, but thereafter the matches ceased.

One of the ground-breaking sporting initiatives that Kiely played a key role in was the establishment of the world's first series of international contests in athletics: the Ireland v Scotland internationals. While team sports like rugby and association football were established at international level in the 1870s, between 1877 and 1895 any moves towards international competition in athletics had been taken by individual athletes or clubs, not by national athletic associations. For example, when Irish athletes competed in championships like the English Amateur Athletic Association's (the 'AAAs'), they did so essentially as individuals, even though some may have worn the emblems of an Irish association or club.

In terms of identifying the first international between athletic clubs, some historians point to the 1895 contests organised between the New York Athletic Club (NYAC) and a London Athletic Club selection. At the time, it was even anticipated in some quarters that Kiely and a few other Irish athletes might 'guest' for the London club. The newspaper *Sport* reported that:

> [*The*] *list includes Horgan, Kiely and Ryan but ... it is hardly likely that they will go. Perhaps one might, but it is not a point about which there is likely to be any great enthusiasm in Irish circles.*[3]

One issue at stake was a desire not to have Irishmen compete on a team that would be essentially portrayed as an English one. Another concern was not to have Irish athletes compete against a NYAC team that itself had a fair smattering of Irish-born athletes in it. In the end, there was no Kiely or other Irish athlete in the London team, and the New Yorkers triumphed easily. The correspondent in *Sport* gushed about the 'American' victory, in which six of the eleven events were won by athletes with Irish backgrounds.[4]

Even considering the New York v London contest an international one, there is no questioning that a full two months before that took place, 'Ireland' had beaten 'Scotland'. This was an eleven-event international contest at Celtic Park, the home of Glasgow Celtic FC, with Kiely centre stage on the Irish team.

This idea was first mooted by the IAAA in 1891.[5] Much of the credit for getting it off the ground went to the efforts and persuasiveness of Irish athlete Tom Donovan, a former Irish all-round champion. Donovan had represented Queen's College Cork in earlier years but by 1895 was studying medicine at Edinburgh University.[6]

This contest was a chance for athletes to represent their nations, both of which were politically part of the United Kingdom. However, both nations had independent identities and proud athletic traditions. One Irish athlete who later refused to represent the London Athletic Club against New York stated that if he competed again in an international contest it would be 'in the colours that won in Glasgow'.[7] There would be no question of representing a 'foreign' team in this battle between what many saw as teams of 'brother' Celts. *The Scottish Referee* caught the moment admirably:

> *Tomorrow at Celtic Park a new departure will be taken in the athletic world, and the first international athletic contest ever held will be* un fait accompli. *That it may be the first of a lengthy series of similar contests between the Thistle and the Shamrock is the fervent wish of all lovers of true athletics. Into contests such as these there is imported no feeling of pot-hunting; selfish cupidity for cups is sunk, and every man strives to do his level best for his country. The very fact of being a representative of the nation's honour is inducement enough to strive for, and* propatria mori, *or put into plain English, 'I'll run till I drop.'*[8]

The Irish team was organised by the IAAA, and the GAA had

nothing to do with its organisation, selection or funding. It is not clear whether the Irish team had a nominated 'captain' in 1895, but it is believed that Kiely routinely served as captain of the IAAA team.[9] He must have been hugely attracted by the prospect of this international contest, having not yet competed abroad.

With great excitement and pride, Kiely and his colleagues

Ireland v Scotland at Belfast, 1900. Kiely is in the front row, third from the left. Others include Denis Horgan, centre of the front row with the large shamrock, Denis Carey two to the reader's right of Horgan, and Peter O'Connor the long jumper, fifth from left in the second row. (*Kiely Collection, Tipperary Museum of Hidden History, original photo taken by Allison's, Belfast*)

arrived at the Alexandra Hotel in Bath Street, Glasgow, early the day before their contest with the Scots. The weather was surprisingly warm and a great carnival was underway in Glasgow that weekend. The Irish team remained relatively relaxed in their preparations. The local newspaper reported that they had (apparently) come over with no intention of beating

Scotland and 'had got slightly acclimatised, for they were here all day on Friday supping ice cream just to keep them cool'.[10]

The first almost legendary impact of Kiely in the Ireland–Scotland contest came in the long jump. Many accounts of this performance exist, such as:

> *Memories cluster round an athletic meeting in Glasgow, in 1895, between Ireland and Scotland. Points were equal on both sides, and one event – the long jump – remained for decision. Ireland relied on a Limerick man to save the day; he was beaten, and the Scots were jubilant, Tom Kiely was an onlooker; so far, he had taken no part in the contest. But with the 'shamrock' trampled upon, his Tipperary heart throbbed, the blood quickened in his veins, and he felt it his duty to throw off the coat – and that was all he threw off – and take a jump. His figures were marvellous, the Scot was defeated, and away to the listening hills went an Irish cheer for the standard-bearer of 'Knocknagow'.*[11]

Another angle on this story suggests that Kiely was already in the changing rooms, thinking he was done for the day, when the call went out to come and win the long jump for Ireland:

> *Kiely's last minute long-jump heroics, which won the title for Ireland, made him a legend. With the dual meet tied at five wins apiece and with Scottish jumpers leading in the final event, Irish officials appealed to Kiely who was finished for the day and dressing in his tent. Rushing to the event without even lacing his shoes, Tom took one desperate leap, winning the event and the day for Ireland. Of such stuff Tom Kiely was made.*[12]

These two versions of the story are typical of the hero worship that attached to Kiely, including the allusion to *Knocknagow*, the 'desperate' leap and the dramatic win with open shoelaces. The reality may not have been quite so amazing on the ground – the newspapers printed in Scotland the day before the contest in 1895 showed that Kiely had always been entered for the long jump, so his participation wasn't as 'out of the blue' as some accounts suggest. He was regarded as a better hop-step-and-jump performer, in fact, but this event was not on the Scotland v Ireland programme.

Coming to the long jump 'cold' in 1895, Kiely not only won it with that single jump, but also broke the Scottish record, or what would today be known as the 'all-comers' record'. The leap of 22 feet 2½ inches was one of Kiely's best ever, all the more remarkable in the circumstances described above and barely one foot short of the then world record.

Although the record itself was broken by Ireland's Walter Newburn just two years later in Edinburgh, Kiely's record, specifically for a long jump with a take-off from grass, lasted a very long time indeed in Scotland.[13] A grass take-off meant that not only was the run-up on grass, but there was no take-off board either. Kiely had become quite an expert on board take-offs, as seen previously when Peter O'Connor turned to him for advice. This Glasgow distance would also have been enough to win the long jump title at the inaugural Olympic Games in Athens the following April, had he been there.

Kiely was a very good hurdler and it was no surprise that he went on to represent Ireland five times in subsequent events against Scotland. Competing against many who were specialist hurdlers, it is quite impressive that he won the race on two occasions, and almost won a third into the bargain.

He won in 1898 and again in 1902, both times at Ballsbridge.

In the hurdles of 1898, for example, Kiely was behind for most of the race, until Stronach of Scotland struck the final hurdle and fell. This allowed the Tipperary man to win in a very respectable time of 16⅘ seconds, and by 2 yards from the other Irish hurdler-cum-weight thrower, Denis Carey.[14] In 1902, an Irish commentator was moved to suggest that Kiely never really trained adequately for events like the hurdles, and was only entered for the event at all because Denis Carey was injured. Yet Kiely won again:

> *Now he gets a fortnight's notice, and he trains for the Hurdles; then he turns up and beats our Highland brethren and P. Harding who beat him at the [Irish] Championship.*[15]

Even when not winning, Kiely impressed in 1901 too. Kiely was by then hurdling in what *Sport* called the 'American style'. This was probably based on Alvin Kraenzlein's 'leg-extended' style, which is essentially still the norm in hurdling, even though injuries are much less likely over modern, weight-balanced hurdles than was the case with the 'solid' variety around 1901. Despite Kiely apparently not concentrating much on hurdling prior to the day:

> *... in the face of his training for weight throwing he ran so fast in the hurdles that Stronach [the Scot] could only beat him by a yard in 16⅗ secs, and that, too, after the Carrick-on-Suir man had almost fallen half-way through the contest.*[16]

Stronach's winning time, and Kiely's 16⅘ seconds in 1898,

were certainly world-class times. Stronach himself was a multiple Scottish champion, a three-time English AAA champion in the hurdles, and a Scottish rugby international. He was to hold the Scottish record in the hurdles for forty-three years. (With metric measurements becoming the norm in Europe, note that the 120 yards hurdles was less than one foot or 30 centimetres shorter than 110 metres.) These 1898 times of Stronach and Kiely would have won the Olympic Games title in 1896 and been close enough to medals in 1904 and at the Intercalated Games of 1906 in Athens too. Those events were run by specialist 110 metres hurdlers, not all-round athletes, so for Kiely to achieve times like that while not even training for the event is quite incredible.[17]

Of course, Kiely's specialism, in so far as he had one, was the hammer. True, he competed in some of the Ireland v Scotland shot put events too, but never with any serious intent, being happy to leave the main responsibility in the shot to his great rival from Banteer, Denis Horgan.

The hammer, as was mentioned in earlier chapters, was in a state of particular chaos when the Ireland–Scotland matches began in 1895. In the USA, the wire-handled hammer was increasingly popular and threatened to eclipse the traditional wooden-shafted hammer used in the British Isles. Even in the Ireland–Scotland context, there were challenges, as the Scots traditionally threw the hammer from a standing position, while the Irish threw it from a circle and following at least two pivots. It was eventually agreed that the Scottish style would be the accepted norm when the event was staged in Scotland, and the Irish style in Ireland the following year. In these circumstances, it was predicted that Kiely would have difficulties in 1895 at Celtic Park:

As the hammer is to be thrown in Scotch style from a fixed mark without a turn, the conditions are naturally favourable to our stalwarts; and good man as Kiely is in the turning business, I do not think he will beat our men at their own game.[18]

Kiely was not very happy to have to adjust to this static style of hammer throwing. The Scottish press gave an interesting insight into his personality, normally so relaxed but steely when it came to competition:

Kiely, an excitable sort of boy and just the kind of man to crack a skull at Enniscorthy or Donnybrook, raised a hubbub about the Scottish style. Kiely would have it his way, and he would throw his own hammer, and he would. 'Tut, tut, man, dear,' said cheery-going [Denis] Horgan; 'just throw it and say no more about it.' Kiely did as he was bid, and as the Scotch officials agreed to allow him his own hammer, the Irish conceded the style.[19]

Sure enough, despite leading for much of the hammer contest, Kiely was beaten by the Scot, Ross, by just 6 inches. The distances were barely over 100 feet, showing how much Kiely's talent relied not just on physical strength but on good technique, which he was unable to use in Glasgow. According to *The Scottish Referee*:

When Ross ... threw 101 feet 6 inches Scotland won the event, Kiely stopping at six inches less, but still vowing he could do better. Given a trial with his own way, Kiely cleared the ring in a trice, very nearly hitting the press-house, and demolishing two bobbies [i.e. policemen] as the hammer flew away at a tangent to the tune of 142 feet 3 inches. 'What do you think of that now?' said Kiely, so pleased that he was about to do it over again. He only desisted on the McCarthy [who appears to have been an Irish 'character' living in Glasgow] remarking that he 'didn't want his wife to be a widdy [widow]'.

Kiely missed the contest in 1896, but when he returned to Scotland in 1897, to Edinburgh, it had been accepted that the Irish style would be the standard hammer-throwing style in Scottish athletics too – although the Highland Games persisted with the traditional Scottish 'standing' throw. The Scots knew what they were in for, and one newspaper joked beforehand:

It is not the case that the SAAA [Scottish Amateur Athletic Association] have been asked by the police authorities to erect a shield in front of Sir Walter's Monument [Sir Walter Scott monument in the centre of Edinburgh] in case Kiely's hammer throw might hit the Bride of Lammermoor or the Fair Maid of Perth.[20]

This time, Kiely won by over 25 feet:

Attention was chiefly directed to the Irishman, Kiely, his reputation as a hammer thrower being widespread. His style was easy, and he let the hammer away beautifully, a fact which the spectators did not fail to notice. Every throw was head and shoulders above those of his fellows, and he easily beat Scotland's best man, McIntosh. His effort of 137ft was 20ft above [the] Scottish record.[21]

In the 1898 hammer event at Ballsbridge, there was drama aplenty when Kiely's first throw saw the head of the hammer come off and land with force very close to a company of Scottish pipers. His winning throw of 146 feet 10 inches, from a nine-foot circle, was a new Irish record, i.e. a record set in Ireland, as the term meant in Kiely's day. This was only 2 inches shorter than the world record throw of John Flanagan in London two years before. However, now that Flanagan was in the USA, employing new training methods and equipment, the Limerick man's best was already at 158 feet, a distance that Kiely was destined never to reach as he persisted with his focus on multiple events.[22]

The first overall Scottish victory in the annual contest came in 1899, amid some controversy because there seemed to be a mismeasurement of one of the jumps. The Irish sensed a mistake had been made but did not object. Kiely won the hammer again, with ease, and one Scottish report spoke of the really high quality of the athletics, in front of 7,000 spectators:

> *A study of the performances shows how really excellent these men are. Indeed, it is questionable whether at the present moment even England could produce a team of athletes who would beat either or both of these teams.*[23]

In 1900, back in Ballsbridge, the Irish won again with Kiely more than comfortable in the hammer. Following his win in Scotland in 1901, the commentator in *Sport* was moved to write:

> *Kiely is of course* facile princeps *with the hammer, and he gave his*

admirers (and they are legion) one more taste of his quality, as he, as stated earlier, put up new Scotch figures with his favourite instrument, the 16lb hammer, doing 145 feet 4 in. It would seem almost foolish to try to write or say anything new about Tom Kiely, but he is simply a wonder ...[24]

The Latin term *facile princeps* essentially means 'natural leader', yet another testament to Kiely's abilities. The Scots too continued to be amazed by Kiely in 1901:

'Whiroo, Hurroo!' and such like exclamations burst from the crowd as J. F. Keily [sic] whirled the 16lb hammer through space, to the wonderment of the beholder, and to the dismay of those within the arena, who gave the Irish giant a very wide berth. He whirled the toy like a twig, and, by covering no less than 145ft 4in, thus shares with O'Connor [i.e. in the long jump] the honour of making one of the two records. This beat his previous record of 141ft 4in, made in 1899.[25]

Kiely made it six hammer wins in a row against Scotland at Ballsbridge in 1902, and then, in 1903, came the day when he was finally beaten. *The Scottish Referee* decided to caption the story of Kiely's defeat with the phrase 'A Giant Overthrown'. Tom Nicholson, the Scot who beat Kiely in 1903, would go very close to an Olympic medal in the hammer at the London Olympics of 1908. He was also a bit like Kiely in that he was a farmer and played shinty, the Scottish equivalent of hurling. He had been gaining on the Tipperary man's distances for a number of years prior to the win in Edinburgh and went through several years unbeaten in the event after 1903 too.

There is no doubt that Kiely's performances in the annual contest had served as repeated lessons in hammer throwing for the Scots. They adopted the Irish throwing style, seeing the benefits of rotating and momentum, and moved to the wire-handled hammer as Kiely had done. Appropriately, when Nicholson did beat Kiely, he did it with Kiely's own hammer:

> *T. R. Nicholson was rather upset when his wire hammer handle gave way. Kiely frankly obliged with his, and then had the chagrin to see the noble Scot defeat him and create a new record ... Nicholson's throw of 149 ft. 4in. established a new record for Scotland, and it is the best throw made so far in this match since it was instituted in 1895. He is the first Scot, too, who has won this event since the Irish style of throw was adopted in 1896. T. F. Kiely has held the throw since 1897 consecutively, so that there must be a spice of chagrin in his overthrow, especially since Nicholson, owing to the handle of his own hammer giving way, was forced to throw with Kiely's.* [26]

There is no suggestion anywhere that the fallen giant did anything but applaud his conqueror. Kiely was a fierce competitor, as already seen in many instances, but was never a sore loser when beaten fairly and squarely, as he was here. In fact, the two throws that Nicholson did with Kiely's hammer were each farther than the Tipperary man had managed, and Kiely eventually lost by over 9 feet.[27] It was ironic that the hammer thrown to beat Kiely that day had been brought by Kiely himself all the way from Ballyneill to Edinburgh.

The 1903 contest against Scotland was to be Kiely's last.[28] As he reflected on reaching the age of Christ (thirty-three), so to speak, he may well have considered that it was time to give up his athletics career. He had increasing responsibilities

The Ireland and Scotland teams in Edinburgh, 1903. Kiely is fifth from the right at the back. (*Courtesy of Scottish Athletics*)

at home and a younger brother, Larry, who was showing real promise and could benefit from his coaching and guidance. He also had committed, his family believe, to a contract to build a cottage in Ballyneill – he regularly did some building work when the cattle dealing and athletics gave him time.[29]

In the end, Kiely was not to compete again in the Ireland v Scotland matches. His contribution to this international series may never have had as dramatic a moment as the day Maurice Davin carried three English heavyweights down the field at Lansdowne Road or sawed off the handle of the Englishman's hammer. However, few could disagree that the cumulative impact of Kiely's performances had a great impact on not only Irish athletics but also the modernisation of athletics in Scotland.

This Scottish adventure was not necessarily the easiest for Kiely to undertake, in practical terms, and it is testament to his steely commitment that he participated in the event so many times. He would eventually represent Ireland five times on Scottish soil, once in Belfast and another three times in Ballsbridge, Dublin. Ballyneill was a long way from all of them. Each contest meant days away from the family farm and cattle dealing, for which he took increasing responsibility as the 1890s progressed. An indication of Kiely's desire to compete in this international contest was retold shortly after his death:

> Early on the morning of the Ireland–Scotland International of 1897 he accidentally cut his wrist with a sharp knife and the blood spurted. With thumb pressed down on the wound to staunch the flow, he waited an hour on the roadside for a doctor who passed daily. When the doctor treated it, Tom made straight for the train [for Ballsbridge].[30]

The date given in this story cannot have been correct as the 1897 contest was held in Scotland, not Dublin. Nonetheless, it demonstrates Kiely's toughness and determination. He would miss only one of the first nine contests, which was almost certainly because of injury, in 1896. Kiely was also made a vice-president of the GAA between 1896 and 1898, and yet never refused to turn out for the IAAA against Scotland in subsequent fixtures. His stature was such that he continued to compete at both the GAA and IAAA championships, and no one deigned to criticise his equanimity.

Kiely's record in Ireland v Scotland internationals 1895–1903[31]

Date and Venue	Result	Event	Kiely's Position	Time/ Distance
20 July 1895 Glasgow	Ireland 6–5	120 Yards Hurdles	3rd	No time recorded
		Long Jump	1st	22 feet 2½ inches (Scottish record)
		High Jump	4th	No height recorded
		Shot Put	3rd	No mark recorded
		Hammer	2nd	100 feet 6 inches
18 July 1896 Ballsbridge	Ireland 7–4		Did not compete	
17 July 1897 Edinburgh	Ireland 7–4	Shot Put	3rd	No mark recorded
		Hammer	1st	137 feet 1 inch (Scottish record)
16 July 1898 Ballsbridge	Ireland 9–2	120 Yards Hurdles	1st	16⅘ seconds

Date and Venue	Result	Event	Kiely's Position	Time/ Distance
		Shot Put	3rd	No mark recorded
		Hammer	1st	146 feet 10 inches
15 July 1899 Edinburgh	Scotland 6–5	Hammer	1st	141 feet 4 inches (Scottish record)
30 June 1900 Belfast	Ireland 7–4	120 Yards Hurdles	4th	No time recorded
		Shot Put	2nd	40 feet
		Hammer	1st	143 feet 6 inches
29 June 1901 Glasgow	Scotland 6–5	120 Yards Hurdles	3rd	No time recorded
		Hammer	1st	145 feet 4 inches
19 July 1902 Ballsbridge	Ireland 9–2	120 Yards Hurdles	1st	17 seconds
		Hammer	1st	139 feet 2 inches
18 July 1903 Edinburgh	Scotland 7–4	Hammer	2nd	140 feet

CHAPTER 5

ADVENTURES IN ENGLAND

With Tom Kiely at the peak of his fame by the age of twenty-five, it was all very well to be able to beat everyone in Ireland, but the real test, he knew, would be to take on the best that Britain, and specifically England, had to offer. There was a sense that the rewards there could be greater too. One Irish athlete in 1895 noted that while entry fees were 'exorbitant' in Ireland, the quality of prizes available at even regional sports meetings in England was far better than most of the prizes available at Irish meetings. According to this athlete, sometimes the value of what was on offer in Ireland was not much more than six shillings.[1]

Kiely was hardly attracted to competition in England by the prizes alone. After all, the logistics of bringing home things like a bedroom suite or an American organ, all of which were mentioned as prizes in the above letter, would have often been impossible. He did, on one occasion, manage to win and bring home a brass bedstead from a cross-channel victory, though relatives have no idea how he managed that. It was given to his brother Larry, who slept beneath it most of his life.[2] On a more serious note, the English Amateur Athletic Association championships (the AAAs) were long-regarded as the top competition in world athletics. It was inevitable that 'Erin's Champion' would want to add to his laurels there as these championships had attracted Ireland's best for many years, including the Davin brothers.[3]

Given that the first AAA championships that Kiely attended were at Stamford Bridge in London, there was a family reason for making the trip too. By the mid-1890s his sister Nell had joined the Convent of Jesus and Mary in Willesden, London as Sister Benignus. Tom likely combined the AAAs with a trip to see her or maybe even to help her settle in north London. Tom is also known to have stayed in the convent's guest suite during subsequent London visits.[4]

Kiely did reasonably well in his AAA debut at Stamford Bridge in 1895, finishing second in the hammer to Corkman William 'Jumbo' Barry who, by then, was a doctor based in Southport. Kiely also appears to have competed in the long jump, though he did not register a mark.[5] The British press was very aware of the quality of Irish athletics and took special notice of the Irishmen winning English titles.[6] Most British newspapers listed both Denis Horgan and Kiely as representing the Irish Amateur Athletic Association. This makes sense because it was the IAAA rather than the GAA that was recognised by the AAA in England, though another newspaper curiously listed Horgan as representing 'Belfast'.[7]

Kiely was not allowed to use the hammer that he'd brought with him to Stamford Bridge. AAA officials, including a vice president and the captain of the AAA, ruled that it had a lead core inside an iron shell. Afterwards, rumours that Kiely had been hard done by circulated in a periodical called *Pastime* and were subsequently carried in Ireland by *Sport*. Kiely was then dragged into a controversy as Barry, the victor at Stamford

Bridge, felt insulted by the insinuation and demanded an apology from the publishers. His letter was printed in *Sport*, as part of its apology:

> *Dear Sir … It is not true that Kiely, in order to comply with the rule, came without his hammer. His hammer, which he produced, could not be used in the competition, it having an iron head filled with lead. If we had been permitted by the AAA the use of such, it is quite probable that Kiely may have justified your expectations of doing a wonderful throw, beating the record by many feet but, for my own part, I can confidently express my belief of increasing it by yards under the same conditions.*[8]

Barry offered to compete again, against Kiely, anywhere and at any time of the latter's choosing, but, perhaps wisely, there is no record of a response from Kiely. Barry's ire was directed against the publishers, and not against Kiely. There is also no question that technical developments in the USA were passing them all out rapidly anyway. Barry himself suggested that the hammer that James Mitchel used in the USA, a lead-headed one with a wire handle and a cross bar grip, had a twenty-foot advantage over the English or Irish ones.[9]

Kiely missed the AAAs in 1896, probably because he had another commitment in London that year, but from 1897 until 1902 he competed at every AAA hammer championship. The AAAs had no all-round competition; the first decathlon would not be held until 1928. There was no triple jump or 56lb event at the AAAs in Kiely's day either. Accordingly, his all-round abilities were not well suited to the AAAs, and he seems to have decided from the outset that trying to compete in several weights events at that level in one day was impossible. Denis Horgan made a similar decision but would go on to win a huge haul of thirteen AAA titles, in the shot put. In fact, outside of five hammer titles, Kiely's only other AAA medal was to be for second place in the hurdles in 1898.[10]

The other commitment that brought Kiely to England in 1896 was a GAA one. The GAA brought off a very successful Irish sports event at Stamford Bridge in April. It was very early in the season for good athletic performances, which probably explains why Kiely was able to win the long jump with a mediocre jump of under 20 feet.

There is no record of Kiely taking part in any of the weight-throwing events on the day and, in all honesty, if he had he would probably have lost out to the emerging giant of hammer throwing, John Flanagan. Unlike Kiely, Flanagan had specialised increasingly and, shortly after Stamford Bridge, he left to join the New York Athletic Club, where his hammer throwing advanced to an amazing level. One reporter wrote:

If the Gaelic Tournament were memorable for nothing else, it will long be referred to in world-wide sporting circles with keen interest, for J. Flanagan of Kilmallock beat his own world's record by more than eight feet. Flanagan threw the hammer several times, and on each occasion his style and attitude were watched with great attention by the public. It was a fine sight indeed, Flanagan being in the peak of condition and a perfect type of graceful muscular manhood. The distance of the throw was 166 feet 4 inches. Immediately after Flanagan's great feat the hammer was conveyed to one of the private rooms on the ground and weighed and measured in the presence of the Press. It turned the scales at 16 lbs exactly and measured a hair's breadth 3 feet 11½ inches.

> *This event was followed by the throwing from the nine-foot circle, and again a world's record was broken – that of T.F. Kiely's – the length of the throw being 147 ft. It was won by Flanagan. The splendid feats had enthused the spectators …*[11]

This could well have been the day that Kiely realised he was never going to match Flanagan again in the hammer. Of course, he could have beaten Flanagan in almost any other event on an athletics programme. Flanagan was joint second in the long jump to Kiely, in fact, but this day showed that the new specialist thrower, complete with wire-handled hammer, had arrived. Pat Davin discussed a lot of the developments taking place in athletics around this time, including in hammer throwing. He wrote:

> *The head of the hammer, formerly of iron or metal, was discarded in favour of lead, but the head of the modern American hammer, like the 16lbs shot, is now made of brass, and the handle attachment is fitted with ball-bearings. It bears about the same comparison to the old hammer as the motor bicycle bears to the 'bone-shaker' of sixty or seventy years ago …*[12]

After the athletics that day, Flanagan and Kiely took part in two GAA matches. In Gaelic football, a team representing Ireland beat a London selection by 3–15 to 0–3. Flanagan played in goal for London, presumably resting after his hammer-throwing exertions, while Kiely was at number 13 for Ireland. There was also a hurling match between Munster and Leinster, where the teams wore uniforms of blue and green respectively and had provincial crests in gold embroidery displayed on their jerseys. Both Kiely and Flanagan played in this, for Munster, in what seems to have been the first ever inter-provincial hurling match. Flanagan obviously had his second wind, as reports suggest he was a star player in this game and scored a number of times. The final score was Munster 5–7, Leinster 2–8.

A second Gaelic tournament was held in London in May 1896, at the grounds of the Universal Sports and Recreation Society Limited, at Kensal Rise in north-west London. This was in aid of the Little Sisters of the Poor, and it saw Flanagan attend and break his own world hammer record.[13] Kiely was not there, again probably because of farm commitments at home. Incidentally, at the AAA championships of 1896, Flanagan won the hammer, with Denis Horgan second.

One further Kiely absence in 1896 needs a brief explanation: the first modern Olympic Games at Athens in early April. There was early Irish interest, from both the IAAA and GAA, in the idea of sending a team to the Games. The great IAAA hurdler Dan Bulger attended the Sorbonne Conference in 1894, which gave birth to the modern Games.[14] April was very early in the year for Irish athletes to be in any kind of form, as the weather conditions generally restricted field events training, meaning the athletics season did not really get started until May. In addition, the GAA felt there were not enough events on the Athens programme, i.e. field events, that Irish athletes were likely to win.[15] In reality, the Olympics did not really capture the imagination of serious athletes at this inaugural stage.

The winning performances in Athens suggest that Kiely, or several Irish athletes, could have won multiple titles had they gone. For example, the winning time in the 110 metres hurdles was 17⅗ seconds, the long jump was won in 20 feet 10 inches and the triple jump in just under 45 feet. Even though there was no all-round championship in Athens, each of these marks was well below what Kiely could do at the time in the individual events.[16] Incidentally, there was no 56lb event in 1896, and a hammer event was deemed too dangerous to stage, given the narrowness of the beautiful Panathenaic stadium used for the Games. When the Olympics later used wider stadia in 1900, 1904 and 1908, John Flanagan won the hammer on each occasion.

In 1895–96, the English AAA purged itself of many athletes judged to be 'professional'. This term itself referred to those athletes who accepted appearance money or bonuses, in addition to expenses for attending meetings. While the AAA's 'decisive and praiseworthy' action was applauded, *Sport* felt that such practices were still to be found in Ireland. The British ideals of amateurism were essentially designed to ensure that sport remained the preserve of 'gentlemen'. Ireland basically subscribed to amateur rules as well, though with more flexibility. *Sport* suggested that in Ireland:

> ... *sensible people will agree that good men of comparatively poor circumstances cannot be expected to pay their railway fares and hotel bills to and at places outside of their particular localities. Of course, the payment of any sum over and above the bare expenses is a thing that every effort should be made to suppress, and would be just as easily checked were expenses allowed as it is at present. It is undoubted that even at the present moment men are being paid not*

alone their expenses but bonuses as well just the same as they were before ...[17]

As mentioned before, Kiely was well able financially to travel and compete when he felt like it, and he was never accused of breaching amateurism during his career. Nonetheless, it is hard to believe that he would have approved of a system which was effectively designed to keep athletics preserved for the gentlemen of Oxford and Cambridge. This sporting snobbery was a prime motive behind the whole amateur ideal of the nineteenth century in Britain, one which Baron de Coubertin initially embraced for the Olympic movement too.

The fact that Kiely continued to travel to the AAAs every year after that, missing time on the farm at very busy times of the year, shows that payment was not what concerned him. Meanwhile, the purging of 'professionals' left the 1897 championships quite short of big-name attractions. As a result, the attendance was well down at Fallowfield, Manchester that year, and things were made worse because: 'The meeting was very badly managed. It should have been concluded at a quarter to six, but was an hour after this before the last event [was] decided.'[18] One newspaper reported that:

Denis Horgan's weight put of 45ft. 4 in. was the best ever done in a championship and these two performances with those of Tysoe in the mile (4 min. 27 sec. against the wind), Kiely in the hammer-throwing, and Leggatt's dual victory in both the high and long jumping, alone redeemed the meeting from mediocrity.[19]

Kiely could beat only what was in front of him and did

so easily, with Denis Horgan almost 16 feet behind in the hammer. The *Irish Independent*'s special correspondent made a slight mistake about Kiely's county of origin here:

> *Kiely's hammer throwing was grand, and he nearly killed one of the judges who thought that he was at a safe distance from the Waterford athlete.*[20]

At the 1898 AAA championships, again at Stamford Bridge, athletics seemed to be on the way up again, as 'a new generation of cracks has come to the front to take the place of those dismissed to the professional ranks by the Association two years ago'.[21] This time, Irish 'national' pride entered the fray with even the unionist *Irish Times* hoping to see Irish athletes victorious over the English:

> *On Saturday, at Stamford Bridge, London, one of the most successful Championship Meetings held in recent years took place. With several Irishmen entered and competing, it was only natural that a big interest was taken in the sports. Four Championships have come to this side of St. George's Channel. The winners were D. Horgan, in 16lb shot, T.F. Kiely, the 16lb hammer, P. Leahy, the High Jump; and W.J. Newburn, the Long Jump.*[22]

The British press seemed to get in on the notion of national identity too. Kiely was styled as 'another representative of the Emerald Isle' in one London newspaper.[23] Another paper seemed more conscious of the national origins of the championship's competitors than it was of their names:

The Amateur Athletic Championships decided at Stamford-bridge [sic] on Saturday, resulted in some fine performances. In the mile a Scottish runner got within one-fifth of a second of the British amateur record time, while in the long jump an Irishman beat the British amateur record by half an inch.[24]

In the absence of photographic evidence from 1898, it could be presumed that Irish athletes were wearing the white vest with entwined shamrocks of the IAAA at this event. Yet, another London newspaper listed several Irish athletes differently. Pat Harding (a Tipperary friend of Kiely's) competed in the 120 yards hurdles for 'Bective Rangers FC' while Kiely was listed as representing the IAAA in that same race (finishing second) but as 'Gaelic AA' when competing in the hammer. It is unclear whether Kiely actually entered as a GAA athlete or

was just known as such by the reporter.[25]

Kiely throwing the hammer at an English AAA championship at Stamford Bridge in either 1898, 1900 or 1902. (*From the collection of Tom Hunt, original source unidentified*)

With his great rival John Flanagan in the USA, Kiely won his third AAA hammer title in a row at Molyneux, Wolverhampton in July 1899, with a fairly modest throw of 136 feet 4½ inches. He also entered the hurdles but hit a hurdle and did not finish. Again, the Irish press basked in national pride: 'Ireland was represented by four great performers, the persons T. F. Kiely, D. Horgan, W. J. Newburn, and P. Leahy. All four won championships for the old country, but their success was as nearly as possible certain before [they competed at all].'[26]

The 1900 championships were back at Stamford Bridge and by this time Kiely is thought to have had two sisters in Willesden, at the Jesus and Mary Convent. Following in the footsteps of Nell (Sr Benignus), Nancy Kiely was, by then, at Willesden too. Tom was in Scotland for the annual match just the week before the AAAs, so he travelled down to London from Glasgow and was reunited with his sisters for a while. He was always very good at keeping in touch with all of his siblings, and was a form of father figure to them. As for the championships, something of a rude awakening was in store for Irish athletics in general. Horgan, along with jumpers Peter O'Connor and the Leahy brothers, were comfortably beaten. The mighty American team was in town, in advance of the Paris Olympic Games, and they really showed how far in advance of the British Isles they were:

After seven years' success in the Weight-Putting, the Irishman [Horgan] had to surrender his title [to] Sheldon, of New York, whose winning performance was especially fine. The other strongman, T. F. Kiely, was also defeated [in] the Hammer by J. Flanagan, the Irish and English ex-champion, who has now made his home America, and competes for the New York A.C. He did the prodigious throw of 163 ft. 1 in., which quite surpasses the previous British record; although it falls short of his American figures.[27]

One small point of note in the hammer was that Kiely beat an American named Truxtun Hare into third place, by just under 5 inches. They would meet again on a memorable 4 July at St Louis in the first all-around championship at the Olympic Games of 1904. It has been suggested that Kiely was somehow off form at this time, and rumours had been rife in Ireland that he would not compete at the AAAs at all, according to *Sport*. The reality was that Flanagan was now a four-year beneficiary of American money, training and technical improvements, and would never again be challenged closely by an Irish-based athlete in the hammer.[28] When the hammer event was held at the Olympic Games for the first time at Paris in 1900, Flanagan won it comfortably.

With no Flanagan in the AAAs field of 1901, however, Kiely was a certainty for the hammer title, and duly obliged (as he and Flanagan were of similar age, it is unclear what the reference to Flanagan as Kiely's 'pupil' is alluding to here):

> *To mention the 16lb hammer is to say that Tom Kiely, of Carrick-on-Suir, won for there is only one man in the world to beat him, and he, the holder of the championship, was absent, and that is John J. Flanagan, late of Kilmallock and now of the New York Athletic Club. If I am rightly informed, Flanagan is a pupil of Kiely's, and the latter is not by a long way the first who 'pulled a rod to beat himself'.*[29]

A pair of British filmmakers named Sagar Mitchell and James Kenyon were at Huddersfield on the day of the 1901 championships and recorded events for posterity. Thankfully, the filmmakers captured a few precious seconds of Kiely that day. The speed of Kiely's rotations and throws relative to his opponents, using by now a wire-handled hammer, is quite clear. Kiely was not only noticeably faster in every movement than the athletes he was competing against that day, but he also made a full rotation more inside the circle than his opponents, increasing his power and throw distance as a result. The film snippet also shows the Tipperary man chatting happily with his opponents outside of the competition and then, when in the circle preparing to throw the hammer, laughing and waving for some officials to move further back in case they got hit.[30]

Kiely's last appearance at the AAAs was in 1902 when once again the competition was held at Stamford Bridge. He won by over 12 feet. In third place that day was American Robert Edgren. He was a sports journalist in New York, who would go on to report on Kiely's activities in the USA before the latter retired. Irish newspapers, including Clonmel's *Nationalist*, reported very little on the AAAs in 1902, linked to a general decline of interest now that the greatest Irish athletes, like Kiely, were ageing or had emigrated.

There was no Kiely at Northampton for the AAAs in 1903, bringing his run of appearances to an end. The *Sporting Life* lamented the absence of many so-called 'cracks' for various reasons. The hammer was won by Kiely's Scottish conqueror, Tom Nicholson, with a wire-handled hammer. Kiely, in all honesty, was in semi-retirement even by 1903. The fact that he finished competing at the AAAs in 1902 is worth bearing in mind, because it makes it less likely that the Association suddenly decided to ask him to represent it at the Olympic Games a full two years after that, as will be discussed in due course.

One segment from the *Sporting Life* in 1903 included a list of the previous twelve years of hammer winners.[31] Naturally, Kiely appears five times. It shows that Kiely's best throws were actually in his last two championships. Greater strength in his early thirties is one consideration, but so too was the wire-handled hammer, which he was by then comfortable using.

The columnist also decided to list the 'attachments' of the athletes, i.e. clubs they represented. Kiely was listed as 'Gaelic AA' twice, 'Suirside AC' once and then as 'Carrick-on-Suir' on the last two occasions. There is nothing all that unusual in this – John Flanagan's wins were ascribed to the 'Gaelic AA' in 1896, to 'New York AC' in 1900, and so on. Kiely did not wear a specific vest or crest of any of these organisations, as far as can be ascertained. It is certain that he wore the vest of the IAAA in 1901 at least, because it is clearly visible on the Mitchell and Kenyon film. There may be nothing in this detail at all, but curiously some Irish athletes were consistently listed as 'Irish AAA': the Leahy brothers from Charleville, for instance. Others were never listed thus. Peter O'Connor wore the IAAA vest in the Mitchell and Kenyon film too but was listed in *Sporting Life* as representing 'Waterford'. One inescapable point in all of the affiliations ascribed to Kiely is that no one ever considered him as just 'British' at the AAAs. His local and/or Irish national identity was always noted in the British press, as in the Irish papers.

The *Sporting Life* feature listed all the various hammer records, whether from a seven-foot circle, nine-foot circle or from none. In the category '16lb from a 9-foot circle', two records are listed, that of Kiely in 1897 (142ft 6in) and Flanagan's from 1900 (163ft 4in). The Kiely throw referred to was at Cappoquin, Co. Waterford, though it was recorded in Ireland as an inch less. Kiely's longer distance from 1901 was not mentioned. The reason must be that the 1897 Kiely throw was with a different style of hammer to Flanagan's but it is impossible to be certain. The difference between the two was almost 21 feet! Time had waited for no one, not even Kiely.

AAA hammer championship results involving Kiely, 1895–1902[32]

Year	First		Second		Third	
1895	William Barry	132 ft 11¾ ins	Tom Kiely	130 ft 2½ ins	James MacDonald	100 ft 3 ins
1897	Tom Kiely	142 ft 5½ ins	Denis Horgan	126 ft 8½ ins	Richard Sheldon	102 ft 2 ins
1898	Tom Kiely	140 ft 1 in	Denis Horgan	125 ft 7 ins	Walter Lawrence	109 ft 11 ins
1899	Tom Kiely	136 ft 4½ ins	Denis Horgan	131 ft 8¼ ins	Nelson Robbie	111 ft 0¼ ins
1900	John Flanagan	163 ft 4 ins	Tom Kiely	139 ft 2 ins	Truxtun Hare	138 ft 9¼ ins
1901	Tom Kiely	148 ft 6½ ins	Ernest May	120 ft 3¼ ins	Henry Leeke II	115 ft 0¼ in
1902	Tom Kiely	142 ft 9¼ ins	Ernest May	130 ft	Robert Edgren	121 ft 0¾ in

CHAPTER 6

FACING CHALLENGES AND CHANGE, 1896–99

The last two chapters have looked at Tom Kiely enhancing his reputation across Scotland and England, but there is a lot more to tell about his established years in Ireland. Being one of Ireland's most famous sportsmen had its pressures, of course. Often, he had to juggle farming commitments with increasing expectations, as well as dealing with challenges to his belief that politics had no place in sport. Yet, fame also brought advantages, such as his being recognised wherever he went, and his being lauded in story and song.

The exploits of the fictitious Mat the Thresher, hero of Charles Kickham's *Knocknagow*, were allegedly the inspiration for James Mitchel taking up hammer throwing. By 1896, by virtue of his domestic and, even then, cross-channel achievements, Kiely continued to be seen as the embodiment of Mat the Thresher. One press reporter wrote: 'Poor Kickham who drew the picture of the immortal Thresher, would have been glad, if he had the genial giant of the present day – the famous Tom of Ballyneill!'[1]

As 1896 dawned, one of the firms which advertised its farm machinery on a weekly basis in the *Nationalist* introduced a 'new' type of plough. It may or may not have been all that

Irish boxing champion and one-time world heavyweight title contender Jem Roche (left), posing with an immaculately dressed Kiely. The more Kiely's fame spread, the more his company was sought. (*Courtesy of Anthony Kiely*)

new as a design, however, as the whole area of patents and design copyright concerning farm machinery in those days was rather 'loose'. That year, though, the plough was called 'Erin's Champion', likely in honour of Kiely.[2]

By now he was being compared, more than favourably, to heroes of old, in a wave of poems and stories. Kiely cut out and kept the following published poem in his scrapbook, written by 'E.K.':

To T.F. Kiely, Irish Champion[3]

'Tis in the gallant county Tipp,
Where best athletes have been;
Where young and old do gaily trip
To every sporting scene.
Where Slievenamon towers o'er a vale
Of Erin's deepest hue –
'Tis here, ye children of the Gael,
Tom Kiely trained for you.

> Athletic fields he made sublime
> And laurels won anew,
> Which sent his name to every clime,
> With fame for Ireland too.
> Athletic standards of our land,
> He raised to high renown,
> The hammer from his Irish hand
> Took the world's records down!
>
> A champion now he stands unique –
> The first in all the lands;
> The world over you may seek
> And matchless now he stands.
> He is the champion best all-round,
> His feats enshrined his name
> With Erin's bravest sons who're found
> High in the ranks of fame.
>
> Till time its course has ceased to go,
> And life its race has run,
> The world's records still will show
> The feats that he has done.
> Beyond all in the world wide
> The fifty-six he wheeled –
> Of all the Gaels he is the pride,
> The idol of the field!

Great literature it may not be, but here was hero worship, linking Kiely with mythological figures of old and with the Irish everywhere. This further demonstrated his placement as the people's champion, the 'wise and simple' man who embodied much of what the Irish felt it meant to be Irish, so to speak. Kiely's career spanned a period when Ireland struggled to find national heroes in politics or society and it is no exaggeration to suggest that the Tipperary sportsman, without ever seeking to, became just such a national hero.

***

Early in 1896, Kiely's roots in Grangemockler and Tipperary GAA dragged him back into the GAA in new ways. His fame saw him elected as a delegate to the GAA's Central Council at the 1896 county convention.[4] The efforts of Kiely and others earlier in the decade had helped revive the club structure in Tipperary. The president of the Tipperary board, D. H. Ryan, was in a position to announce at the same convention that:

> *... a few of us have saved the Association in the County from the throes of death, and now we have been privileged to see the valiant sons of gallant Tipperary bring home in triumph the hurling and football honours of Ireland.*

Although he played on several Tipperary football teams, Kiely was not a member of any of the All-Ireland winning teams referred to above. He continued to play with Grangemockler and was appointed one of the GAA's national vice presidents, representing Munster, from 1896 to 1898.[5] It is hard to imagine him engaging to any high degree in GAA politics at national level, and the extent of his attendance at Central Council meetings is unclear. Newspaper coverage of meetings does not list attendees, and the minute books of the Central Council held at Croke Park date from after this period. One contribution from Kiely that has survived, however, referred to a proposal that the GAA should formally involve itself in the organisation of a national commemoration of the centenary of the 1798 Rebellion. Among the voices which opposed this, and ultimately won the day, was Kiely's:

> *Opinion was divided as to whether or not this '98 Committee was a national or a political body, Tom Kiely holding that it was political while James Nowlan of Kilkenny claimed that it was national. In the end it was decided not to nominate any GAA men to the Committee but GAA clubs were left free to take part in the Commemoration if they wished.*[6]

Kiely was probably mistaken in his fears that the 1798 centenary would become politicised. Around the country, committees sprang up to celebrate Wolfe Tone and others, and the example of Clonmel itself must have eased Kiely's concerns. In April 1898, just prior to national commemorative celebrations of 1798, the *Nationalist* reported:

> *The movement has sprung directly from the patriotic spirit of the people, and that noble spirit will certainly carry it out in every detail, in a manner befitting the memorable occasion, and worthy of the best record of the Premier County.*[7]

Keeping with GAA issues, a local football match played at Carrick-on-Suir in early 1897 gave another example of the competitiveness of Tom Kiely. Grangemockler defeated Carrick Commercials by four points to two, and Kiely was Grangemockler captain. The winners got a set of gold medals and the runners-up got silver. Kiely's captaincy included

him insisting that substitutions were not allowed when the
opposition lost one of their players:

> On the change of sides, Mr P. Daly (Commercials) got hurt and had to
> leave the field so that the Commercials had to play with 16 men, TF
> Kiely refusing to allow another in his place ...[8]

In 1897, delegates from the South Tipperary division at the
annual county convention included Maurice Davin and Kiely.[9]
Soon enough, Kiely was embroiled in yet another serious row:

> In the 1896 final Arravale [Rovers] and Grangemockler met again
> before a huge crowd in Horse and Jockey. The Mocklers led at half-
> time by 0–3 to nil but Bob Quane notched a point for the champions
> before adding a goal ten minutes from time. Grangemockler objected
> to the goal and to the legality of one of the Arravale Rovers players
> and refused to continue. They appealed to the County board but at the
> hearing of 20th November they were unable to produce any evidence
> and their appeal was lost. The club were suspended until 1st January
> 1897 for leaving the field. Grangemockler refused to enter a team in
> 1897, 1898 or 1899.[10]

Arravale Rovers walked off the field at Deerpark in a previous
encounter with Kiely's team, following a refereeing decision.
That match had been replayed, so Grangemockler felt aggrieved
by their treatment on this next occasion. They lodged an appeal
to the county board, costing £1 to submit, claiming that the
spectators at Horse and Jockey had interfered with play just
prior to a crucial Arravale Rovers goal, and that the Rovers had
an illegal player on their team. The appeal failed, however:

At a subsequent meeting of the Council in Tipperary the Grangemockler deputation were ruled out of court, and the club suspended for three months, whereupon Mr Kiely immediately resigned his position on the Council.[11]

Several clubs in South Tipperary clearly sympathised with Grangemockler. *Sport* declared:

I can state on sound authority that nearly all the clubs in that portion of the county do not intend to affiliate this year ... The South Tipperary clubs also complain of insufficient representation on the Council, and in connection with this it may be well to state that there are only two members representing that portion of the county whilst there are three members from Tipperary town, where there is only one club affiliated.

This row, in addition to the old football injury previously referred to, and his desire to concentrate on his athletics career, meant that Kiely was rarely found in championship football games after 1897. He continued to referee matches occasionally for the Davins at Deerpark, however, including a hurling game between Moycarkey (Tipperary) and Mooncoin of Kilkenny.[12]

Despite the non-appearance of his club in Tipperary championships, Kiely was re-elected as one of the GAA's national vice-presidents (representing Munster) at the 1897 annual convention in Thurles. This occurred *in absentia*, as Kiely is not listed among the attendees, reinforcing the notion that he was happier to leave the politics of the GAA to others.[13]

***

Returning to look at Kiely's athletics career in these years, 1896 was not an exceptional year and he competed very little up to August. In addition to his international activities and GAA commitments that year, there were also injuries and new farming responsibilities. In 1896, William Kiely bought the lease on a second farm, at Curraghdobbin, just north of his seventy-eight acres at Ballyneill. The valuation records for Tipperary South Riding show that this second farm had just over 104 acres, with the land having a rateable annual valuation (RAV) of £89 and the buildings having rates of £9 per annum.[14] William's surname is spelled 'Kyly' in the records. The local press announced:

> *Mr Thomas Rockett, auctioneer, Carrick-on-Suir, put up for sale a valuable farm in Curraghdobbin, consisting of 104 acres statute measure, the property of the late Mrs Rockett. After keen competition Mr J. F. Quirke, in trust for Mr William Kiely, Ballyneill, was declared the purchaser at £1,000 and auction fees.[15]*

Almost certainly because of increased farm duties, Kiely failed to attend the IAAA championships on Whit Monday that year. It clashed with a GAA tournament in London, but Kiely was not at that either.[16] With a new farm to worry about, extensive buildings to do up, and having already been to London at Easter with the GAA 'invasion', Kiely had very little time left for athletics in 1896. His brother Willie was still no more than twelve, so of little use on the extended Kiely farms as yet, while sixteen-year-old Larry seems to have continued into secondary education, so would also have likewise been of limited help on the farm.[17]

Kiely wearing the vest of the Irish Amateur Athletic Association.
(*Original source unknown*)

Kiely's eventual return to athletics in 1896 was at the Dublin Metropolitan Police (DMP) Sports in late July. *Sport* was delighted: 'One of the most pleasing features of the meeting was the reappearance of Kiely in the athletic arena, and it is to be hoped that his return will be a permanent one.' Kiely won the hurdles, somewhat luckily, and then the hammer. With more and more changes taking place to the hammer, such as throwers changing from wooden handle to wire handle and from iron head to lead, things were in danger of becoming chaotic and made the proper keeping of records very, very difficult. Kiely won the DMP hammer event with 135 feet

9½ ins, which was put in doubt as a possible record because he had used a leaden-headed hammer. *Sport* explained:

> *[This] point has not, I believe, been yet satisfactorily cleared up. The English Association allowed the leaden head at their championships, and the IAAA, though supposed not to recognise them, permitted their use at the international contest [Ireland v Scotland]. Why can't this thing be settled once and for all!*[18]

Kiely remained in Dublin and entered the GAA national championships, held at Jones' Road the day after the police sports. On Saturday, therefore, he had competed at a police sports under IAAA rules and then on Sunday he was under the GAA.[19] Kiely's relatively poor long jump, added to no mark in the triple jump and not entering the hurdles all suggest that pre-existing injuries had not healed. This injury had less impact in weights events, so he entered six!

Kiely's GAA titles that day were in the 56lb with unlimited run and follow, and two in the hammer. The two hammer titles came about because one event used a lead weight with wire handle, thrown from a nine-foot circle, and the other event allowed an unlimited run and follow but with a wooden-handled implement. Interestingly, Kiely threw the wooden-handled hammer 143 feet 2 inches and only managed 134 feet 8 inches with the wire and lead one.[20] Clearly he had catching up to do in using the new technology at this juncture, especially with his great rival John Flanagan now in the USA, improving all the time and specialising in the hammer while Kiely remained a multi-eventer.

In August 1896, Kiely was at Clonmel Sports but

performed poorly, with just two seconds and a third. At another meeting he threw the hammer from inside a seven-foot circle a distance of 140 feet 4 inches, noted at the time as a 'world record' but there is uncertainty about this claim.[21] He did certainly break an Irish record for throwing the 56lb with unlimited run and follow at Carrick-on-Suir, hoisting the weight 36 feet 6½ inches.[22] However, again suggesting that injury, or illness, had come against Kiely, he did not compete in the 1896 all-round championship, even though it was held very nearby, in Tipperary town. That day, there were just three entries and the contest ended in dispute over refereeing decisions.[23] This may be why the GAA did not hold an all-round competition in 1897.

***

Things improved for Kiely in athletics during 1897: he was back at the Ireland v Scotland match, the AAAs and at meetings as before. At Queen's College Sports (May) he won the hammer. The following month he took the IAAA hammer title with a wire-handled hammer, throwing a distance of 139 feet 10 inches, described as 'a record for Great Britain' although no performances with a lead and wire-handled hammer had yet been verified by the joint IAAA–GAA records committee. Kiely threw 144 feet 4 inches in an exhibition event, but it is unclear whether that was with a wire- or wooden-handled hammer.[24] The *Nationalist* celebrated 'Another record for Tipperary' anyway, while *Sport* added an extra half-inch as 'the popular T.F. Kiely gave a grand exhibition with the hammer and he was enthusiastically applauded when he broke the record'.[25] For records purposes, throws outside of competition could not be verified, as is still the case in all athletics events.

Kiely sought out new venues too. In late June he was at the market town of Cappoquin in Co. Waterford, winning the long jump with 22 feet, the 56lb with 34 feet 7 inches and, according to the *Nationalist*, 'broke the Irish hammer throwing record by the fine throw of 142 ft, beating his previous record by 2ft 2in. Flanagan's world record is 150ft.'[26] This must again refer to a mark with a wire-handled hammer, as Kiely had done more than 140 feet with the wooden-handled hammer several times previously. The Cappoquin mark was subsequently recorded as 142 feet 5 inches in a 1906 publication.[27]

At Clonmel on the August bank holiday of 1897, Kiely won the 56lb with unlimited run and follow but was only fourth when the same weight was thrown from a standing position because his athleticism and speed were less useful from a standing position. He also won the 120 yards hurdles championship of Ireland.[28] Then, at Wexford on a Thursday evening, 'Kiely won the hurdles easily and broke the record in the 16lb [wire-handled] hammer throwing, in which he put the hammer 143ft ¾ in.'[29] Kiely's work with this new type of hammer was leading to steady improvement – his Wexford mark was over 8 feet better than he had thrown in May. It was predicted that he would be invited to the USA to take part in the American national championships.[30] Kiely did not go, in the end, but his fame was such that America felt its all-around athletes would not be a match for him, whatever about hammer specialist John Flanagan, now domiciled in New York:

Land and Water [*a popular outdoor recreation magazine of the era*] noted in August 1897, Page 45, that Kiely can 'run, jump and take the hurdles like a stag and handle the weights almost as well as [James] [sic] Flanagan himself. He doesn't know when he's tired and only leaves an athletic field when there is nothing left on the programme for a man to do.'[31]

Later still in 1897, Kiely competed at Cahir Sports, where he won a suit of serge, presented by Messrs Mulcahy, Redmond and Co. of Ardfinnan. This was for winning the hammer event, with 'the fine throw of 144 feet 2 inches, making a new record'.[32] Again, this must refer to a throw with a wire-handled hammer, meaning that by the time Kiely threw the hammer 145 feet at Clonmel that October, he had improved across the season by over 10 feet with the new hammer design.[33]

After more successes at Carrick-on-Suir, Kiely's final fling in the 1897 season was at the GAA championships, which had been postponed to late September at Tipperary. This proved to be his second-best performance ever at a national championships, as six titles were won. He won the hurdles, long and triple jumps, and two hammer events. He also broke his 1896 record for the 56lb by half an inch.[34]

***

By 1898, the new range of equipment, rules and techniques had completely confounded both record-keepers and long-standing athletics enthusiasts. Kiely, by this time, had ceased maintaining his scrapbook, so there is no clue as to what he thought of all the variations and permutations in weight throwing. Broadly speaking, he had made the leap to modernity by moving to wire-handled hammer throwing, and he had mastered rapid double rotations when throwing from a circle. In fact, the aforementioned video evidence from Mitchell and Kenyon suggests that by 1901, if not sooner, Kiely was doing two-and-a-half rotations at high speed inside a seven-foot circle at Huddersfield while his rival hammer throwers were doing no more than one-and-a-half, and at a much slower speed.[35] The problem was that sports meetings in Ireland persisted with both old-style and new rules, so that what an athlete threw and how he threw it could vary from place to place and week to week, depending on local tradition. The athletics correspondent in *Sport* bemoaned the new directions:

> *Records are going every day, but I believe in very few of them, especially Flanagan's with the hammer. No one would attempt to put down a tin tack with the hammer that he is using ... If we are going to throw a hammer or a 56lbs weight, in goodness name let us do so, but not a fantastically designed missile which was never intended for any other purpose than to deprive old-time athletes of legitimately earned laurels with legitimate weapons ...*[36]

Kiely carried on regardless in 1898. He won the hammer at Queen's College Sports with a throw 10 feet below his previous best and finished third in the long jump with 21 feet 2 inches. That day, Westmeath man Walter Newburn broke the long-standing Irish long jump record of Pat Davin by jumping 23 feet 4 inches.[37] The hammer title was also an IAAA national title, though Kiely missed the main IAAA championships a few days later.

In July 1898, the village of Windgap, just a few miles from Ballyneill, advertised its cycling and athletics sports, referring to T. F. Kiely as 'starter, etc.'[38] While this was almost certainly a tactic to increase attendance, both GAA and IAAA rules frowned on any competitive athletes acting as starters or handicappers at sports meetings. (A handicapper basically decided on how much of an advantage some athletes might be given when competing against others in handicap events – though if a handicapper was also a competing athlete, there would be an obvious conflict of interest. Thus, Kiely did not compete in the sports meeting at Windgap, or wherever else he acted as handicapper.) The Anner Sports (near Clonmel) and Kilcash Sports (near Ballyneill) both had Kiely as handicapper and starter. Again, Kiely was obliging local meetings by lending his name and prestige, possibly at times when he was not training much or in good enough form to compete himself, though he reportedly 'managed affairs as handicapper and starter, with efficiency and despatch [*sic*]'.[39] Later newspaper reports suggest that the GAA overall had difficulties in getting people to act as handicappers – too much of that burden tended to fall on administrator supreme Frank Dinneen – and the association may just have been happy to have Kiely's help at the time, regardless of regulations.[40]

Ever the competitor, Kiely wrote to the Thurles Sports committee that August, saying that 'Leahy of Charleville' and he were anxious to try for triple jump records at the upcoming Thurles Sports, and requesting that the ground be level and properly prepared.[41] In the end, Pat Leahy won that event without a record, with 48 feet, but it is not clear whether Kiely took part. At those same sports, Kiely threw another 'record' of 154 feet 3 inches, presumably with a wooden-handled hammer.[42] There is a suggestion that Kiely also broke his own 56lb for distance record in Cork in August 1898, throwing 38 feet 11 inches, but a contemporary source for this has not been located.[43]

Throughout 1898, Kiely's wire-handled hammer throwing improved. Kiely's greater use of a wire-handled hammer was bound to impact on his performance eventually. Once mastered, the wire handle meant that the hammer's centre of gravity was further from the thrower's hands. This meant that speed of foot was as important as strength in the circle, with the thrower acting as a fulcrum and his rapid rotations adding power and, hence, distance. The triangular handle was much easier to grip than a wooden one when rotating in the circle. It required less adjustment of the hands while rotating, allowed the weight to be swung further from the hands and so generated more force. The use of ball-bearings in the attachment of the handle to the hammer head made it also less likely to break on impact than the old wooden-handled hammer, which allowed no 'give' on impact with hard ground.

With the new hammer, he reached 146 feet in an exhibition throw at Limerick Sports in June, and added 10 inches to that in competition at Ballsbridge on 16 July.[44] At Cahir Sports on 25 July, sporting ecumenism was very much in evidence. Among the patrons were local gentry and 'Colonel Clowes and Officers of the 8th Royal Hussars', Sergeant Sullivan of the Royal Irish Constabulary (RIC) was the field officer, and yet the event was a GAA one, with Frank Dinneen, the national secretary, in attendance and assisting with the programme. That day, Kiely broke the world record for the 16lb hammer from a nine-foot circle, throwing it 151 feet 11 inches.[45] To this day, this is the only record still attributed to Kiely in the old AAA records. That in itself is fascinating, as the event was a GAA one and yet the collaboration on records within Ireland at that time ensured that Kiely's distance was accepted by the IAAA and then by the English AAA.[46] It will probably never be beaten either because the standard circle has been of seven-foot diameter for over a century at this stage.

Sadly, the Nenagh National and Literacy Institute Sports later in the summer carried signs of challenges ahead. Kiely won three events there, two in jumping and then the 56lb throw. There was no hammer event, which was linked to crowd safety, and an absence of competitors able to compete with Kiely. The hammers were now travelling a lot further than they had even ten years previously, and the new wire-handled hammer could be a real threat. The wire-handled version encouraged fast rotations in the circle, which made misdirection more likely – all in an age when the huge safety cages of modern hammer throwing were not even dreamt of. It was no coincidence that *Sport*, while praising the great organising and athletic work of Kiely at Carrick-on-Suir Sports in August, also commented: 'They will want to enlarge some of the grounds if Tom Kiely is to throw the hammer anymore. This time he sent it from a seven-foot circle 147 feet 1 inch …'.[47]

The Carrick Sports was the first time when all three Kiely brothers competed at the same sports meeting. Tom, naturally, won the hammer in what was described as a new record; his brother Larry was placed third in the same event. On closer examination, a 'W. Kiely' is also found, winning a confined 300 yards handicap race. This appears to have been a race for youngsters, as one of the younger Davins finished second. Willie Kiely received 10 yards odds for the event, two less than Master Davin got.[48] Larry would have been about eighteen at this time, with Willie just fourteen.

Just prior to the Carrick Sports of 1898, Kiely reached 147 feet 9 inches, presumably with the wire hammer, at the GAA championships in mid-August, where he also won the hurdles title. Having missed the competition since 1895, he must have looked forward to the restoration of the all-round championship by the GAA later that year. Unfortunately, this was postponed in early September because of inclement weather. Then the re-fixed date of 30 September was deferred, so it was 16 October before the event was finally staged, at Tipperary.

On the day, only five competitors turned up. The weather again was miserable and local papers wrote of a chaotic day, scheduled to open at 1.30 p.m.

It was an hour and a half later, however, when a start was made and at this stage the field presented a desolate appearance, the attendance consisting of the competitors, a body of policemen and a handful of spectators.[49]

Kiely won his fourth all-round championship in 1898 without even a canter. In a nine-event programme, although he failed to score at all in two of the first three events, the 100 yards and the high jump, Kiely finished first in every one of six further events so that, with one event remaining, he had more points (thirty) than the rest of the field combined.[50] As usual, when he did not need to, Kiely did not bother to run the last 880 yards race and the championship came to a close with that. This day also saw Larry Kiely appear at the all-round championship, where he competed in the 100 yards only before withdrawing.[51]

The sparse attendance and weather were factors, but at this point the GAA was doing little good for the all-round championship anymore. The IAAA had abandoned the all-round first, but the GAA squeezing the championship into the end of the year like this, having not run it at all for two years, was a disaster. Even the Irish persistence with awarding points based only on placings in each event had come to be problematic. Kiely was viewed on both sides of the Atlantic as the greatest all-rounder of his day, but the Irish scoring system took no account of times or distances, so it was impossible to compare his performances accurately with those of American champions.

**

1899 was a fairly standard season for Kiely, though his only Irish titles that year were in weights events – the IAAA hammer and the GAA hammer and 56lb throw, with unlimited run and follow. In the case of the GAA hammer event, Kiely's distance of 156 feet 2 inches was noted as beating his previous record of 151 feet 11 inches, and is still considered his best-ever throw.[52] *The Freeman's Journal* noted that he 'threw with the wind' on that occasion at Thurles, but this may have been a euphemism for 'downhill' or some other circumstantial advantage which made it unreliable as a record.[53]

Domestically, Kiely's 1899 efforts were very concentrated

around local sports meetings. This may be explained by his farming commitments as his father became increasingly inactive on the land. In late June, at Nenagh, the Constabulary Sports drew 10,000 spectators, who saw Kiely perform heroics, before going to the AAAs in Wolverhampton. The local press complained that he did not train or specialise enough, but added that, nevertheless:

> *Beyond doubt Ireland's greatest athlete is T. F. Kiely, and we question if the assertion, that as an all-round athlete he is unrivalled, could be safely challenged. His reputation as an athlete of extraordinary versatility has no doubt prompted his selection as captain of the Irish athletic team to visit America next July.*[54]

Yet again, plans to visit America did not materialise, but in August, Kiely won prizes at Cahir Sports, Bansha and Youghal, where a reputed hammer throw of 156 feet 9 inches was not ultimately ratified.[55] In September, he was at Kilsheelan Sports and was both secretary and competitor at Carrick-on-Suir Sports. He was at Ballyluskey for the sports in October. With the exception of Youghal, none of these places was more than thirty miles from Ballyneill. In most cases, Larry Kiely competed on the same programmes. At Carrick, incidentally, Tom did break a (British) hammer record on level ground, when he threw from a seven-foot circle and managed 152 feet 5 inches. Larry was third in that event, with the ever-present Denis Horgan splitting the brothers Kiely.[56]

No all-round championship was held in 1899, or indeed in subsequent years either. It is claimed that the GAA dropped the all-round championship after 1898 because they could

Larry Kiely on the extreme right, lining up beside Tom in what appears to be the hurdle race at the Munster championships in 1902 at Dungarvan. The man in the bowler hat behind the upright athlete is Dan Fraher, owner of the field. (*From the collection of Tom Hunt, original photograph by Edmund Keohan of Dungarvan*)

find no one left who wanted to compete against Kiely. In reality, Kiely would never again win an all-round title on Irish soil because neither athletics body wanted the bother of promoting it. Kiely was still willing and able, but he no longer had an all-round championship to compete in – a case of having the Prince but no *Hamlet* for him to perform in.

Tom Kiely in classic pose at the sportsfield in Ballyneill, with an old-style wooden hammer. (*Kiely Collection, Tipperary Museum of Hidden History*)

The silver belt for the IAAA all-round championship. As he did not have to return it, Kiely didn't bother getting his name engraved for his third victory in 1894. (*Kiely Collection, Tipperary Museum of Hidden History*)

One of Kiely's 1896 GAA
athletics medals.
(*Kiely Collection, Tipperary
Museum of Hidden History*)

The 1897 AAA hammer medal
won at Manchester.
(*Kiely Collection, Tipperary
Museum of Hidden History*)

A studio photograph of 'Erin's Champion' taken by Lauder Brothers of Dublin. (*Kiely Collection, Tipperary Museum of Hidden History*)

The 1904 All-Around World Championship and 'Olympic' medal won at the St Louis Olympic Games. (*Kiely Collection, Tipperary Museum of Hidden History*)

The 'loving cup' presented to Kiely on behalf of Irish-America before he left the USA in 1904. (*Kiely Collection, Tipperary Museum of Hidden History*)

The illuminated address presented to Tom Kiely by the GAA on his return from St Louis. (*Kiely Collection, Tipperary Museum of Hidden History*)

Tom Kiely with Martin Sheridan on the day of
their great athletic contest in Dungarvan, 1908.
(*Courtesy of Waterford County Museum*)

An elderly Tom Kiely.
(*Kiely Collection,
Tipperary Museum of
Hidden History*)

The Kiely memorial at
Ballyneill, erected with
funds raised by a local
committee, and here adorned
with decorative wreaths on
the occasion of the 150th
anniversary of Kiely's birth.
(*Author's collection*)

Tom Kiely of Lisheen points to the Olympic gold medal won by his grandfather at St Louis. Now with a green ribbon, this is on display in Tipperary Museum of Hidden History.
(*Courtesy of John Crowley and Tipperary Museum of Hidden History*)

From left: Tom Kiely's running shoes, the 1904 'loving cup' showing American and Irish motifs, and the gold watch that the Irish-American club presented to Kiely in 1906.
(*Photographed by the author at Tipperary Museum of Hidden History*)

CHAPTER 7

ON TOP, BUT NO FURTHER, 1900-03

For many athletes who specialise in weight throwing, it is often the case that their peak years of throwing come in their early thirties, due to the benefit of years of physical conditioning. Tom Kiely continued to be a top-class athlete and continued to win championships and break records. However, the years of his career from 1900 do convey a sense that his best years were behind him. In fact, only fourteen of his fifty-three Irish championships were won after 1899.[1] It is not easy to understand why this relative decline occurred, but it certainly makes the achievements of later years even more remarkable, as will be seen later.

His family life was evolving too. By 1900, all of Kiely's sisters except for one had become nuns or were close to making that decision.[2] William Kiely was now domiciled in the farm closer to Ballyneill, leaving his son Tom at Curraghdobbin. The census returns for early 1901 make interesting reading. In the Ballyneill farmstead it recorded William aged seventy-two, Mary aged fifty-nine and twenty-year-old Larry. At Curraghdobbin, Thomas Kiely was recorded as '30', although he was actually five months short of being thirty-two, and was listed as the head of the family. Also residing there were

Willie aged eighteen, their sister Maggie who was twenty-eight and two servants, John Lonergan and Annie Fitzpatrick. Maggie would marry later in life and live in Dungarvan as Mrs Slattery.[3]

Curraghdobbin was the main centre of Kiely farming activity by this point and Tom was the overall 'head of family' in a real sense, if not yet legally so. What the census does not record is that even Mary Kiely is believed to have lived quite a deal at Curraghdobbin too, as William had become increasingly difficult to live with, and so Larry was entrusted with minding the Ballyneill farm more and more. The 1911 census confirmed that Mary and William were by then living in separate houses.[4] Having two servants at Curraghdobbin in 1901 demonstrates the prosperity of the Kielys. The servants were also vital to the running of the farm, of course, as by now both Tom and Larry were highly active athletes.

The census shows that the Kiely house at Curraghdobbin was one of only three first-class houses in the area. It had between seven and nine rooms and a total of nine windows at the front of the house. The Ballyneill farmhouse was slightly smaller but was still one of the largest recorded in that townland.

Regardless of census returns, both Kiely farms were legally held in William Kiely's name, one a leasehold from the 'Earl of Clonmell' (*sic*) and the other from land agent Rodolphus Scully. The only time that Tom Kiely's name appears on a property transaction during these years is in 1903, when he purchased a labourer's cottage in the area. The records state that this cottage was purchased from a William

Burke, with no land, and that the building had a rateable annual valuation of £1.[5] Kiely's grandson, Tom, believes this may well have been a cottage purchased by Kiely to support a young woman from the district who had given birth to their daughter around this time. They did not marry, and William would have vetoed that in any event as the young woman was without property. Tom is said to have given the young woman and their daughter financial support, and his grandson Tom has been very happy to meet his relatives descended from that relationship up to the present day.

Although he had not yet married, Kiely was no stranger to female company and was one of the most recognisable athletes in Ireland, strikingly handsome, relatively sociable and well-to-do. This was reinforced in the *Nationalist*, where the (male) writer drew favourable comparisons between Kiely and a Greek god:

> … *as for Apollo, my honest, unbiased opinion is, that neither in build nor general appearance – taking in fact, the entire tout essemble* [sic] *– would he at all compare with Tom Kiely as we have often seen him in the initial stage of making or breaking a record, Apollo would, indeed have been vastly improved if he had gone in more for dumb-bell and Indian club exercise than he appears to have done …*[6]

***

Ever a competitor who disregarded political or religious affiliations, towards the end of the 1890s a meeting in Belfast gave another insight into Kiely's steely character. This time he competed in the face of Orange Order opposition to a Sunday athletics meeting at a soccer pitch. That participation would have offended Orangemen and, conversely, quite a few of the more extreme GAA nationalists too because of the venue being a soccer pitch. Yet:

The tournament organised by the Red Branch Hurling Club on the Celtic Football Club Ground at Belfast on Sunday last was a signal success. Everything possible to crush the initial effort of the club was done by the Irish Football Association, the Orangemen and Sabbatarians without number. Efforts were made to have the sports proclaimed by the Lord Mayor of Belfast. Even the Lord Lieutenant was invoked to come to the rescue. Notwithstanding all of this, no less than seven thousand persons assembled and cheered to the echo the splendid performances of Kiely and Leahy.[7]

Moving forward, as the Kiely brothers prepared for the 1900 season, it was predicted that Tom was going to concentrate on breaking weights records, and that young Larry would be a star too, once he perfected his hammer-throwing technique:

[A]s we are told that young Kiely is an athletic jewel of the brightest ray, we may fully expect another gem to sparkle in the crown of Tipperary's athletic glory. He is a big upstanding athlete – a foe similar to his brother Tom, and should, indeed, make his nine-foot circle a very warm corner. He is presently perfecting his system of throwing by 'spinning' within the chalk line with a twelve-pound weight, and in this way he cultivates a lightening-like delivery.[8]

Tom Kiely was more active than usual in the early months of the 1900 season, competing in May at sports meetings in Mullinahone and Nenagh. In the latter, he won at slinging a

56lb weight and in the hurdles and came second to Pat Leahy in both the running long jump and the hop, step and jump. Kiely was still content to compete in as wide a range of events as possible.

The Paris Olympic Games were expected in early September and had the Irish sports writers anticipating a great showdown between Kiely and John Flanagan, now representing the USA.[9] There were plans for a group of IAAA athletes to attend the Paris Olympic Games and that Kiely would be among them. With no all-round event scheduled for Paris, it is not likely that Kiely was very interested. In any event, the death knell to any such plans was sounded while Irish athletes, including Kiely, were at the AAAs in London in July 1900. The IAAA and its athletes were very surprised to be told that the Paris Games were starting not in September but the following week. 'Belvedere' noted in *Sport*:

> *I cannot account for the misconceptions over the Olympic Games at Paris today. Everyone thought, because it was advertised, that September 2nd was the date, and I hold letters to that effect. However, one new disappointment more or less won't make much difference …*[10]

In the end, Pat Leahy of Charleville was the only Irish athlete (i.e. not representing America) of note to make it to Paris. There, he performed heroics, despite sea sickness and a late arrival, to win second in the high jump and third in the long jump.[11] As for Kiely, having been away from home competing at both Glasgow and London in early July, it was time to get back to Curraghdobbin and Ballyneill.

A feature of Kiely's activities through 1900 up to July was

that he did not take part in many hammer contests. Everyone may have been anticipating a great hammer clash in Paris between Kiely and Flanagan, but it is not at all certain that Kiely was preparing for that. The IAAA championships saw him only run, and lose, in the hurdles, and there was no hammer entry in Mullinahone, Nenagh or when the sports were eventually held at Youghal on 30 June. Only at Pallasgreen Sports in early July did he throw the hammer, and he did so unspectacularly. When Kiely and Flanagan met at the AAAs in London, Flanagan won quite easily, as has been shown in a previous chapter. Perhaps Kiely had no real intention of competing in Paris, aware that there was to be no all-round championship there.

It was really only after his success at the Scotland match and failure against Flanagan in London that Kiely threw the hammer with significance at home in 1900. At the Dublin Metropolitan Police Sports on 14 July, Kiely was third in the 28lb event and second in the 16lb shot put; there was no hammer event on the programme. At the RIC Depot Sports, in aid of the Queen's Jubilee Fund and the RIC widows' and orphans' fund, Kiely won the hammer, but the press gave no distance. He also competed in long jump and hurdles without success.[12] In August, Tom beat Larry in the hammer and other events at Compsie Sports, but Larry competed on his own at Clonmel just a few days later. No obvious reason for Tom's absence has been found, though he was back later in August winning five events at Cashel, just two at Carrick-on-Suir and then four more at Kilcash Sports.[13] The new Olympic hammer champion, John Flanagan, visited Ireland that month too, and won the hammer event at Kilmallock

Sports with 160 feet 5 inches.[14] Kiely was not there as the date clashed with the Carrick-on-Suir Sports, which he was centrally involved in organising.

***

The return of Grangemockler footballers to the Tipperary championship in 1900 did not entice Kiely back to the playing field. Probably the most interesting development for Tom and Larry in 1900 was the GAA's effort to reinvigorate athletics by organising inter-county competitions. On 23 September, at Dan Fraher's field in Dungarvan, athletics teams representing Tipperary and Cork met. Tom was the Tipperary captain, and co-selector along with John Bourke. The two met at Magner's Hotel in Clonmel to pick the team.[15] The entire event came about because of a challenge issued by Cork and taken up on behalf of Tipperary by Tom Kiely.

A crowd of between 8,000 and 9,000 saw 'Magnificent Tipperary' win a comfortable victory. Six special trains were laid on for spectators that day.[16] There were thirteen events on the programme, and the winner of each event got four points for his team, second place got two points and third place got one point. Tom won five events: long jump, 16lb hammer, hurdles, 56lb unlimited run-up and the hop, step and jump. Therefore, on his own, he won twenty points. Larry was runner-up to Tom in the hammer, gaining two more points. In the end, Tipperary won by 63½ points to Cork's 27½. Cork missed the presence of Denis Horgan, certainly, and the event is otherwise notable for the fact that John Holloway, future competitor at the St Louis Olympic Games alongside Kiely, was on the Tipperary team too.[17]

The Tipperary athletics team which defeated Cork in 1900. Larry Kiely is third from the right at the back. Tom is in the centre of the front row with the sash and beside him, moving to the reader's right, are John Holloway, Paddy Ryan and Pat Harding. (*From Dinneen, Frank B.* Irish Athletic Records, *1906, p. 271*)

Although Kiely continued to win many prizes, he really did not improve his performances much after the age of twenty-nine. Many cited his continued insistence on competing at many different events, but that was Kiely's decision, one which he never wavered from. What is undeniable is that, from 1901 onwards, Kiely threatened only one further Irish hammer record. At Tipperary Sports in 1901 the hammer event was won by Kiely, with what seemed an incredible throw of 164 feet 6 inches. *Sport*'s reporter suggested that 'if all matters be right this is an Irish record'.[18] In so far as this can be verified, the record was not subsequently ratified.

Sports meetings were also changing, with an increasing number of them promoting cycling as well as athletics, and often the weight-throwing events were left off the programme. Kiely did not attend the 1901 Queen's College Sports as it had no weights events on the programme that year.[19] Later, at the sports at Clonmel organised by Clonmel Cycling Club, eight of the twelve events were devoted to cyclists. Kiely competed only in the hurdles, finishing second.[20]

In terms of Irish championships, May and early June for the IAAA championships had never suited Kiely's farming schedules. Despite this, he won one hammer title at Ballsbridge in appalling weather in 1901, on a day when his one-time pupil Peter O'Connor broke the world long jump record with a leap of 24 feet 9 inches.[21] By 1901, the GAA had lost interest in Irish athletics, by and large. The all-round championship was dead, and the GAA athletics championships were a disaster:

> *The date of the fixture was changed so often that nobody could regard any announcement in connection with it as a certainty, and when a day was finally decided on [29 September, in Limerick], very little notification of the event was given ... Although the weather was so bad that a postponement was clearly inevitable, the meet got under way, but after a few events had been concluded it was decided to adjourn sine die.[22]*

The postponed events were never re-fixed. Kiely won two GAA titles in 1901, simply because these had been farmed out to sports meetings earlier in the year: the 56lb title at Portlaoise on 8 July and the hurdles at Tipperary in August. No other events in Kiely's repertoire were rescheduled. Larry won a hammer title for the near-forgotten discipline of throwing the hammer with unlimited run and follow, at Cashel on 4 August.[23]

All the while, American techniques and training were leaving Irish athletics behind. While the Mitchell and

Kenyon video evidence shows that Kiely was using two-and-a-half turns in the circle before letting the hammer go, his one-time pupil John Flanagan had perfected three full turns in New York.[24] This and other adjustments to technique had an inevitable impact on his distances by 1902:

> *Flanagan winds the hammer more over his head than any other athlete we have seen at that exercise, and when his body revolves it does so almost as quick as lightning; as a consequence he keeps all his power together and covers very little ground. Kiely swings the hammer as he does the 56lbs, round his body, never up over his head, and he spreads himself out in the ground in the unlimited run style and covers quite a space. This, we believe, is not as good a style as Flanagan's and does not show the same command of the weight that the latter's style does …[25]*

Otherwise, in 1902, Kiely was still competing at local meetings, in places such as Nenagh, Clonmel, Fethard, Callan and Tipperary. He also won the AAAs and the match against Scotland, both in the hammer. Only once did he throw over 150 feet all season, at the IAAA championships in Cork:

> *T. F. Kiely was, of course, at the head of affairs in the 16lb hammer, and won easily with 150 ft 3½ ins, which was his fourth try. The hammer was landing on spongy ground, and at the fourth try went deep into the soil. While being extracted the handle was broken, and the competition ended. Kiely was, however, awarded the championship. It was certainly hard on Kiely that the event should have thus ended … for he was bound to make a new record with his succeeding throw …[26]*

That missed throw might have been irrelevant anyway.

Later in the year came the news from New York that John Flanagan had broken the world hammer mark again, hurling the weight 171 feet 9 inches at Celtic Park.[27] The Americans, and specifically the Spalding company, were even rectifying the issue of hammers breaking when hitting the ground, using ball-bearings to lessen the tension between hammer head and wire handle.[28]

Health problems beset Kiely again in late summer 1902. He spent much of his time outdoors with the cattle and it was not at all uncommon for him to get a drenching in inclement weather. This contributed to the occasional bouts of illness, undoubtedly. Despite these health setbacks, Kiely won several Munster athletics titles at an inter-county event in Dungarvan, where Larry Kiely and the giant Tom Phelan of Mullinahone were also prominent competitors. Phelan has been described as a pupil of Kiely's just as Peter O'Connor in the long jump and John Flanagan in the hammer were

Kiely on the right, with two other athletes. The tall man in the centre is Tom Phelan. Note that Kiely is clearly wearing an IAAA vest. This image is from the 1902 Munster championships, organised by the GAA. (*From the collection of Tom Hunt, original photograph by Edmund Keohan of Dungarvan*)

at different stages.[29] Phelan would go on to win six national titles in throwing the 56lb weight and when pictured beside Kiely, he almost dwarfed the Ballyneill man. In the surviving photograph of Phelan and Kiely from those Munster championships in Dungarvan, it is also noteworthy that although he was at a GAA event, held in a field owned by Dan Fraher, one of the most prominent GAA men in the country, Kiely had no qualms at all about wearing an IAAA vest on the day. There was no political statement being made here, just a reinforcement that Kiely was focused on his sport, nothing more.

The week after the Munster championships in Dungarvan, at the 1902 GAA national championships, held in Limerick yet again, Kiely won the 56lb throw and hurdles, and was second in the long jump and shot put. The biggest shock was Kiely losing the two hammer events (from a nine-foot circle and with unlimited run and follow) to Paddy Ryan. The *Sport* columnist again criticised Kiely for entering too many events, but added:

> To do more justice to the Carrick man, we must state that he was in anything but good health for the past fortnight. Even at Dungarvan [the previous week], where he annexed several events, he was complaining … what a falling off there was in Kiely last Sunday when compared to his throwing during the season …[30]

Referring to Kiely's performance at Limerick, his local paper commented on him being 'in wretched form in the early part of the day … entirely off colour' at the 1902 GAA championships.[31] Those championships echoed the decline in GAA athletics already alluded to, with the added complication that gambling appeared to have become an increasing difficulty.[32]

A legend emerged about Kiely in 1902 which has been often repeated, concerning an incognito appearance on the field at an All-Ireland football final. The earliest source of the story found during research for this book is the semi-autobiographical *The Big Sycamore*, written by Fr Maurice Browne under the pen name of 'Joseph Brady'. Fr Browne was a relative of the woman who would eventually become Kiely's wife and in his book, Grangemockler was called 'Mullinaglock', a place with a famous football team, and one alleged extra panel member:

The eighteenth man was the most famous of all, for he won world-wide fame as an all-conquering athlete – Tom Kiely. I put him down as the eighteenth man, because his father was such an industrious man that he did not allow his son to waste his time by going to football matches. There had to be a conspiracy of silence among the neighbours when Tom played. He was selected once to play in an All-Ireland final in Dublin. Tom dared not ask his father's permission to travel with the team on Saturday. He milked thirteen cows as usual on Saturday evening and started out on foot to catch the night train at Fethard, a journey of twelve miles.

He skirted Slievenamon, passed by Cloneen, and reached Fethard by midnight. A friendly porter found him a place in the van. Tom lay down to rest on a mail bag. The train reached Dublin at five o'clock on Sunday morning. Tom heard an early Mass, took breakfast, and made contact with the footballers in the city. Having played the game of his life, he returned by night mail from Dublin and reached home in the early hours of Monday morning. Tom was remarkable on the football field not so much for his expert kicking, as for his ability to soar into the heavens above the heads of his opponents and fist the ball farther than any other player could kick it.[33]

Fascinating as this story is, it has proven impossible to verify. There are some elements of well-known information in it, but much of the story is difficult to believe. Tipperary reached two All-Ireland football finals during the years of Kiely's career. The first was the 1895 competition, when he and Grangemockler played no championship games and the county representatives were Arravale Rovers, and the second was the 1900 competition, when the final was played in October 1902. As discussed, Kiely was in very poor physical form, or was ill, in the autumn of 1902. Furthermore, there had been no mention of him on any local football team for over five years by 1902.

Other details make no sense in the context of Kiely's life. By 1902, Kiely's sporting activities no longer needed to be hidden from his father, and the Kielys had very few, if any, milking cows on their farms then. The idea of Kiely walking to Fethard to get a mail train also makes little sense, as it would have been much simpler to get a train from Carrick-on-Suir station, a few miles away, to Waterford, and then on to Dublin. Many people in any GAA crowd in 1902 would have known Kiely, as he was one of the most recognisable sportsmen in Ireland, and yet not one contemporary newspaper or account mentions this figure on the Tipperary team.

Tipperary's team in the 1902 final (held at Terenure) was backboned by county champions Clonmel Shamrocks, with players from a few other clubs. Grangemockler had five players involved, none of them resembling Kiely.[34] Crucially, the photograph of the winning team has nobody in it resembling Kiely, although one list of the Tipperary panel does include a Kiely who played club football for Clonmel Shamrocks.[35]

***

The feeling that Kiely's career was in its twilight was reinforced in 1903. His loss in the hammer event at the Ireland v Scotland match, and his non-appearance at the 1903 AAAs, have been mentioned elsewhere. He continued appearing at sports meetings close to home. At Callan, Paddy Ryan won the hammer, but Kiely did not compete in the event. Instead he entered and won the 56lb and finished second in a handicap hurdles to John Holloway. At Waterford, where there may have been no hammer event, Kiely won the hurdles and Larry took the prize for the long jump.[36] Kiely may have been struggling again with an injury, though he won an IAAA hammer title again on 1 June, with a very modest throw. In fact, Kiely had not intended to compete at all that day but the fact that future Olympic hammer champion Paddy Ryan failed to arrive for the start of the hammer event left the field open for him to score a relatively easy victory, with his brother Larry in third place.[37]

Kiely's form seemed to improve, as usual, later in the year. At the GAA championships, uninspiring as the whole event was, Kiely won three more national titles. These were in the hurdles, the 56lb throw and the hammer, where his 145 feet 7 inches was more than enough to beat a field that badly missed Paddy Ryan's quality.[38]

The final good day of the 1903 season for Kiely was at Queenstown (now Cobh) on 27 September, for yet another

Kiely is on the extreme right of this image, which was taken at Dungarvan in 1902 at the start of a hurdles race, possibly a heat. (*From the collection of Tom Hunt, original photograph by Edmund Keohan of Dungarvan*)

Kiely preparing to put the shot at the 1900 Tipperary v Cork match in Dungarvan. This was the only one of the six events entered that he did not win. (*From the collection of Tom Hunt, original photograph by Edmund Keohan of Dungarvan*)

Tipperary v Cork competition. He won four events: the long jump, hammer, hurdles and 56lb with unlimited run-up. He was second in the shot to Denis Horgan and also second in the hop, step and jump.[39] Tipperary won the day once again, due in no small measure to Kiely's performance.

Perhaps on that day in Queenstown, Kiely looked out over the Atlantic and wondered what might have been. He had turned down invitation after invitation to go to the USA. Yet he had seen others carve out athletics careers and break records that he would never again break in Ireland. His score of twenty points in the match against Cork, and relatively good form at the GAA championships that month might have suggested to him that he was not done for yet. Perhaps a letter from his old Clonmel friend William Prendergast in New York convinced him. The World's Fair and Olympic Games in St Louis would, finally, bring Kiely to America.

CHAPTER 8

ONE REMARKABLE DAY IN ST LOUIS

In 1904, the USA was the only major country which really promoted all-around athletics, and at the age of almost thirty-five, Tom Kiely decided he was going to take on the American champions of several previous years in their own back yard. This was the stuff of legend, billed as the 'All-Around Championship of the World' at the Olympic Games in St Louis, Missouri. That said, it was a story grounded in a well-worked-out 'plan of campaign' by Kiely and several other Tipperary men.

Having resisted many calls to go to the USA, all the way back to the Chicago World Fair's athletic contests in 1893, Kiely finally set sail in late May 1904. The main appeals had come from relatives and Irish-American sports administrators. By 1904, the Greater New York Irish Athletic Association (GNYIAA) was well established in Long Island City and was fast becoming a great athletics club. Among its key people was Clonmel man William Prendergast. His role in Kiely's American exploits, and indeed in his life after athletics, was very important.

William Prendergast was already an established figure in Irish sporting administration when Kiely took part in his first athletics meeting. As seen earlier, Prendergast was a central figure in planning the 'Gaelic Invasion' of the USA in 1888. Like others on that trip, the young Prendergast saw the great attractions and opportunities in the USA and decided not to return immediately to Ireland.

Prendergast came back temporarily to south Tipperary in the early 1890s and served as a member of Clonmel Corporation. He also officiated at a Deerpark Sports meeting in 1892, where Kiely was one of the secretaries.[1] Prendergast eventually went back to the USA and became a US citizen in 1895.[2] He joined the New York Police Department and was based at Oak Street Police Station. As a very lucrative side-line, he also began to buy small properties and renovate them, aware of the growing opportunities for real estate development in New York. Prendergast then became the treasurer of the GNYIAA and played a huge role in formulating the share offer which financed its impressive stadium at Celtic Park, Long Island City. The builder of the main stand at Celtic Park was another Clonmel man, named Dwyer.

Prendergast tried several times to get Kiely to New York:

To raise funds, Frawley [a fellow GNYIAA leader] and Prendergast sought another Irish athletic 'invasion'. They contacted Patrick Davin and Tom Kiely in Ireland and hoped to have a party in New York for the 1899 Labor Day Games. The tour failed to materialize, and another effort was made in early 1900, which ended with a few individual athletes coming.[3]

Celtic Park was attracting more and more of the world's top athletes for special appearances or as guest members of the GNYIAA. By 1904, the club had a number of world-class performers and Olympic champions in its ranks. It was also attracting many athletes who had no Irish background at all, but who felt at home in its lack of social snobbery. The first African-American and the first Jewish-American to win Olympic titles were both members of the GNYIAA, later called the Irish-American Athletic Club (I-AAC).

By 1904, Kiely had no easy decision to just leave for America. What helped was that his two brothers were now well able to look after things while he would be gone. Larry was twenty-four and Willie was approaching twenty-one. Among other 'pull' factors, Kiely knew that there were several relatives and others from south Tipperary in New York who had been long-standing friends at home: fellow athletes like the Hardings, and William Fleming of Carrick-on-Suir who would act as his manager in the USA once he arrived in early summer.

It has been mistakenly suggested, including by this author in the past, that Kiely sold some of his prizes to pay for the fare. Kiely family members today feel this was unlikely, as they can locate the most valuable prizes that Kiely won, or can testify that he gave away others, for example, for use as prizes at local sports meetings. The prize-selling theory also forgets that Kiely was a well-off cattle farmer and could have afforded the fare himself without difficulty.

More importantly, there are the immigration records. Kiely landed in New York on 2 June 1904, on board the *Teutonic*, having left Queenstown on 26 May. The record of 'Passenger number 12978', Thomas F. Kiely, aged thirty-five, saw him describing himself as a labourer, with the word 'Farmer' written above it. The ship's manifest suggests that Kiely travelled alone, with no obvious travelling companion on board. At Ellis Island, he gave his final destination as New York. He declared that he had $50, although a line had been drawn through $60 in the same box. The $50 was the amount deemed necessary to prevent immigrants from being an immediate burden on the resources of the USA. One of the questions asked was 'By whom was Passage paid?' To this, Kiely answered 'Friend'. To the question of 'Whether going to join a relative or friend', he gave the name 'William Prendergast', with an address at 159 East 92nd Street, New York.[4]

The obvious implication here is that Kiely's passage to America in 1904 was paid for by William Prendergast. The deeper question is whether Prendergast's generosity was linked to a hope that Kiely would compete at Celtic Park and for the GNYIAA in 1904. The club was on the crest of a wave and bringing the world's most famous all-around athlete to its venue would be a glorious reinforcement of what *The Gaelic American* had written about it:

> *No athletic organization in America has done more for the encouragement and propagation of Irish athletics and athletics in general than the Greater New York Irish Athletic Association ... When the property at Laurel Hill, L.I. was purchased in 1897, there was much headshaking among the wiseacres, who failed to see what a splendid field there was for a properly managed Irish athletics organization in Greater New York ... Over $50,000 have been expended on the club house and grounds since then. Its track is one of the finest owned by any athletic association in the United States.[5]*

Celtic Park had to wait only a week before Kiely did indeed

appear there, with a huge crowd attracted by the prospect of seeing Ireland's greatest athlete:

> 'Kiely Day' was the means of attracting over five thousand sport enthusiasts to Celtic Park on Sunday afternoon when the Kickham Athletic Club tendered a reception to Thomas F Kiely, the champion all-around athlete of Ireland, who is to be Ireland's competitor in the All-around Athletic Championship of the World, to be held in July at the St Louis Exposition. Kiely … is the holder of forty world's records, and the winner of eighty championships and 1,500 prizes …[6]

This occasion was a sports 'picnic' organised by the Kickham Athletic Club, and Kiely's attendance was advertised and used to swell the crowd, just as in Ireland. The admission charge of 25 cents per head, plus alcohol sales, would have made the event worth several thousand dollars to the organisers. Having landed in New York just a few days beforehand, Kiely was not in good physical condition and his weight had dropped from 185lb to 177lb, due to the rigours of his sea crossing. While *The Gaelic American* felt the Irishman had done well in the weight throwing events, his 'sea legs' came against him in the hurdles, 'besides he had a bad cold, and, to him, the excessive heat proved the severest of handicappers'. *The New York Tribune*, with much less reason to view Kiely with green-tinted glasses, agreed that: 'after his ocean trip … he acquitted himself well … but none of his performances yesterday give any idea of his prowess as an athlete, as he was fully seven pounds below his normal weight'.[7]

Kiely's form was still a major disappointment. *The Gaelic American* consoled itself with the hope that it was too soon to expect Kiely to have recovered from the voyage, adding: 'Had it not been for the fact that Kiely was to exhibit at the games proved such a "draw", the champion's manager told the *Gaelic American*'s reporter that he would have scratched his man.' Kiely's manager, William Fleming, was also chairman of the Kickham Club, which explains his desire to have him at the club's picnic, whatever about other meetings.

Fleming then decided to focus for the next few weeks on getting Kiely as fit as possible for the St Louis all-around championship on 4 July. This caused problems, as Celtic Park had already been promoting other meetings in advance, using Kiely's name. In late June, *The Gaelic American* carried an advertisement for the Irish Revolutionary Brotherhood Veterans games on 26 June. It announced that the 'Putting Heavy Weight Contest' would be 'Between T.F. Keily [*sic*], Ireland's Greatest Athlete, and John Flanagan, Champion of America.'[8]

In the Sun's *report of I.R.B. Veterans games at Celtic Park on Sunday the following paragraph appeared: 'For the past week or so the management of the games spread the news around town that Kiely and Flanagan would meet and their names adorned the programme to substantiate the report. Kiely did not appear, however, and when asked last night by the reporter of the* Sun, *said he never intended to compete, that he never promised to meet Flanagan, and the use of his name on the programme was absolutely unauthorised.' This statement is absolutely incorrect. Kiely promised David J. Naughtin [President of the IRB Veterans Association], in the presence of P. J. Conway [President GNYIAA], Martin Cowan and William Fleming to appear at the games and he kept his word.[9]*

Kiely and John Holloway (with the large shamrock on his jersey) pictured at St Louis. (*Photograph courtesy of Con Casey, original source unidentified*)

On this occasion, it seemed that Kiely appeared, as he had promised, but did not take part in any events at Celtic Park. He must have been used to sports committees at home trying to attract spectators by putting his name on the programme, but the American levels of interest still put unwanted pressure on him. John Flanagan was by this time a specialist hammer thrower, while Kiely had nine other events to train for.

There has been much debate about what country Kiely was 'representing' as he headed for the all-around championship at the St Louis Games.[10] Sometimes, normally very authoritative sources can be misleading: 'Offered a free trip if he would compete for Great Britain, thirty-five-year old Tom Kiely refused, paid his own way, and competed for Ireland.'[11]

There were only three athletes at the St Louis Games who were technically citizens of Great Britain but were not members of the American or other national teams: Tom Kiely and John Holloway from Tipperary, and John Daly from Galway. They were three Irish individuals, not an Irish 'team' in the modern sense. However, there is no doubt that these three Irish-born athletes considered themselves Irish rather than British. They were mainly known as GAA athletes and were certainly not there as representatives of Britain, nor had any of them been asked to represent Britain.

In the build-up to St Louis, there had been much talk of an Irish team going, particularly in the USA itself, for example:

'*Strong Team of Irish Athletes for World's Fair*' ran the New York Sun's *headline of April 8, quoting World Fair and Olympic athletics chief, James Sullivan's prediction that the GNYIAA would bring a party bolstered by visiting Irish athletes, 'some of whom have international reputations,' including Horgan, O'Connor, Pat and Con Leahy, John Daly and Jack Holloway. By the end of April, Conway [Leader of the GNYIAA] suggested that 15 would compete, and a tug-of-war team would also go.*[12]

It is worth remembering that the only 'national' team that Kiely had ever represented in competition was Ireland, in the annual matches against Scotland. That said, the lines were a little more blurred in St Louis and indeed the concept of athletes firmly representing 'nations' was still very loosely understood at the International Olympic Committee (IOC) in 1904. This, along with whether or not Kiely's win constitutes an Olympic victory, will be discussed further in Chapter 12.

**

The commitment made by Kiely to Prendergast and the GNYIAA must have included an expenses arrangement. It is difficult to imagine Kiely remaining in the USA until October, as he did, but arriving with no more than $50 in his pocket. Patrick Redmond has suggested that:

> Kiely, like others before him, just took himself over to the States and travelled down to St Louis. It is probable that Kiely would have accepted the GNYIAA's aid, but either his membership was submitted too late or he was compelled to compete unattached.[13]

The reality may be somewhere in between. If the GNYIAA paid Kiely's fare, the association could make it back many times over through Kiely's drawing power at Celtic Park. Even Redmond has confirmed that no newspaper in the USA suggested that the GNYIAA had signed him. Kiely's focus was on the all-around championship on 4 July, and nothing else. This would explain his reluctance to compete at Celtic Park Sunday after Sunday before then or to join the GNYIAA team that won the AAU junior and senior athletics championships at St Louis less than two weeks before the all-around championship.[14] Kiely later declared, of all the American clubs wishing to 'sign' him: 'I declined their offers, and decided to win or lose as the representative of Ireland.'[15]

Legend has it that Kiely announced himself in St Louis as competing 'for Tipperary and Ireland'. It is obvious that Tom Kiely was representing Tom Kiely, first and foremost, and then Tipperary and Ireland. The officials at the St Louis Games would have had no difficulty with that, as athletes were not compelled to represent national teams in 1904. They would have been very glad indeed to have such a famous non-American competitor in what was termed the 'World's Championship' all-around competition at the Olympic Games.[16]

A page from the *St. Louis World*, 4 June 1904.

When the seven elite athletes appeared on Francis Field, St Louis for the 'All-Around Championship of the World', there were five Americans and two from 'Tipperary and Ireland'. The AAU all-around championship had traditionally been held on 4 July and now followed the Olympic gymnastics competitions at St Louis. Indeed, two of the competitors,

Max Emmerich and John Grieb, had just finished first and second respectively in a 'triathlon' called 'Combined Exercises, Field Sports'.[17]

Although the championship was held at the height of summer, the weather was atrocious. One account noted that: 'The ground was so deep in mud that they had to shovel out the seven-foot circle for the hammer event to give the men grip for their spiked shoes, making them throw uphill.' The same account also reported that Kiely later commented that Francis Field that day was 'No place for a non-swimmer'.[18] Possibly the most comprehensive contemporary and local account of Kiely's victory in the all-around championship wrote of how:

> The meet was run off under adverse circumstances due to the rain. The contestants, judges and spectators at one time were compelled to retire from the field, so heavy was the rainfall. The men were at the field event by 1:45 o'clock and had only finished the 100 Metre [should read 'Yard'] run and the shot put when the rain began. This was somewhat of an advantage to the contestants, as they received at least three-quarters of an hour's rest.[19]

It is difficult to imagine that the contestants needed much of a rest after just the 100 yards (91.44 metres) and the shot put. However, after three events Kiely had a serious challenge on his hands. Finishing last in the 100 yards must have been a surprise, given his well-known basic speed over hurdles. The adjudication in America, as in Ireland, saw only the winner's time in each heat recorded, and other placings were based on an estimate of their distance behind the winning time. In the

100 yards, Kiely was placed last because he was judged to have been 11 feet behind Truxtun Hare's winning time of 10.8 seconds, whereas the joint runners-up in the other heat were 4 feet behind Ellery Clark's winning time of 11 seconds.[20] What aggrieved Kiely particularly was being penalised a yard at the start, for what would today be called a 'false start'. He claimed later, exaggeratedly, that this cost him forty-eight points in his score.[21]

Kiely's shot put was also disappointing, though his last competitive shot-put performance, in August 1903, had not been much further than he achieved in St Louis. He complained later that

A picture purported to be of Kiely in the high jump at St Louis, 1904. Given that his jumper bears the crest of the GNYIAA, it is unclear whether this is from the all-around contest or the Irish Sports. (*Original source unknown*)

having to put the shot from a circle, rather than the square used in Ireland, had been an added difficulty.[22] Nor would the position improve after the athletes returned to the field for the high jump. All the jumpers struggled in the conditions, but Kiely's 5 feet even was still a disappointment. As far back as 1893, Kiely had occasionally jumped as high as 5 feet 7 inches.[23] John Holloway, a long-time friend and fellow Tipperary man, did well in winning the high jump with 5 feet 6 inches and was in third place after this event, with Kiely trailing in last.

After the deluge, the local newspaper noted that the water on the track was an inch deep in some places. The fourth event, the 880 yards walk, proved a turning point, though Kiely later described how competitors 'were obliged to walk in three inches of mud on account of the track being new, and the continuous rain that was falling':[24]

> *The walk was the feature track event, Kiely and Holloway crossing the tape at the same time, and judges decided to give to both the same number of points. They made the half mile in 3 minutes and 59 seconds. Ellery Clark led the bunch at the start and for half a lap, when Holloway began closing on him. When in the stretch, Kiely got a fast gait, and with Holloway crossed the tape.*[25]

Kiely then won the hammer with 120 feet 7 inches, the poor distance being testimony to the conditions. Kiely had thrown the hammer over 143 feet even on his mediocre day at the Kickham Sports in New York three weeks before.[26] Kiely himself suggested after the all-around contest that missing one of his throws because he had left the field to change his shoes and having to use an unfamiliar style of hammer were further challenges he encountered on the day.[27]

At this stage, the conditions and fatigue began to take effect on some of the competitors, and two were gone by the end of the sixth event. John Grieb, for instance, 'made three balks and did not score in the event. He would swing the hammer around his head, but would either let it drop at his feet or throw it a short distance and fall out of the ring.'[28] Ellery Clark was reportedly suffering from bronchitis all day, though the local newspaper was not alone in its suspicions about the 1903 American all-around champion who: 'after he saw that there was little chance of him winning or landing a place in the championship, retired after the hammer throw'.[29]

It is too simple to suggest that Kiely's strength in the weight throws was the difference between winning and losing in the end. After the hammer, he was still only third overall, behind Hare and Gunn, and there was only one weight event among the last five. In reality, it was a combination of his weights ability, his technical expertise and a dogged determination which would see Kiely win the championship. For example, the pole vault was certainly not an event that ever featured in the Irish all-round championship. Not once had he been found competing in this event at an Irish sports meeting. Yet, Kiely cleared 9 feet to beat Hare by a clear foot and finished just 6 inches behind Holloway, who had been an Irish pole vault champion.

Kiely was now in second place, a position he consolidated by winning the hurdles in 17.8 seconds. That was a relatively slow time for Kiely, but again the conditions played a significant part. With three events left, Adam Gunn was now the Tipperary man's obvious rival. Gunn had won the pole vault and lost the hurdles to Kiely by just 3 feet, so he was ahead of the field overall by 235 points. He was a Scot who had settled in Buffalo and won the US all-around championship in 1901 and 1902. He and Kiely would become good friends subsequently.

Only now, in event eight, did Kiely strike the front, winning the 56lb weight with a throw of 29 feet 3 inches. Gunn, a lighter man, struggled and saw Kiely edge ahead overall, by just thirty-one points.

Then came the long jump, or 'broad jump' as it was termed in the USA, as event nine. Of course, this is where

Kiely's versatility and technical expertise, i.e. his 'all-round' athleticism, saw him jump a creditable 19 feet 6 inches in the mud, just 5 inches behind the event winner Hare but a crucial 16 inches ahead of both Gunn and Holloway.

Kiely led by a huge 159 points from Gunn with only the mile run remaining. Hare was in third place and Holloway fourth. Kiely had never liked middle-distance running, but when he had to, he was well able to get around the track. As Hare and Holloway led the way and would finish joint first at the tape in the mile, Kiely jogged around and made sure that his main rival was kept in his sights all the way. Eventually Gunn finished the mile in third place but only 6 seconds ahead of Kiely. Kiely's time, 5 minutes 51 seconds, seems desperately slow by modern standards, but as he never ran this event if he could help it, this time remained his fastest ever recorded over the distance.[30]

'Erin's Champion' was now the all-around champion of the USA and, by American definition, of the world too. There were no national anthems played, nor flags raised, but Kiely received his medal, inscribed with 'Amateur Athletic Union of the United States MDCCCLXXXVIII' on the front – the AAU was founded in 1888 – and 'All-Around Athletics Champion of the World' on the back, with a bar above the ribbon stating '1904 Universal Exposition Olympic Games: St Louis'. The first response of the USA to Kiely's win in St Louis was a relatively matter-of-fact one, the Robert Edgren column in the New York *Evening World* merely reporting:

St Louis 4 July: Thomas F. Kiely, of Ireland, won the all-around championship of the world, formerly held by Ellery H. Clark of

Boston, from five other noted athletes in the games held to-day under the auspices of the A.A.U.[31]

This short note, accompanied by a list of results in each event, was syndicated to other newspapers across America, in places with no obvious link to either Kiely or to Irish America.[32] This undoubtedly helped increase awareness of Kiely, although the main response to him in the early days after 4 July was still to come from Irish America. In some respects, this victory was the crowning glory of the career of the man who has been called 'the greatest athlete of Ireland's greatest athletics period'. However, there is another story to be told, the story of how this victory impacted not only on Kiely and Ireland, but more immediately on Irish America.

After his victory, Kiely wrote home with the news. This envelope from the Lindell Hotel, St Louis, was used to send a letter to Sister Camillus in Dungarvan, though such was his busy schedule as world and Olympic champion that it was not written until late July, by which time he had reached another hotel in Chicago.
(*Courtesy of Tom Kiely of Lisheen*)

The 1904 all-around championship, by competitor and event[33]

Event	Tom Kiely	Adam Gunn	Truxtun Hare	John Holloway	Ellery Clark	John Grieb
100 Yards	3rd heat 1 (6th) 713 pts	2nd heat 2 (tied 4th) 720 pts	1st heat 1 (1st) 790 pts	2nd heat 1 (2nd) 769 pts	1st heat 2 (3rd) 748 pts	2nd heat 2 (tied 4th) 720 pts
Shot Put	3rd 10.82m (35ft 6in) 448 pts	1st 12.21m (40ft 1in) 668 pts	2nd 12.09m (39ft 8in) 648 pts	6th 10.01m (32ft 10in) 320 pts	5th 10.26m (33ft 8in) 360 pts	4th 10.54m (34ft 7in) 404 pts
High Jump	Tied 5th 1.52m (5ft) 480 pts	2nd 1.65m (5ft 5in) 640 pts	Tied 5th 1.52m (5ft) 480 pts	1st 1.68m (5ft 6in) 672 pts	Tied 3rd 1.62m (5ft 4in) 608 pts	Tied 3rd 1.62m (5ft 4in) 608 pts
3 event total	**1,641** (6th)	**2,028** (1st)	**1,918** (2nd)	**1,761** (3rd)	**1,716** (5th)	**1,732** (4th)
880 Yards Walk	Tied 1st 3 min 59 sec 717 pts	4th 4 min 13 sec 647 pts	5th 4 min 20 sec 612 pts	Tied 1st 3 min 59 sec 717 pts	3rd 4 min 11 sec 657 pts	6th 4 min 49 sec 467 pts
Hammer	1st 36.76m (120ft 7in) 706 pts	3rd 31.40m (103ft) 495 pts	2nd 36.28m (119ft) 687 pts	5th 27.51m (90ft 3in) 342 pts	4th 29.11m (95ft 6in) 405 pts	No mark ------- 0 pts

Pole Vault	**3rd** 2.74m (9ft) 472 pts	**1st** 2.97m (9ft 9in) 616 pts	**4th** 2.44m (8ft) 280 pts	**2nd** 2.89m (9ft 6in) 568 pts	No mark ------- Withdrew	No mark ------- Withdrew
120 Yards Hurdles	**1st** 17.8 secs 670 pts	**3rd** @14ft 600 pts	**2nd** @3ft 655 pts	**4th** @16ft 590 pts		
7 event total	4,206 (2nd)	4,441 (1st)	4,097 (3rd)	3,978 (4th)		
56lb Weight	**1st** 8.91m (29ft 3in) 684 pts	**3rd** 7.22m (23ft 8½in) 418 pts	**2nd** 7.59m (24ft 10in) 475 pts	**4th** 5.98m (19ft 7½in) 222 pts		
Long Jump	**2nd** 5.94m (19ft 6in) 612 pts	**Tied 3rd** 5.53m (18ft 2in) 484 pts	**1st** 6.07m (19ft 11in) 652 pts	**Tied 3rd** 5.53m (18ft 2in) 484 pts		
One Mile	**4th** 5 min 51 sec 534 pts	**3rd** 5 min 45 sec 564 pts	**Tied 1st** 5 min 40 sec 589 pts	**Tied 1st** 5 min 40 sec 589 pts		
Total	**1st** 6,036 pts	**2nd** 5,907 pts	**3rd** 5,813 pts	**4th** 5,273 pts		

CHAPTER 9

THE AFTERMATH OF ST LOUIS

The mere presence of 'Erin's Champion' among the Irish communities of the USA in 1904 had a hugely positive impact. The Irish had endured decades of economic and social challenges after making their way to the USA. They were still not accepted in many areas of urban America, a fact not helped by political corruption and cronyism in New York, certainly. To have an Irishman come over, be hailed as the 'World's Champion' and tour many American cities gave a huge boost to Irish America. Tom Kiely's achievement reinvigorated people's Irish identity and helped show America that the Irish were now an established part of American sport and society.

In its first edition following the all-around championship, New York's *The Gaelic American* was in raptures. This newspaper was controlled by the Fenian John Devoy, assisted by future 1916 Rising leader Tom Clarke, and was always on the lookout for opportunities to promote Irish nationalism. During the summer of 1904, it serialised the Charles Kickham novel *Knocknagow*, and many in America, just as in Ireland, were inspired to see in Kiely the embodiment of Mat the Thresher. The newspaper wrote of Kiely's altruism and patriotism:

He was always eager to assist the promoters of small meetings and has frequently competed four or five times in a week. His individuality, and his prestige, has done more to uplift athletic Ireland than any man excepting Maurice Davin, of Carrick-on-Suir. Kiely's wealth of laurels has been no detriment to the sacrifices he has made in the interest of one of the heritages of his race – the instinct of sport.[1]

By the following week, the use of Kiely's name to help advertise and promote meetings began again. A preview of a Christian Brothers fundraiser at Celtic Park announced that Kiely, 'who has postponed his departure for Ireland until after the event', would appear along with John Flanagan, Martin Sheridan and John Holloway (fourth in the all-around at St Louis).[2] Kiely, unsurprisingly, was nowhere near New York when this news was published in mid-July, nor would he be for some time. His win on 4 July had made him a celebrity, more than ever, among Irish-Americans, and he later described the reaction, in his own matter-of-fact style, to Sister Camillus in Dungarvan:

Well I won the World's Championship on 4th July & the Irish people here went crazy over my victory. I've had more invitations than I could fulfil in a year.[3]

Before taking up any invitations, there was St Louis to see properly, staying for a time as a guest of the Chief of Police, Mathew Kiely, who was a native of Newcastlewest, Co. Limerick.[4] Furthermore, the AAU had organised an 'Irish Sports' day, involving athletics, hurling and Gaelic football matches, and Kiely intended to compete there. This time, he

Kiely's letter home from the USA to Sister Camillus.
(*Kiely Collection, Tipperary Museum of Hidden History*)

was listed as representing the GNYIAA, as was his companion from the all-around championship John Holloway.

This represents the only time that so-called 'Irish Sports' featured at an event organised under the Olympic Games banner. The decision to hold Irish Sports had, in fact, been taken years before, when the Olympics were originally fixed for Chicago. When the Games were changed to St Louis, the Missouri city's large Irish population meant that Irish Sports remained part of its programme. Understandably, unlike Kiely's all-around victory, being confined to Irish athletes meant that these Irish Sports have never been accepted as 'Olympic' events in the record books.[5]

The Irish Sports were also held at Francis Field on 20 July. Tom Kiely won five athletic events and was second in one. Holloway won two events, was second in two and third in another, so that the newspapers gushed afterwards that Kiely and Holloway between them had scored more 'points' than the rest of the competitors combined.[6]

Kiely's five winning performances in the 'Olympic Irish Sports' were as follows:

- 120 yards hurdles: 17.2 seconds
- Two hops and a jump: 43 feet 9 inches
- 16lb hammer throw: 139 feet ½ inch
- 56lb weight throw: 29 feet 6½ inches
- 42lb stone throw: 23 feet 8½ inches.

Some of these figures give a good insight into the impact that the conditions had on Kiely's all-around performance on 4 July. Back then, in the mud and rain, his hurdles time was over half a second slower than on the Irish Sports day. Kiely's hammer win on 4 July was almost 18½ feet short of what he did in the Irish Sports. Even finishing second in the broad jump, his jump at the Irish Sports (20 feet 9¾ inches) was over 15 inches further than on 4 July. John Holloway's jumping improvement was even more remarkable. He had broad-jumped 18 feet 2 inches on 4 July, and yet beat Kiely with a leap of 20 feet 10¾ inches at the Irish Sports.

While details of the different events are sketchy, one incident during the Irish Sports certainly caused some amusement:

In the hammer throw, when Kiely came up for his third trial in the preliminary round, he threw the hammer high, and everyone waited breathlessly for it to drop, as they fully expected him to break the record. The hammer failed to drop, however, as it had by some freak caught on a heavy wire which stretched from the grandstand to the pavilion in the center of the track and hung suspended in mid-air. As the hammer throw was a special event for which no preparation had been made, and this was the only hammer on the grounds, the event was hung up until, in response to the promise of a reward of a dollar, a small boy shinned up one of the supports of the grandstand and unfastened the wire ...[7]

While in St Louis, Kiely certainly took the opportunity to visit the World Fair and take in everything he could about this massive event. His letter to Sister Camillus also mentioned catching up with people from home, a Mr Dunne and a brother of William Duggan, the latter from Carrick-on-Suir. The Kiely family believe that the great Irish tenor John McCormack sang at a reception in Kiely's honour. McCormack, in 1904, was one of the performers at the 'Irish village' which had been constructed as part of the World Fair attractions. It is at least likely that the two great Irishmen met there.

Today's Kielys also remember Tom and his brother Larry, later in life, joking about knowing the Roosevelts in America. This could have transpired in one of two ways. The US President in 1904 was Theodore Roosevelt. He was of Irish extraction on his mother's side, a member of the American Irish Historical Society and a great admirer of the Irish-American athletes of Celtic Park.[8] Theodore Roosevelt's daughter, Alice, presented medals to athletes at various events in late June, though it has been impossible to verify whether she was still in St Louis when Kiely was there.[9] It is just as likely that Kiely met the Roosevelts in New York later, as his cousins lived near the Roosevelt home on Long Island. Theodore Roosevelt would certainly have wanted to meet Kiely. He went on to invite the entire American athletic squad to his home at Oyster Bay, Long Island, after the 1908 Olympics, and particularly celebrated their Irish heritage on that occasion.[10]

While wandering around the World Fair, another story about Kiely was born and, thankfully from the perspective of historical research, was documented at the time:

On last Thursday evening, at the conclusion of the meet in connection with the Irish Sports at the Stadium, Kiely, accompanied by Chief of Detectives Desmond and Chief of Police Kiely, started in to do the Pike [a major public concourse at the Fair site]. Being embarrassed somewhat by the weight of his grip, in which were all his running clothes and the five gold medals which he had just won at the Stadium, Kiely left it in charge of the man at the cigar stand in the Irish Village and proceeded on his way rejoicing. On his return, however, he found that someone had made away with his grip and left him minus both medals and track clothes. A search was made, but the missing property could not be located. Consequently, he was compelled to exchange clothes with Holloway in each alternate event, and both could not appear at the same time. The mere mention of 'Irish village' is almost enough to make Kiely fight.[11]

What is difficult to explain, however, is that the same newspaper report used this event to explain why:

It was noticed that Kiely and his compatriot and brother athlete, John J. Holloway, representing the Greater New York Irish A.A. never appeared on the track together, although in all previous meets the contests between them in the jumps had furnished the best features of the day's sports. Instead, they alternated in their appearances.

The problem with this story is that the Irish Sports were held on 20 July, which was a Wednesday in 1904. Thus, if Kiely's clothes were stolen on a Thursday, the following day, he would certainly have had at least five medals in his bag. However, there is no record of Kiely or Holloway competing in any other sports meetings or events in St Louis, so the events that they had to change clothes for after his medals were stolen remain a mystery. One non-Olympic gold medal in Tipperary museum's Kiely Collection is filed as a St Louis prize, but the St Augustine's club that presented it was a Boston one at the time and was almost certainly won by Kiely when he visited his Boston relatives later in the 1904 trip.

The two known photographs of Kiely from St Louis do not help to clarify this story much either. One seems to show him wearing a GNYIAA vest with its easily recognisable 'winged fist' crest, performing the high jump. If this is Kiely, it must be from the Irish Sports day when he was listed as a GNYIAA representative, even though the results do not list Kiely as being in the first three in the high jump. That may well be, as the third placed athlete in the Irish Sports did 5 feet 3 inches, which may have been beyond Kiely. Whether it is his own or Holloway's vest is impossible to say. The other photo shows Kiely and Holloway standing together in St Louis. In that, Kiely has an off-white singlet with an undecipherable crest above his heart, while Holloway has a striped jersey with a large shamrock on the front of it. That photo is more likely to have come from the all-around events on 4 July, when neither of them was likely to have been wearing a GNYIAA singlet.

***

As something of a celebrity in the USA, Kiely's views on athletics and related matters were sought out. At a time when sport, and particularly athletic sport, was becoming increasingly scientific and specialised, the Irishman appeared to be a breath of fresh air:

[He] is able to go on the field with no apparent training, enter ten or a dozen events and exert himself to the utmost in all of them with apparently no ill effects to himself.

'What is the secret of my ability to remain in active athletics at my age?' said Kiely, in response to a query. 'I am 34 years of age and have been in athletics as long as I can remember. The secret of retaining my activity and vigour is that I have lived a regular life, and have never dissipated ... The American trains hard when the season rolls around and is in the finest of condition when he steps on the track. But before the season is over, he is likely to be found over-trained and stale. When the season is over, he relapses into his loose methods of eating and drinking and does not put on a spiked shoe until the next spring.

The Irish athlete keeps in training all the year round but never does much heavy work. When he enters a meet, he does it not for the medals or for the purpose of breaking or establishing records, but to have all the sport out of it that he can have. If he makes a fairly good showing, he is satisfied. This has been my experience and general method, and to this I attribute my unfailing good health. I train in moderation the year round and need very little work to get in shape for a meet. Nor do I feel any ill effects after my exertions, because of my perfect condition.[12]

Kiely travelled to various cities when in the USA in 1904. His letter to Sister Camillus was written on the notepaper of the Palmer House Hotel in Chicago, though he mailed it from there on 30 July in an envelope that he had acquired at the Lindell Hotel in St Louis. These were not small or basic hotels. In his letter to Camillus, Kiely said:

I visited Milwaukee and Chicago. I spent a fortnight at St Louis. The Fair is magnificent and I cannot describe its splendour here. I am to visit Buffalo, Syracuse, Boston and Philadelphia ere I return to New York. I expect to return home the end of August or early September ...[13]

It is known that Kiely, for a time, stayed in a small hotel or boarding house on the lake shore in Chicago, run by two Miss Halpins from near Clonmel. They had emigrated to Chicago some years before and bought a boarding house there.[14] Kiely also wrote that he was staying with a Fr Fielding (from the diocese of Ossory originally) in Chicago for part of his time there.

It is not clear whether Kiely made his way from St Louis to Chicago via the town of South Bend, Indiana, or whether he just met someone from the famed Notre Dame University elsewhere. Kiely was too old for college by 1904, but people in the USA were aware that he had a brother at home who had been showing considerable promise. Larry Kiely won an Irish hurdles title, and had three second placings in weights events, during the summer of 1904. One way or another, Notre Dame was interested in offering Larry a scholarship, as Kiely informed Camillus:

Larry is having a good time this season. He can get into Notre Dame University, in Indiana, free, & get educated to any profession or stay a year or two & go for the all-round c'ship & represent the University. I don't know what he shall do.

It is fascinating to realise that the Americans were so advanced in their policies of grooming promising athletes as far back as 1904. Larry never went to Notre Dame, perhaps because of commitments to the home farm, but he did become a high-class athlete in his own right and competed at the 1908 Olympic Games in London.

When the Christian Brothers Sports (mentioned earlier in this chapter) were eventually reported on in *The Gaelic American* of 6 August, Kiely was still touring America. He had travelled on from Chicago to Buffalo and elsewhere throughout late July and well into August. He seems to have taken part in some competitions, winning a few prizes, but his main interest was in seeing the USA and meeting up with friends and acquaintances. When he went to Buffalo, in upstate New York, Kiely and his manager, William Fleming, were warmly welcomed:

Kiely is in Buffalo as the guest of the Irish Nationalists and was met by a committee of that society, headed by James M. Walsh. Among the first to greet Kiely was Adam Gunn, the young Scotch athlete, of Buffalo, who held the AAU championship in 1901 and

1902, and who pressed Kiely closely at St Louis for first honors last month.

'Under a little different circumstances this time,' laughed Gunn.

'Yes indeed' said Kiely. 'Will I ever forget that competition in St Louis, mud to your knees and drenching rain throughout the period. It was enough to stop any man, and hours of it, too ...' Kiely declared Gunn to be 'easily the best athlete he had encountered on this side'. [15]

Kiely was the guest of Irish nationalist groups in the American cities he visited. The committee in Buffalo endeavoured to secure his attendance at the Ancient Order of Hibernians field day on 6 August but owing to unspecified previous engagements Kiely was unable to oblige. He had already missed the Christian Brothers Sports in New York, and subsequently there would be no Kiely appearance at the senior Metropolitan championships in late August, the GNYIAA's own revival of the 'Tailtin [*sic*] Games' on 5 September or other events in Celtic Park.

Most significantly of all, there was no Kiely in St Louis when the main individual athletic events of the 'Olympic Games' were held, and where athletes of the GNYIAA such as Martin Sheridan and John Flanagan won gold for the USA in fields which were largely drawn from the USA alone. Only one athletic event held between 29 August and 3 September was won by a non-American, and he was from just over the Canadian border: Etienne Desmarteau in the 56lb weight throw.

The likelihood is that Kiely decided that he had won what he had come to win, the all-around championship, and that he felt the later 'Olympic Games' in St Louis were for event specialists. In most events that he was a top performer in, specialists like Flanagan (hammer), Desmarteau (56lb) and Meyer Prinstein in the long/broad jump were achieving distances beyond the capacity of the now thirty-five-year-old all-rounder, and he knew that. He had places to visit and people to meet, so he happily left those Games to others. His job was done.

The Washington Times, not an Irish newspaper in any way, carried a lengthy interview with Kiely on 7 August 1904. It referred to his greatness in no uncertain terms:

> *... Kiely is undoubtedly the brightest star that athletic firmament has ever known ... Never in the history of athletics has anyone achieved the enviable reputation that Thomas Kiely retires with. To have won over 1500 prizes seems to our youthful athletes as a taste of paradise. These were won in all branches of athletics: running, jumping and weight throwing ...*[16]

In the same article, Kiely spoke of the all-around win and what it had taken to achieve it:

> *Several of the events were new to me and I had been some time out of some of the others; consequently my task was a hard one. Anyone who understands athletics can see that the program of the AAU championships is the severest test that an athlete can be put through but when one has to go through it in five hours in the face of a blinding rainstorm on a new track soaked with water and mud is something more than I care to attempt again. I doubt if any of us who went through it on July 4 will do many brilliant performances during the remainder of the season. For me, I have achieved the height of my ambition and retire from the track with deep regret. I*

also wish to mention the fact I have met with nothing but the highest courtesy and sportsmanlike treatment from officials and opponents while [here] for the championships and truer sportsmen than Messrs Gunn of Buffalo, Hare of Pennsylvania and Holloway of New York [the Bansha man was a member of the GNYIAA] I have never met.

Kiely had stated, clearly, that he had retired from athletics. That may be the best explanation of all for his non-appearance at further competitions in the USA during 1904. Interestingly, he highlighted the sportsmanship of fellow competitors Adam Gunn, Truxtun Hare and John Holloway, but made no reference at all to Ellery Clark. Clark had not endeared himself to Kiely at St Louis, being both arrogant and a quitter in many people's eyes. Their paths would cross again, unfavourably, in 1906.

While it is not clear when exactly Kiely arrived back in New York from his pan-American travels, he certainly spent a few weeks there before his departure for home, a full month after his letter to Sister Camillus had planned for. He had many friends to visit in New York, like William Prendergast, but he also had cousins in Brooklyn and Long Island to see. Tom met up with the children of John Kiely of Mullagh, while in New York, as shown in the portrait photograph taken at the time. John Kiely, thought nowadays to have been Tom's uncle, was the man who had fled to America after the killing of a bailiff, as mentioned previously, but is thought to have died during a cholera epidemic soon after. Subsequently, his wife, Johanna (nee Hickey), and three of her five children left Ireland for America when the children were adults.

The best evidence of all that his friends in New York and

Kiely with his American cousins. On the left are John and Nelly Kiely
(Long Island) and on the right is Thomas Kiely from Brooklyn.
(*Kiely Collection, Tipperary Museum of Hidden History*)

the GNYIAA were fully understanding of Kiely's American
travels, and absence from some of their sports events, comes
from the manner in which they eventually said 'goodbye'
to him. Advertisements appeared announcing that a grand
reception and presentation was being organised for 'TF Kieley
[*sic*], Champion Athlete of the World', scheduled for Sulzer's
Harlem River Park and Casino on Saturday 24 September.
The Gaelic American announced:

> *A massive silver cup will be presented to this sturdy athlete on
> this occasion. Police Commissioner William McAdoo will preside
> at the reception and State Senator John J. Frawley will make the
> presentation speech.*[17]

A special organising committee of Irish-American dignitaries
was assembled, involving GNYIAA officials, a fine smattering

of New York police and firemen, and Kiely's fellow Tipperary athlete Henry Harding as one of the committee's secretaries. They in turn wrote to others inviting them to become involved:

The affair has been placed in the hands of a Committee of competent Irishmen of this City, who desire to know if you would honor them with your co-operation, and allow yourself to be placed as one of the General Committee.[18]

Kiely spent almost four months in America. At Sulzer's Harlem River Park, three days before he left for Ireland, he received a 14-inch-high 'loving cup' from Police Commissioner William McAdoo 'on behalf of the many friends he has made during his stay in this country'.[19] That same cup was valued in 1904 at $1,000, equivalent to £250 or so in 'Tipperary money', enough to buy possibly forty good acres of land if it were sold at home.

Not only did Kiely take the cup home with him, but, despite its monetary value, he never sold it afterwards. It carried the names of those who had celebrated his achievements in Harlem, including the great athlete James Mitchel, who had been one of Kiely's inspirations when he began his career. The cup rests today in the Tipperary Museum of Hidden History at Clonmel, courtesy of the Kiely family. On its front, etched in huge letters, it reads: 'Thomas F. Kiely of Ireland – All-Around Champion of the World – won at the Olympic Games, St Louis U.S.A.'

At the reception, Police Commissioner McAdoo said that Kiely had shown himself to be the greatest athlete in the world. He added that Kiely typified many of the best qualities of the Irish people; he was a fine representative of the race. Not only did Kiely possess skill and physique, but he displayed moral and staying qualities. McAdoo stressed that physical and moral courage, as Kiely had shown, where what made the Irish race invincible.[20]

No details remain of what Kiely himself said on the night, although it seems that he was unsure about retiring now, as he promised the attendance that he would return to compete in the USA someday.

Kiely with a group of New York dignitaries, 1904. Back, from left: M. McCarthy, J. C. Landy, J. Phelan, M. Harding (District Chief, Metropolitan Fire Department), W. O'Keefe (Supervisor, 4th Ward). Front row, from left: Thomas King (Captain, MFD), Kiely and Thomas Clancy (First Assistant Chief, MFD). (*Kiely Collection, Tipperary Museum of Hidden History*)

When the morning came for Kiely to leave for home on board the *Celtic*, he was accompanied to the dock by William Prendergast. The *New York Daily News* summed up the impact that the athlete had had on American opinion:

> *Of two men who walked up the gang plank of the* Celtic, *which cast off her lines at 9 o'clock this morning, there was one who possessed what the almost unlimited wealth of the other could not buy. He who was accompanied to the dock by scores of friends, and was given a parting ovation seldom recalled, was Thomas F. Kiely, world's champion athlete, who returns to his native land, the Emerald Isle. The other was William Waldorf Astor, former citizen of the United States, but a subject now of his majesty King Edward, who boasts of wealth beyond computation.*[21]

William Waldorf Astor had effectively renounced his American citizenship to become British and would ultimately gain a peerage for his loyalty to his new country. Kiely, on the other hand, was his own man, doing things his own way. Yet he had helped enhance the reputation of Ireland, and its citizens living in America, very significantly over the summer of 1904. He was now returning to Tipperary and Ireland as a world and Olympic champion.

CHAPTER 10

WHAT SWANSONG? KIELY'S LAST YEARS IN COMPETITION

Before he left the USA to return to Ireland in 1904, Tom Kiely had given ambivalent and sometimes conflicting messages about retiring from athletics. People back in Ireland, especially in GAA circles, expected that the victory in St Louis was to be Kiely's last great achievement. The Central Council of the GAA, which still struggled to spell 'Kiely', noted:

> It was decided that an address be presented to Mr T.F. Keily [sic] on his landing at Queenstown, the president, trustees and sec to attend as a deputation to present the address. Messrs Dinneen and O'Toole were appointed to draft the address for next meeting of Council to be held in Dublin on July 30.[1]

GAA members organised celebrations for Kiely's homecoming, both at Queenstown and in Carrick-on-Suir. One Tipperary newspaper wrote of the arrival of Kiely at Queenstown, of the particularly warm greeting between Kiely and Maurice Davin, and of how an illuminated address was presented to the champion by the GAA. Queenstown Sports Committee,

Cove [*sic*] National Hurling Club and the Gaels of Tipperary town and district also presented addresses.[2] In reply to the GAA, Kiely said:

> *My Friends – I thank you for the splendid address you have presented me. It shall be a treasured souvenir of your friendship and goodwill after fifteen years connection with the GAA. I wish I had deserved all the nice things that have been said and written about me for the past months. Now that we have got this championship, I hope to see it remain here, and I expect the GAA will do its part towards attaining that end.*

Kiely informed reporters that he had gained ten pounds in weight since he arrived in the USA (though the voyage over had seen him lose most of that amount through sea sickness). Then he gave his clearest indication yet that he was not retiring:

> *He said he was in first class condition and had no intention of giving up the track though he might give up all-round athletics and go in more for weight throwing. It was, however, quite possible that when the time came to defend the title of the world's championship he would enter provided not [sic] more suitable candidate was found in the meantime.*[3]

Always of an independent mind, Kiely may well have had enough of the adulation and crowds before he even left Queenstown that day:

> *The man himself had little time for personal adulation and his*

patience with the trappings of celebration had been exhausted by the time he returned to Carrick-on-Suir. On the day of his return, the townspeople waited at the railway station with the brass band prepared to provide the conquering hero with an appropriate welcome. Unfortunately for the welcoming party, Tom Kiely, independent to the last, disembarked from the train at the edge of town and walked home through the fields to Ballyneill![4]

If the presentation of addresses was not necessarily something that came at the end of an athlete's career, the collection of money for what was called a 'testimonial' might seem more like a farewell. In fact, the idea of a collection for Kiely began in at least two separate quarters immediately after his win in St Louis and without any reference to whether he was due to retire. The *Nationalist* led a special Tipperary testimonial:

The Nationalist will subscribe, and help in every way, for it is only right that the Premier County should suitably honour this splendid Tipperaryman, born and reared 'neath the shadow of Slievenamon, and who, by his prowess, has added luster [sic] to our county, and to Irish manhood, by winning the proudest title in the highest athletic arena of the world.[5]

The GAA's Central Council also felt inclined to raise funds to thank Kiely for the manner in which he had represented Ireland and the GAA. This conveniently overlooked the fact that the athletic body which had promoted an international dimension up to this point was the IAAA, and the only vest worn by Kiely in such international competitions had been that of the IAAA. The problem was that, by 1904, the GAA and IAAA were at loggerheads again, and gone were the days of collaboration on record-keeping and support for each other's meetings. This may also explain why there was so little official IAAA reaction to Kiely's win, because he was seen as more of a GAA man, despite his support for both associations over the years.

This sort of divisiveness must have frustrated Kiely enormously. The GAA's later action, organising a football match with the intention of giving some of the proceeds to Kiely as its own 'testimonial', may have embarrassed him greatly too:

> The Inter pro challenge for the benefit of the Keily [sic] memorial and distress in the City, half of gate receipts to be equally divided. The match was fixed for Jones' Road on January 29th. Mr Stephen Holland to act as referee.[6]

When the game eventually came off, in front of 15,000 spectators, it was billed as a fundraiser for the poor of Dublin, and there was no further reference to it being for Kiely.[7] Kiely may have disassociated himself from it, as he had by January 1905 definitely decided to continue competing. Receiving such a public testimonial could have threatened his amateur status.

One final point about this *Nationalist* testimonial deserves a comment. Despite having five sisters who, by this time, were nuns, during close to six months of the *Nationalist* calling for contributions, churchmen were slow contributors to the Kiely testimonial. Father C. F. Ryan, the curate in Drangan, and Archbishop Fennelly, whose £3 was the largest individual

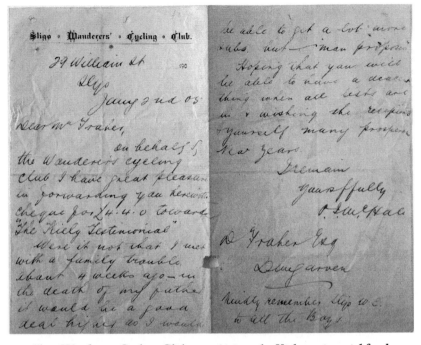

Sligo Wanderers Cycling Club gave £4 4s to the Kiely testimonial fund.
(*Kiely Collection, Tipperary Museum of Hidden History*)

donation of all, were the only clerics on the *Nationalist* list.

It has been suggested that because of the involvement in the GAA of Archbishops Croke and Fennelly, priests in Tipperary fully participated in GAA activities.[8] However, it is fascinating to note how a pair of female readers of the Clonmel newspaper berated the clergy for its lack of contributions. One, 'a Clanwilliam girl', hoped 'to see more priests helping in the movement', while another, a 'Tipperary mother', wrote more cuttingly:

> *It would be well if more of our good soggarths, and particularly those under the jurisdiction of the great patron of athletics in Ireland [i.e.*

Croke], would throw themselves into the project. We know that every soggarth is proud of Tom's mother, and we have confidence in movements in which the soggarths lead.[9]

***

In 1905, 'the Champion' was found yet again on his way to various sporting meetings. He missed the IAAA championships in June but was at the GAA championships in Cork. There, on 23 July, Kiely won the Irish title in slinging the 56lb weight with an unlimited run and follow, was second in the hammer to future Olympic champion Paddy Ryan, and was also second (to James Burke of Dunmanway) in the hurdles. In that event, Kiely was only beaten by inches even though he stumbled and almost fell at the last hurdle, with the winner's time recorded at $16\frac{4}{5}$ seconds, an impressive time indeed.

Kiely went to quite a lot of sports events in the northern half of the country in 1905 – places like Dundalk, Ballina, Belfast and Sligo. Ballina, of course, would have allowed him to call to his sister Benignus's second convent home, at Gortnor Abbey, Crossmolina. In Sligo, he was hard-pressed to make the event, despite many hours of rail travel:

Kiely competed at the Queenstown Sports on Sunday, got to Limerick that night by the mail, and started before 7 a.m. for Sligo. He was in the train until 2.15 PM that day, and yet when he tried the 56lb from stand, without run or follow, he broke the long-standing Irish record by Dr J.C. Daly, by four inches on the second attempt …[10]

In this case, the writer suggests that Kiely would have thrown farther than the record of 27 feet 2 inches had he arrived in

Sligo the evening before, and then gives an insight into Kiely's stubbornness: 'However, no one can tell the champion his business, and we expect he will not be content with the Sligo record when he again takes the notion.'

For several of these 1905 meetings, Tom and Larry Kiely travelled and competed together. They tied in the long jump at Dundalk Sports, doing 23 feet 7 inches in what must have been a handicap event, because that distance was never one reached by Tom in his prime. Larry beat Tom in the 16lb shot, and by 5 yards in the hurdles, but then Tom beat Larry in the hammer.

What the Dundalk visit also showed, to the correspondent of *Sport*, was that even in mid-1905, Kiely was eyeing up an opportunity to get back to America and the all-around championship of the AAU. In a reported conversation with local man Stephen Holland:

Kiely gave himself away, because he was never responsible for that statement that he intended to retire after his win in the World's championship. 'Indeed,' says he, 'it would be impossible for me to leave the boys [i.e. his fellow athletics competitors], and I would go to sports if only to look on. I must compete, and when I am in the field in competitions, I feel as fit as I did ten years ago. I must wipe out some weight records next year, but I am watching the next World's Championship, and I do not care to give up all-round training until I find out when it is to be held. If it not be held next year or the year after I will go in for weights, when I expect to surprise a few people.

Kiely must also have been encouraged by his late season form in 1905, such as at Dungarvan on 17 September, a day when he threw the hammer 154 feet 2 inches, his best-ever throw from a circle.[11]

When 1906 dawned, the chances of Kiely continuing his athletics career domestically were compromised by a renewed outbreak of 'bans' between the IAAA and GAA, whereby any athlete who competed at one organisation's meeting was automatically banned from meetings run by the other. Kiely's great rival, Paddy Ryan, was banned from the IAAA in mid-1906 because he competed at a GAA meeting. With Larry now a top-ranked athlete, the Kiely brothers faced an awkward decision. There was no dispute or difference of opinion between the brothers, but they effectively went separate sporting ways at this time. Larry continued to enter IAAA meetings, winning a number of national championships, representing Ireland in the Ireland v Scotland matches, and eventually being selected in the hurdles on the 1908 British and Irish Olympic team for London. There would have been no opportunities like those were he to attach himself to the GAA alone.

Tom Kiely, on the other hand, was 'done' with the AAAs and the Ireland v Scotland matches, and had always been more a GAA athlete than an IAAA one in terms of the number of championships he appeared in. It has been difficult to locate any IAAA responses to Kiely's success in America, but there has equally been no evidence located of a rift between the IAAA and Kiely, although almost certainly he would have disagreed with the new ban. That was just adding more and more difficulties to what was already a troubled and declining national athletics scene – *The Irish Times* called it the 'decadence' in Irish athletics.[12]

***

With the athletics divisions in Ireland, and the GAA being realistically much more interested in hurling and football than in athletics, Kiely decided on a return visit to America in 1906. He arrived at the port of New York on 26 May with the intention of competing at the AAU's 'All-Around Championship of America' in Boston on 23 June. This gave him four weeks to recover from any ill effects from the voyage. This time, he stayed in Flushing, as New York had expanded in that direction. William Prendergast had a house in the Bronx and at least one house at 262 State Street, Flushing, New York.[13]

Prendergast had speculated on Long Island property, especially a large tract of marsh land outside of Flushing that he picked cheaply with a partner, while also possessing property in Sunnyside now wanted by the Pennsylvania Railroad.[14]

Kiely found Irish America as anxious as ever to use his name as a draw for various sports meetings, and he was in trouble more or less straight away in 1906 for apparently making promises to appear and then not doing so due to simple misinformation:

[He] had promised not to compete before Beantown, but appeared at the Men of Galway Games the day after his arrival. Five thousand fans were hoping to see him, but unfortunately he had been told by the organisers in the morning that the event was cancelled due to heavy rain. However, when a huge crowd braved the downpour, the day went ahead without Kiely, amidst a disgruntled crowd.[15]

Since his triumph in July 1904, Kiely had watched the emergence of a new giant of athletics in the shape of Mayo man

Martin Sheridan. Sheridan won the discus at the individual Olympic championships of the St Louis Games held later that summer, and then earlier in 1906 he had triumphed in several events at the Intercalated Olympic Games in Athens. More significantly, he was a very serious all-around athlete and many expected that the AAU all-around title of 1906 would be fought between Sheridan and the newly arrived Kiely. This wasn't to be, though the two competed at the same sports meeting in Celtic Park within a little over a week of Kiely's arrival: the *Evening World* reported that Sheridan won the discus and Kiely took the 56lb weight throw. They did not compete against each other, unsurprisingly, as Kiely rarely if ever threw the discus, and Sheridan was not known as a 56lb specialist either. The paper added that 'The winners hold the world's records for each of these events, a further proof of their right to possess the proud titles they hold.'[16]

Sheridan had won the AAU all-around title comfortably in 1905 and would do so again in 1907 and 1909. In Athens that April, he had intended to participate in a pentathlon but tore his leg with his spikes while training for the jumping events, causing him to withdraw.[17] This injury was slow to heal, so that Sheridan competed on the card with Kiely in Celtic Park with his leg in bandages and it hampered him markedly.[18] He was in no condition to take part in the all-around championship a couple of weeks later, and did not go to Boston at all.

It has been suggested by a historian who is certainly no fan of Ellery Clark's that this individual used his Bostonian connections to have the all-around championship dates brought forward from early July. The alleged intention was to catch Sheridan unawares. However, Clark was to find his nemesis from 1904, 'Erin's Champion', arriving from Tipperary instead to take him on.[19]

On 23 June 1906, at the Technology Athletic Field, Brookline, Boston, Kiely competed in his second AAU all-around championship. His main rivals were Ellery Clark and a young man of twenty years named John Bredemus. A mere 300 spectators turned up for the event, as the weather was worse even than at St Louis in 1904. The conditions alone make it impossible to compare the total of 6,274 points scored by Kiely with Sheridan's world record from 1905, of 6,820 points.

This day, perhaps more than most, saw Kiely's competitive spirit bring him through, in the face of the weather and other circumstances. In the hammer, for example, he used his old-style non-revolving Irish hammer for all but his last throw, and when he used the American hammer he threw it 142 feet 10 inches.[20] With that throw gaining 973 points, referee James E. Sullivan of the AAU announced that Kiely had achieved the largest number of points ever won in a single all-around event.[21] (At that time, scoring in the all-around was based on how close an athlete got to a world record. A world record in any event was worth 1,000 points.) Then, Kiely's best 56lb throw of 33 feet was ruled a foul because his foot touched the painted throwing circle. Sullivan admitted that Kiely's distance would have stood had the organisers installed the normal metal rim around the circle. As his Spalding company made these rings, the suggestion may have been a clever marketing ploy on Sullivan's part, i.e. that venues buying the rings would be more likely to have throwers break records.

The challenges did not end there. Kiely won the broad jump with a relatively poor effort of 19 feet 10½ inches, running and jumping against the wind. Boston was the hometown of Ellery Clark, and even American press sources suggest that he was given more leeway than was fair in his efforts to beat Kiely. He more or less trotted to victory in the 880 yards 'walk'; one reporter declaring simply that Clark 'ran' the walk.[22] He then insisted on having the hurdles event started before Kiely had even the time to put his spikes on. The Tipperary man was unimpressed:

> *I wanted to take half a minute or maybe a minute to change into my other shoes. Your Boston man Clark said no and I ran the hurdles in me stockin' feet. And I beat 'em. In me stocking feet! I beat him in the All-Round of course. Ye should be proud of him here, the poorest specimen of a sportsman that I ever met.*[23]

Kiely won anyway, by 5 yards, without touching a hurdle.[24] Clark retired from the competition soon afterwards. In the pole vault, Kiely skipped his last attempt in order to save himself for other events. Then he was so comfortably ahead before the last event, the mile, that he did not bother to extend himself, allowing Bredemus an easy win.[25] Of course, the trotting Kiely gained nothing like the points he might have done in the mile if he had really cared about those points. Winning was all that mattered, though it is tempting to speculate how many points Kiely could have gained in an all-around contest in the USA if he had ever really pushed himself in all ten events or had gone there in his mid-twenties.

These details all add up to the notion that given better

circumstances, the almost thirty-seven-year-old Kiely could still have come close enough to Sheridan's world record. In any event, Kiely was once again crowned AAU 'All-Around Champion of America' – not quite as grandiose as the 1904 title, with its extra Exposition and Olympics titles, but a magnificent achievement for a semi-retired athlete, nevertheless. The significance of the AAU all-around championship was shown by the end-of-year US newspaper listing of 'America's National champion in amateur athletics – Thomas F. Kiely'.[26] Even the spelling was correct.

Kiely's victory was hailed in Irish-American New York as a sort of victory for the ordinary Irishman over upper class Bostonians:

> *Clark, of Boston, was favourite, and all the city papers were represented by photographers and reporters, yet the result of their energy and activity was absent from their evening issues. There was not a line in any of the Boston papers that night. They lacked the plucky spirit of the Irishman that travelled 3,000 miles for the competition … Clark ran in the half mile walk. One of the officials warned him several times, yet at no period of this contest did he walk square heel to toe … Clark, who is the son of a Boston millionaire, rode to the field in an automobile accompanied by his wife, who remained an interested spectator to the close …[27]*

Kiely did not stay in the USA quite as long as he had done in 1904, but his 1906 trip still continued for over a month after his victory in the AAU championship. He was found mostly in and around New York once he had won in Boston. In early July, he competed at the Clan na Gael Sports in Celtic Park, where the largest gate receipts ever taken at the venue were recorded. Kiely competed only in the 56lb event, and was second to John Flanagan:

> *Tom Kiely, the all-around champion of America, was second to Flanagan. Kiely was not fully recovered from the effects of his all-around struggle the previous week, but could not let such a gathering pass without competing.*[28]

Then it was announced that a testimonial day in honour of Kiely, involving the Tipperary football team, would be held at Celtic Park, with the headline 'Giant Kickers to Honor Tom Kiely – Famous Football Team of Tipperary to Give Champion a Testimonial'. There were also promises that Martin Sheridan and John Flanagan would be there to compete and honour Kiely.[29] It is logical to take this 'testimonial' as involving a financial outcome, probably a portion of the gate receipts, to be

The watch presented to Kiely when he was at New York's Celtic Park in 1906. He wore it all his life.
(*Kiely Collection, Tipperary Museum Hidden History*)

given to Kiely, in addition to a gold watch which he wore for the rest of his life. The normal admission fee to Celtic Park was 25 cents per adult, and the usual attendance would run to thousands of people. In the end, this event took place at the Tipperarymen's Association annual games at Celtic Park. Thomas F. Walsh, described as the Montana mining king, another native of south Tipperary, presented the association with all the prizes for the games. As for the football match, the esteem in which Irish America held Kiely was well demonstrated, though it is less clear how good a referee he was:

> *Tom Kiely, the American all-around champion, was invited to referee the Tipperary-Kilkenny game. Kiely agreed to assist in the running off of the meeting, but he declined being referee on the plea that as he was a Tipperary man it would not be fair to Kilkenny. Edward O'Shea, the Kilkenny captain, implored Kiely to arbitrate, stating that he and his team could rely on the Carrick man for fair play ...* [30]

Kilkenny led by seven points to five at half-time. Then, in the second half, things went awry:

> *The men were in the middle of a very exciting game and had been playing about ten minutes of the second half when some of the spectators broke into the enclosure and interfered with the players. O'Shea, the Kilkenny captain, called his men off, and the referee gave no decision.*

It is generally believed that Kiely eventually left the USA on 15 August 1906, after further appearances in Chicago and Milwaulkee.[31] In the latter, it was announced that:

> *The annual picnic of the Milwaukee [Ancient Order of] Hibernians is taking place today Judge O'Neill Ryan will be the orator of the day and a feature will be the presence of Tom Kiely champion all-around athlete of the World.*[32]

Thanks to the increasing syndication of news reports in the USA, curious stories of Kiely were carried in newspapers where there were no athletics meetings and very few Irish living either. One such story may give an insight into Kiely's sense of humour. As far apart as Omaha, Nebraska, and Walla Walla in Washington State, it was reported that:

> *Thomas F. Kiely, the noted Irish weight thrower, had been told that the Irish were very popular in America. 'I can readily believe that', Mr Kiely replied. 'The Irish are popular everywhere. The secret of their popularity is tact. An Irishman sat at home with his wife one evening, he reading the newspaper, she doing various household jobs. Finally, the lady rang for the maid and said: "Here, Anna, take this postcard and put it in the letter box outside."*
>
> *"Surely, my love, you can't think of making this poor girl run down three flights of stairs and up again for the sake of one postcard. Just give her a quarter and let her fetch me two bottles of beer and three cigars at the same time."'*[33]

As he left the USA, Kiely again spoke of plans to retire. In fact, he was never to compete in either the USA or Britain again but continued to take part in a few athletics meetings in Ireland:

> *Mr. Kiely says he will then retire from all contests for the all-around championship and that he will not come to this country again for athletic events, although he expects to take part in some in Great Britain.*[34]

Before the next season began, however, the Kiely family was rocked by the news that Katie had died of severe bronchial problems in her Ursuline Convent on the outskirts of Antwerp. The *Nationalist* reported in October 1906 that:

Intelligence has been received with regret in Dungarvan of the death in a convent in Wilbrick [sic] in Belgium, of Miss Kate Kiely, sister of Mr T.F. Kiely, the Irish athlete and world's champion, and of Sister Camillious [sic], of the Mercy Convent, Dungarvan.[35]

Subsequently, the newspaper added that Katie had been due to take her final vows in November, but instead she took them on her death bed. It also commented that she had been the fifth daughter given by the family to the service of God.[36] The reverend mother at the convent, Mère Lydia, was an Irishwoman. She wrote some very lengthy letters to Sister Camillus at the Mercy Convent in Dungarvan, and among other things the letters suggest that the deep faith of the Kiely sisters had come from their mother in the main:

[Katie] said, smiling, my mother, my dear mother, tell her that I am not sorry to leave the world. I know very well, she said, that my mother will conform herself to the will of God, as do I, and so will my father and brothers and sisters. Tell, she said, mother and family to pray for me and I shall not forget them when in Heaven …[37]

A later communication spoke of sending on mementos from Katie, one for each family member. Katie had been an artist, so Mère Lydia wrote of sending paintings and drawings of hers to the Kiely sisters, and one painting each to William Kiely, Tom and his brother Willie, while Larry got his late sister's watch. Again, the implication in the second letter is that Katie had been particularly close to, and influenced by, her mother:

I gave [her] mother the big cross Katie had in her bed and two little
framed pictures, the Sacred Heart of J[esus] and M[ary] on which
dear Kit looked always, during her illness, until the last morning.[38]

***

Life went on in 1907, a year when Kiely won his last two
Irish championships, GAA ones in Thurles on 28 July. There,
he won the hurdles in a time of 16⅘ seconds, and then beat
Paddy Ryan to win the 56lb weight throw. Ryan won the
hammer, but for an unspecified reason Kiely did not enter
that event at all.

In 1908, Kiely waved his brother Larry off to the Olympic
Games in London, where he contested the hurdles without
reaching the final. Kiely had finished with athletics, or so it
seemed, until a certain Martin Sheridan arrived in Ireland.
Sheridan was the star of a stellar American team at the
London Games. After them, he visited Ireland to see his
relatives and do a Kiely-style tour of various places before he
returned to his New York home. For reasons discussed in the
next chapter, by mid-1908, Kiely was living in Co. Waterford,
not too far from Dungarvan, and a special contest was arranged
between the newly arrived Sheridan and the 'retired' Kiely, at
Dan Fraher's field just outside Dungarvan.

Their meeting was widely seen as a challenge between what
might be termed the 'returned Yank' and 'Erin's Champion' to
decide which of them was entitled to be known as all-round
champion. There was, of course, no logic to this comparison.
Sheridan was in his prime at twenty-eight and had just won
his ninth Olympic medal in London, while Kiely was thirty-
eight, retired and, as will be seen, had other things to deal with

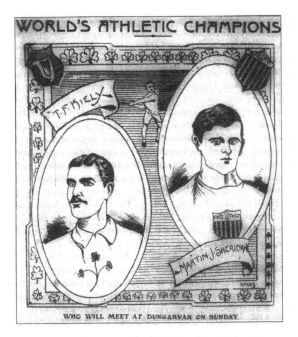

A drawing advertising the great Kiely–Sheridan duel at Dungarvan,
from the Irish *Weekly Freeman*, 15 August 1908.

that summer. Yet the challenge went ahead and with special
trains carrying spectators from far and wide, local newspapers
reported an attendance of 10,000.[39] So great was the focus
on the Kiely–Sheridan 'duel' that many reports since have
completely ignored the fact that there were seven other events
and lots of other athletes in Fraher's field that day.[40]

Sheridan's favourite event, the discus, was not included in
the five tests, apparently because Kiely opposed it. He had no
intention of being 'nice' to his friend and rival, which should
not surprise anyone at this point in the story. Kiely had never
really thrown the discus and would have had no hope against
the three-time Olympic discus champion. The five-event
contest was based entirely on weights events – the 16lb shot,

16lb hammer (Irish style), 56lb, 28lb and a less common 7lb event.[41]

The 16lb shot was the first event on the programme and was, somewhat surprisingly, won by Sheridan by almost 6 feet. Kiely won the hammer, as expected, but not before he threw the old-style Irish hammer 150 feet 3 inches, breaking the twelve-year-old 'world' record for the implement, which he had set himself. Sheridan had probably never thrown such a hammer competitively. As the crowd surged and gambling intensified around the field, the next two events were shared too. Kiely threw the 28lb weight 32 feet 2 inches but Sheridan reached 33 feet exactly. The 56lb (unlimited run and follow) test came next, and Kiely on his sixth attempt reached 34 feet 5 inches. Sheridan's best registered mark was 34 feet 3 inches.

The scene could have hardly been more dramatic. With the final event to come, the two giants of Irish athletics were tied at two events apiece, and it all came down to a rarely seen event, throwing a 7lb weight. Kiely was twice Irish champion at throwing the 7lb weight, but that had been back in 1892 and 1893, and the event had not even featured at a national championships since 1896.[42] It is quite likely that Sheridan had never thrown this weight in the USA, although it might be argued that this weight was closer to what Sheridan usually threw in the discus (between 4lb and 5lb) than to anything Kiely was used to. It is hard to believe that either man thought himself a specialist in the 7lb event, and yet this would decide who was to be the 'World All-Round Champion' in the eyes of everyone in Dungarvan and Ireland. Then:

To the crowd's dismay the referee Frank Dinneen, allegedly a very fair man, ruled that both athletes fouled all three efforts with the 7lb weight and he declared the contest void. The crowd apparently did not take the referee's decision too kindly, and are reported to have left the ground in a rather angry mood. But, in view of the high regard in which Dinneen was held generally in athletic and sporting circles, it would be uncharitable to believe he would have discredited himself by unjustly ruling against either athlete.[43]

The story goes that Sheridan and Kiely protested vigorously and asked to be allowed a further three throws each. Dinneen, it is recorded, stuck to his guns, declared the 7lb weight event a 'no result', and the overall contest a draw. According to one source, eventually peace was restored:

Both men expressed themselves satisfied with the judgement of the referee, but neither seemed to realise on the day that he was in fact correct in not proceeding to a second round as they should have qualified in the first three tries to entitle them under the rules to three more [i.e. fouling three times each meant that neither athlete could be permitted three further attempts. This is still a basic rule in field events.].[44]

Few if any people won their wagers that day in Dungarvan, and Frank Dinneen was loudly criticised by supporters of both athletes for not producing a winner. In other ways the result was perfect. Neither champion had been beaten, and an honourable balance had been achieved with Kiely's age and retired status offset by Sheridan's limited experience with the specific weights used in the contest. 'Erin's Champion' was still Erin's Champion, and yet the greatest American Olympian of

Mary O'Donnell, wife of Tom Kiely.
(*Kiely Collection, Tipperary Museum of Hidden History*)

the day had finally had a chance to compete against his hero on Irish soil. Two rematches were hurriedly planned before Sheridan was due to return to the USA, but at Dundalk (23 August) and Ballina (6 September), Kiely was injured and only threw the hammer for demonstration purposes on both days.[45] He really only went to these distant places to honour Sheridan, in many respects the 'new Tom Kiely', and to bid him farewell.

On the evening of the Ballina Sports, an address of welcome

to Mayo man Sheridan was read on behalf of Ballina's Council after the sports, at a banquet in the Imperial Hotel, Ballina. The address also singled out Kiely, who must have been in attendance. Despite his injury that day, the address recalled how 'On a former occasion the Ballina public witnessed Mr Keily's [*sic*] athletic prowess with much interest and pleasure.'[46] Sadly, Sheridan died of respiratory complications or the Spanish Flu in 1918, so the pair of champions never met again.

The back injury which hampered Kiely in Ballina came against him subsequently, and his last recorded appearance at a sports meeting was later that autumn, in Co. Cork. Realistically, Kiely had retired from athletics in 1907 and now, having bid adieu to Martin Sheridan, he had other things to busy him. For example, barely a week before he took on Sheridan in Dungarvan, Kiely had finally given up his life of bachelorhood and married Mary O'Donnell at the Pro-Cathedral in Dublin. That, in itself, was a story and a half.

CHAPTER 11

FROM 1908 ONWARDS

As mentioned earlier, Tom Kiely was no shrinking violet when it came to female company. By 1906 or earlier, he had already met his future wife (Mary O'Donnell) on a couple of occasions. There is a version of the story of Kiely's return to Carrick-on-Suir after St Louis in 1904 which suggests that he slipped off the train before it arrived in Carrick so that he could call to see Mary. One of Mary's cousins was also a sister-in-law of William Fleming, who had been Kiely's manager at St Louis.[1]

Mary's surname was O'Donnell, though she was often known in Carrick-on-Suir as Mary Fitzgerald. This was because when Mary was a young child, her father, Patsy O'Donnell, came home from Mass one day to find his wife dead on the floor. She was pregnant at the time, but the child she had been pregnant with died also. Patsy subsequently emigrated to America and left Mary behind to be brought up by her mother's mother, Mrs Fitzgerald. Accordingly, Mary was commonly known as Fitzgerald; she was also a relative of the famous Browne family of Grangemockler, mentioned in an earlier chapter.[2]

The Fitzgeralds had a farm at Mullagh, on the Ballyneill side of the Davin farm at Deerpark, and also ran a coach and horse business in Carrick-on-Suir. Mary herself was effectively an orphan, however, and without a dowry. It has been seen that William Kiely disapproved of his son's involvement with another young woman a few years previously on similar grounds, so it is no surprise that he disapproved of Tom marrying Mary.

Mary was working in Dublin as a nanny in 1908 and basically the couple decided to get married there, with no family members from home in attendance. They were married by celebrant Fr James Flavin on 29 July 1908, at the Pro-Cathedral on Marlborough Street. The only witnesses were Joseph Kinahan and Julia Kavanagh. Joseph Kinahan, according to the 1911 census, was a native of Queen's County (now Laois). He was a clerk who lived in Marlborough Street, so he may well have been attached to the Pro-Cathedral in an administrative capacity. Julia Kavanagh was from Dublin city and wife of the verger at the Pro-Cathedral. Fr Flavin lived in the priests' house at 82 Marlborough Street, while both Joseph Kinahan and the Kavanagh family lived in houses attached to the Pro-Cathedral.[3]

The marriage was subsequently entered in the official registry as 'Marriage No. 196' on 21 September 1908 by Laurence Keogh, registrar. Mary's surname was mis-recorded as 'McDonnell', but there is no doubt that this is the record of their marriage. Thomas F. Kiely was listed as being of full age, a bachelor and farmer, son of William Kiely, farmer, while Mary McDonnell [sic], was termed a spinster of full age, and daughter of Patrick McDonnell.[4]

Kiely family history has it that Tom and Mary lived a few months in Dublin, and that William Kiely banned his eldest son from their farms around Ballyneill. There is also a story of

Tom presenting a set of medals, in the form of a large necklace, to his wife on their wedding day, though family members do not feel that either of them was that kind of 'romantic'.[5]

Meanwhile, whether he wanted it or not, twenty-four-year-old Willie Kiely took over responsibility from Tom for the Curraghdobbin farm, with Larry in charge at the old Ballyneill farm. Tom rented a small farm in Co. Waterford, in the general area of Kill, enough to fatten some cattle and make a living. There is no sense at all of any difficulties between the Kiely brothers themselves. In fact, it is thought possible that Willie and Larry contributed some funds towards the purchase of a new farm by Tom, just north of Dungarvan, around 1909:

> *Mr T.F. Kiely, the well-known athlete, has purchased by auction for £470, the farm known as Fruit Hall [sic], containing 124 acres, near Dungarvan.*[6]

The farm was, in fact, known as 'Fruit Hill' and had previously been owned by the Wall family, who were relatives of the Kielys. It had some spectacular views of Dungarvan bay and the Ring peninsula. It is highly likely that Kiely's friend, Dan Fraher, and possibly the funds of William Prendergast in New York, were on hand to assist in the purchase too. For certain, Tom had funds put by from the various testimonials that had been presented to him, not least in the USA in 1906.

Fruit Hill became the Kiely family home for many years. The area around it, known as Bohadoon, was somewhat hillier than the farms at Ballyneill. The farm's name came from the prevalence of wild fruits, such as hurts and sloes, growing on the hillside around it. Much of the farm was good land with the bonus of being close to the fine market town, port and railway station of Dungarvan. Kiely concentrated initially on rearing draught horses there, and their grazing activity helped to clear some of the scrub and furze into the bargain. He continued dealing in and fattening cattle, and eventually the couple had ten or so dairy cows, which were often milked by Mary.

Tom also went to various fairs to buy the cattle for himself and for his two brothers back in Tipperary. Family friends from Árd Mhuire, Carrick-on-Suir, the Healys, often called to visit the Kielys at Fruit Hill. They sometimes took Tom's calves to markets and fairs, paying him his dues on the way back from the fairs. Mrs Healy would take the eggs and fowl from Mary under the same conditions and sell them too at the fairs. Tom was particularly known for his ability to identify which cattle he and his brothers owned, from among often large groups of unbranded cattle at various droving 'stations'. The Kielys traditionally employed families who specialised as drovers, including the Forans, Goughs and Hogans.[7]

By the time of 1911 census recording, Tom and Mary Kiely had a two-year-old daughter, Mary Rose, and a son of just eight months whom they had named William. They would go on to have a family of ten children, eight of whom survived early childhood. The children were Mary Rose, William Francis, Catherine (Kate), Millie (Camillus), Ita (who died from meningitis at twelve), Esther, Tommy and Larry. Another two children, Bridget and John, died young.

***

When the First World War broke out in 1914, it presented an opportunity to Tom Kiely to sell horses to the British Army. Many of these were bought in the west of Ireland, as he had done with the cattle, and he would occasionally get a telegram from an agent to alert him when some good horses became available. The horses were broken and trained for work at Fruit Hill, and generally sold on to a dealer and exporter named Rod Shanahan of Kilmacthomas, about fourteen miles away. Horses were in huge demand once the Western Front was established towards the end of 1914:

> *On the eve of the War, the British Army possessed only 25,000 horses, but by 1917 it had 591,000 horses and 213,000 mules. Horses were as critical to the war effort as the heavy artillery, machine guns and the millions of men. All breeds were needed. Ploughing horses and former pullers of newly electrified tramcars were bought up by the British Army through a network of army agents, dealers, and vets from farmyards and at horse fairs all around Ireland … Herds of horses were driven through the streets of Ireland's ports to haul weapons, supplies and the wounded through the mud and shellfire of the trenches.*[8]

Eventually, 65,000 horses went from Ireland to the war. Kiely and his drovers brought his horses to the Shanahans by road. Rod Shanahan's son provided a vivid memory of the horses making their onwards journey to Waterford port, along the roads in the dark of night:

> *Horses were brought to Waterford by road during the night, leaving usually around 1 AM … The horses were driven by two drovers on horseback. Four jobbers on horseback went ahead and between two*

and four men would take charge of the side roads. Once the horses reached the city, more men were sometimes required to keep order. The horses then were held in Widgers' yard before being loaded onto the boat. In most cases they were slung onto the boat with a crane ...[9]

Old William Kiely died in 1915, leaving Tom technically 'free' to return to Ballyneill or Curraghdobbin. Well settled in Co. Waterford, however, Tom did not disturb or try to lay claim to either of his brothers' interests, but instead purchased another farm, just beside the village of Ballyneill itself. The records show that in 1916 Thomas F. Kiely took over the leasehold interest of the farm, known locally as Ballinaduirce, from a Jane Cleary. There were just under 106 acres and the rateable annual valuation of the land was £86. The valuation records contain a number of notes in the margins. Some of these are indecipherable, but they show that ultimately the valuation of the buildings for rates purposes was reduced to £3, because some of the outbuildings were down.[10]

No one ever lived in the Ballinaduirce house or buildings after that.[11] Tom and Mary continued living at Fruit Hill, on the other side of the Comeragh mountains, and his brothers helped to look after things on the new Kiely farm. The total acreage in the hands of the three Kiely brothers at this point was close to 400. The valuation records show that by 1926, Tom's brothers Willie and Larry held 195 acres of land inherited from their father.[12] Sadly, their mother died in 1917, but at least she had the knowledge that her sons were united and prospering. Although in her early seventies, she had worked hard all her life in difficult circumstances, prompting one of her grandsons to suggest that it was often the case that the Kiely women were the real farmers, while the men were cattle dealers.[13]

Though a strong farmer, Tom Kiely's fame as an athlete may help explain that for the duration of the turbulent times between 1916 and 1923, he was left alone at Fruit Hill, untroubled by revolutionaries, Black and Tans, Regulars or Irregulars.[14] Kiely's status as 'Erin's Champion' also saw him selected in 1924 as one of the standard bearers at the opening of the Tailteann Games in Dublin. A photo of the occasion shows Kiely carrying the national flag, immediately behind two youngsters with Irish wolfhounds. True to form, he is carrying it aloft, held in just one hand. In the advance planning for the Games, it is possible to see a nice long-term impact of Kiely's all-round efforts too. Even though no all-round championship had been held in Ireland since 1898, the minutes of the organising committee recorded:

A letter was read from Mr Dan Shea of New York, asking that the All-Round Championship or Decathlon, would be placed on the programme. This event was agreed to.[15]

All the Kiely girls were sent to boarding school, mostly under the watchful eye of their aunt in Willesden, or latterly when she was based at Gortnor Abbey in Mayo. Boarding school may not have been quite to their tastes, and one if not two of them left and returned home, despite their father travelling over to England on a few occasions to 'sort' things out.[16]

Then, in the mid-1920s, Kiely left Fruit Hill and bought Graigue (often spelled 'Craigue'), just north of Carrick-on-Suir, though situated in Co. Kilkenny. When William

Kiely leading the parade of athletic champions, carrying the flag, at the Tailteann Games 1924. (*From the collection of Tom Hunt, original source unidentified*)

Prendergast visited from the USA in 1922, he is thought to have been involved in the negotiations to buy Graigue, because his family came from Killonerry nearby. On the 160 acres at Graigue, former home of the Blackmore family, Kiely got more into cattle dealing and into stocks and shares and was, as a result, more financially secure.

One of his main investments was in Imperial Tobacco, even though he never smoked himself, and he also had shares in Great Universal Stores (a pioneering mail order company), American railways and in oil. Prendergast is thought to have been instrumental in getting Kiely into the stock market, having made a fortune himself in New York, between real estate and shares.[17] Kiely's grandsons can remember an outside toilet at Graigue, where the toilet paper consisted of reams of old stockbroking reports, hung from a hook on the wall.[18]

Graigue had a big house with a square courtyard and a lodge. There was a big orchard too, with apples, pears and gooseberries, about five acres of fruit in all. Lord Ponsonby was the local charitable and positive landlord, and the general milieu of Graigue was strongly Protestant. Kiely got on very well with everyone.

During the Economic War 1932–38, neighbouring small farmers couldn't sell their cattle so a number of them had big debts. They were haunted by bailiffs and debt collectors. A lady who had been a neighbour of Kiely's in Graigue told his grandson Tom about a day that the bailiffs came to seize what her family had. She was sent across the road to fetch 'the Champion'. She had always called him 'Sir'. When Kiely came over, he wrote a cheque to pay off the bailiffs, and that was the end of it.

Kiely continued to attend sports meetings, including the second staging of the Tailteann Games in 1928. Then, the newly crowned Olympic hammer champion, Pat O'Callaghan, was also one of the honour guard, along with Tom, Peter O'Connor and John Flanagan. Flanagan came back from the USA to live again in Co. Limerick. O'Callaghan came from Denis Horgan's home area around Banteer.

At Graigue, Kiely continued to breed horses, though not to the same extent as during the First World War. He always kept a good horse for himself and used it for many journeys to meet his brothers and see how the other farms were doing. His wife kept a fine black mare for use on the trap. However, one day he decided to visit a neighbouring farm to look at a horse and he took the mare. While talking to the farmer, they didn't realise that the mare (in season) had been 'entertained' by the farmer's stallion, a famous sire called 'Sandyman'. Subsequently, a very lively foal was born. He was sold as a three-year-old to the Oblate fathers in Pilltown, who hoped to use him to draw milk to the creamery. He proved a little too lively for that kind of task, however, and one day the trap came home with nothing on it, the horse having bolted and upturned everything, including the driver. Eventually, he was sold for £10 to the army equestrian team, which turned him into a famous show-jumping horse, called 'Ballyneaty'.[19]

In 1932, Pat O'Callaghan won his second Olympic hammer title, at Los Angeles, and had settled as a doctor in Clonmel. He and Kiely became the best of friends, though it was a friendship based on mutual respect and frequent disagreements too, about sport, politics, greyhounds or whatever. Anthony Kiely told a lovely story of meeting O'Callaghan later in life and, when 'the Doc' heard him laugh, he remarked that Anthony had his grandfather's laugh. O'Callaghan also knew how fiercely competitive and determined Tom Kiely had been, in order to achieve what he did, and commented to Anthony at one point that if Kiely and Muhammad Ali had ended up in a dark room some time, with the door closed, his money would have been on Kiely to come out in one piece.[20]

When the family came to Graigue in the 1920s, Kiely bought his first car, a Morris 6, which was quite a curiously coloured orange and black machine. Just as he had always had a good horse available, Kiely also made sure he had a good motor car, and later had an Armstrong Sidley and a Morris 8, bought from Sam King of Clonmel. He never drove himself, and his usual 'chauffeur' in later life was his daughter-in-law Aggie.

In the early 1930s, Kiely bought a seventy-eight acre farm at Mullagh from the Fitzgeralds (his in-laws).[21] In 1942, he bought nearby land at Ballynagrana, in what seems to have been two lots totalling around sixty-one acres. He later renamed this farm 'Shawfield', possibly recalling a sporting venue in Scotland that he had visited in his younger days, and to distinguish it from nearby Shawvilla. The Land Registry recorded on 4 November 1942: 'Thomas F. Kiely of Mullagh, Carrick-on-Suir, County Tipperary, Farmer, is full owner of the property.'[22] Kiely then sold his interests in Graigue, meaning that all his land holdings were located in and around

Kiely pictured at the Garda Síochána Sports in Clonmel, 1929. Back row, from left: unidentified man, Pat O'Callaghan, Kiely, Percy Kirwan, J. J. Ryan, General Eoin O'Duffy (then head of the gardaí and Olympic Council of Ireland), Dan Fraher, Peter O'Connor, Pat Davin and P. Stokes. Front row, from left: unidentified man, P. J. O'Reilly and J. Anthony. (*Kiely Collection, Tipperary Museum of Hidden History*)

Ballyneill, and he and Mary came to live at Shawfield.

Kiely also acted as a judge at numerous athletics meetings and got involved in greyhound racing on occasion too. Anthony Kiely remembers the excitement during the late 1940s when his grandfather had two winning dogs at Kilcohan Park, Waterford, on the same evening. At that stage, because the Kielys had moved to Shawfield, most of Tom's greyhounds had the prefix 'Shawfield' too.[23]

By the 1940s, all of Kiely's daughters had gotten married, all with £1,000 in dowries, thanks mainly to profits from his investments. They were all very well educated, but none had much interest in going further, e.g. to college.

At Shawfield, Tom walked every day, hail, rain or snow. He used to go down by Davins' to chat with Pat sometimes, then come up a boreen back to the Clonmel side of Davins' and then up through Mullagh, to check in on the cattle, etc. He would then go home for his dinner in the middle of the day. In the afternoon, he would walk down the Mullagh road towards his son William's house. From there, he would head west and count his cattle in Ballinadeirce, near the house he built for Jack Strapp in 1904, before going on to the village of Ballyneill itself. In Ballyneill there was the pub, a place that Tom hated because of the role alcohol had played in his own father's difficulties, and the village shop owned by Hickey's (relatives of the Kielys).

In the parlour at Hickey's every Friday, Tom would sit by the fire. Eventually, his brother Willie would arrive from Curraghdobbin and Larry from the original Ballyneill farm to discuss cattle dealing and business. None of the three would go into the pub, but the shop owner, Mr Hickey, would

Kiely and a friend with one of Kiely's
'Shawfield' greyhounds. (*Courtesy of
Anthony Kiely*)

go and get three small bottles of Guinness for the brothers, who would have them at Hickey's fireside. In the shop, Tom would pay for the three small bottles one week, Larry the next and Willie the third week.[24]

The early 1940s saw the three Kiely brothers getting on well, as they always had, and each one of them a man of independent farm means. However, there was some trouble in store, in the form of the Emergency, and the demands of a Compulsory Tillage Order. The Emergency Powers (No. 12) Order, 1939 (Compulsory Tillage Order) obliged every occupier of ten or more statute acres to cultivate an area equivalent to at least one-eighth of such land. Then an Amendment Order (No. 53), in 1940, required farmers to cultivate in 1941 one-fifth of such land:

The requirement was gradually raised until in 1944 and for some years afterwards the tillage quota amounted to three-eighths of the arable land, with an allowance for tillage newly laid down to grass. From 1944 it became compulsory to grow wheat with the quota for each holding varying from one-tenth of the arable land in the best wheat growing counties to one-twenty-fifth in the least suitable areas.[25]

This legislation did not go down well with Kiely and did not endear De Valera's government to him in any way. He and his family had been cattle dealers, and there was significant extra cost involved in having to grow crops on a portion of their land. One of his grandsons recalled that Kiely subsequently felt well pleased when he heard that one of the Fianna Fáil government members had been kicked by a horse and injured, because he blamed that government for compulsory tillage.[26] This incident may even have prompted him to call one of the racehorses he bred 'Irish Minister'.

Two grandsons remembered Tom's son William going to England, buying a harvester at a sale after the Second World War and cutting corn in Shawfield and elsewhere. Everyone came to see the contraption. Shawfield's compulsory tillage acreage alone was fifteen acres and the requirement continued for several years after the Second World War. At one point, the fuel (tractor vaporising oil, otherwise known as TVO) was getting scarce and Tom himself came up to the house at Shawfield for the TVO, leaving his son Willie in the combine harvester. Tom collected seven gallon drums of the fuel, and carried the drums, one in each hand, from the van that his daughter-in-law Aggie drove him in through a back field to the combine harvester.[27] The weight of each seven gallon drum roughly equalled a 56lb weight, in each hand. Kiely by that time was over seventy-six years old.

The Kiely sons seem to have inherited their father's strength too. There was another day at Shawfield when they

Kiely with John Duggan and a horse bred by Kiely, 'Irish Minister'.
(*Kiely Collection, Tipperary Museum of Hidden History*)

got a little tired of a man who had repeatedly driven up to the entrance gate, and then parked his ass and cart there while he continued on to the house on foot. This left the main entrance blocked, of course, so one day two of Tom's sons, Larry and Tommy, unhooked the cart, tied a rope under it, and hauled the cart up into an overhanging tree. When the 'visitor' returned to his cart, the ass was tied to a fence and his cart was nestling in the tree.[28]

Tom and Mary Kiely were wonderful grandparents. One grandchild recalled visits to Shawfield on Sundays, finding his grandfather listening to GAA matches on the big crystal radio in the kitchen, and Mary always smiling and making huge apple tarts. Shawfield had an orchard, and the kids were allowed to play and take apples home, sometimes being taken out there by their grandfather. The front parlour was recalled too, laden with many of the trophies that Tom had won during his career. When the grandchildren were leaving, invariably 'grandfather' would press a shilling, big money in the late 1940s, into their hands as they said goodbye.[29]

As this narrative approaches the year of his death, 1951, it is useful to look at Tom Kiely's position a little more closely. Having been 'cast out' for marrying Mary O'Donnell in 1908, he had more than made a success of life in financial terms. By 1942, he owned three farms and had 'money in the bank'. After the Second World War, he took the decision to hand over the three farms formally to his sons. Tommy got Ballinaduirce. Willie was in Mullagh where there was a slaughterhouse beside the house, enabling Willie to keep his butcher's shop in Carrick-on-Suir supplied. Tom's third son, Larry, was formally given Shawfield and the Land Registry documents record, on 1 June 1949:

(a) The right of Thomas F. Kiely during his life to reside in the dwelling house and to be suitably supported

(b) The right of Mary Kiely (wife of Thomas F. Kiely) during her life to reside in the dwelling house and be suitably supported. Note. These Burdens rank in the same priority.

Laurence Kiely of Shawville [sic], Ballynagrana, Carrick-on-Suir, County Tipperary, Farmer, is full owner of the property.[30]

In reality, despite officially divesting himself of these properties, Kiely remained very much as head of the family and took an active role in the affairs at all family farms. His death, when it came, was quite sudden. One Saturday, his sons were rounding up cattle, sorting out drovers, etc., for the fair day the following Monday in Carrick-on-Suir. Tom was in the thick of proceedings, and then declared, quite suddenly, that they would all go in and get Nanny to make the tea. Everyone was surprised, but all went in.

As they all gathered with their tea, Tom had been looking at the newspaper for a long time, until Mary went over to him. He had had a stroke and was paralysed all down his left side. He could still speak but was put into bed and the doctor was sent for. On Sunday morning the doctor came again and told the family that Tom wouldn't last long. That evening, Fr Harty, an old acquaintance from his Fruit Hill days, came from Dungarvan to give him the last rites. True to form, Tom said to him: 'Haven't you anything better to be doing?' He died a couple of hours later, around 2 a.m. on the Monday morning.[31] Mary Kiely lived on until 1971.

The Champion was no more. He had lived a full and long life, enjoyed himself and achieved incredible things both on the sporting fields and in business. He was the first great sporting star of modern Ireland, and the last of the old breed of Gaelic champions too. His career bridged the period when sport moved from being purely 'amateur' to being organised, regulated and modernised. Kiely managed to straddle both cultures. Had he gone to America, as many did, or gone to more than one of the Olympic Games of his day, he might well have become much more widely known as one of the giants of modern athletics.

That said, there is no denying that he was a giant of modern athletics, and that Kiely himself would have changed very, very little in his career or his life. He persisted in being an all-rounder when few others were, and he represented both Irish athletic associations when many sought to polarise them. He defied the political, religious and social norms of his day when they clashed with his own sense of the right thing to do, whether in sport or in life. Ultimately, Kiely was his own man.

Kiely was described subsequently as 'the greatest athlete of Ireland's greatest athletics period' and as 'The golden boy of Ireland's athletics Golden Age.'[32] An American sports historian of modern times has called him 'The greatest athlete in the isle's [i.e. Ireland's] history.'[33] Pádraig Puirséal, writing as 'Moondharrig' some months before Kiely's death, recalled 'how the GAA seemed at its Last Gasp, but the darkest hour produced Frank Dinneen – and World's Wonder Tom Kiely'.[34]

His death brought a host of tributes to his greatness. William Dooley wrote:

> *His passing brings back memories to old-timers of the phenomenal range of his activities on track and field which placed him on such a pedestal that, during the entire course of his long career he was never once beaten in an all-round contest.*[35]

In Co. Waterford, where the Kielys had lived between 1909 and the mid-1920s, a County Council meeting was adjourned as a mark of respect, and Mrs Kiely was written to with the resolution, passed in silence, that the councillors sought to:

> *… express their deepest sympathy on his [i.e. Tom's] recent death, and that we place on record our appreciation of the fame which he brought to this county, by his outstanding achievements in the athletic field.*[36]

A cousin of Mary's wrote from Rome: 'I have heard with deep regret of poor Tom's death. May God rest his soul.' The sender was Michael Browne, originally from Grangemockler but then of the Vatican, where he would become Cardinal Browne before the end of that decade. Tom's good friend Fr Harty said the funeral Mass at St Nicholas' Church in Carrick-on-Suir, as Kiely's Shawfield residence lay just inside that parish. He was laid to rest afterwards in the family plot at Ballyneill, in a double plot which held his parents and would, in time, have the graves of Mary and several of their descendants as well.

The local paper announced Kiely's death:

> *The death of the renowned Thomas F. Kiely at his residence, Shawfield, Carrick-on-Suir, at the ripe age of 82 years, removes from our midst one of the world's most famous athletes of other days, a man who in the nineties was supreme as an all-round athletic champion not only of Ireland but of the whole world wherever organised athletic conditions were known ... It is no exaggeration to say that Tom Kiely was the greatest all-round athlete that Ireland ever produced.*[37]

At the house in Shawfield after the funeral, Millie Casey and other members of the Kiely family served food and drink. Peter O'Connor was there, having remained a friend since the 1890s when Kiely had given him advice about how to long jump from a board take-off. That year, 1951, O'Connor was celebrating a half-century of holding the Irish long jump record, a record that had been a world best for two decades of that half-century. As he stood in a corner of the parlour and reflected, he said: 'T.F. would turn in his grave if he saw all the alcohol.'[38]

Having seen the determination, the independence and tolerance that characterised Tom Kiely all his life, one suspects that he would have been a bit harder to ruffle than that.

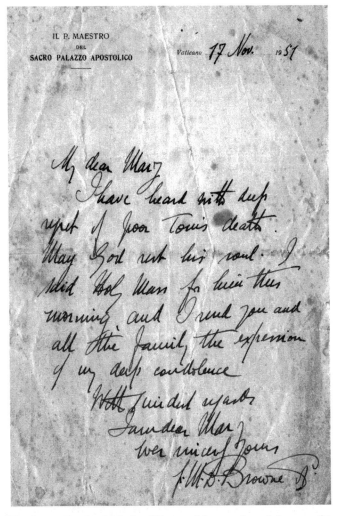

The future Cardinal Michael Browne's letter of condolence to his cousin Mary, on the death of her husband, Tom, in 1951.
(*Kiely Collection, Tipperary Museum of Hidden History*)

CHAPTER 12

TOM KIELY'S OLYMPIC LEGACY

In looking at the legacy of Tom Kiely, two key questions about his St Louis exploits have caused debate for over a century in sports history circles.

One question concerns whether the gold medal he won at St Louis was for an Olympic title. That has been broadly accepted for over half a century but occasionally resurfaces. It needs to be 'put to bed', so to speak, here.

The second question is whether he was representing Ireland or Great Britain. This is still a very live issue.

THE ST LOUIS GAMES IN CONTEXT

The first thing to be said is that we must not try to impose modern expectations of what 'Olympic' means onto a 1904 event. The St Louis Games were the official Olympic Games but were largely entrusted to the organising skills of one powerful individual, and he had a number of fingers in one pie, so to speak. St Louis had few of the features that are nowadays synonymous with the Olympics. There were, for example:

- no national teams (national Olympic committees nominated athletes from 1906, though it is argued that Germany and Hungary sent official teams to St Louis)

- no standardised team uniforms (partially instituted from 1908)

- no national anthems (standardised in 1932)

- no winners' podium (introduced in 1932)

- no standardised medal design across all events (introduced in 1908)

- no Olympic rings or flag (introduced in 1920).

To understand the St Louis Games and hence Kiely's involvement there, you need to strip away all of the above from your expectations. Then, imagine having the events spread out over five months, include a cornucopia of events for their crowd-pulling, novelty or commercial appeal, and add to the mix a concurrent World Fair, otherwise known as the Universal Exposition. Now you have an idea of what to expect from the St Louis Olympic Games. These Games were in some respects reflecting what had happened at the Paris Games before them. They were of their time, but they were Olympic Games and modern analysis must not try to impose today's norms on historical events. St Louis had the added complexity of having very few of the International Olympic Committee (IOC) in attendance, and the IOC never issuing an Official Olympic Report.

The St Louis Games were initially intended to be the Chicago Olympics, having been officially awarded to that city in 1901. The problem was that the US Congress approved funding for the World Fair at St Louis on 3 March 1901, to commemorate the centenary of the 1803 Louisiana Purchase. Subsequently, mainly for logistical reasons, St Louis scheduled its World Fair for 1904. A clash of fixtures, so to speak, between the Fair and the Olympic Games looked inevitable.

World Fairs, including the ones at Paris in 1900 and at Chicago in 1893, traditionally included significant sporting, and specifically athletics, competitions. St Louis organisers appointed the head of the US Amateur Athletic Union (AAU), James E. Sullivan, a man of Co. Kerry extraction, encountered in earlier chapters, as the 'Chief of the Department of Physical Culture Section of the Louisiana Purchase Exposition'.[1]

Sullivan, who was also *de facto* head of the Spalding sporting goods company, viewed the AAU as the sole certifying agent for sport in America and he pointed out that 'it will be impossible to hold a successful [Olympic] meeting without the consent of that body'.[2] In his St Louis capacity, he immediately set about ensuring that major AAU championships would be held there. He spread the programme out, as Paris had done, in order to ensure that there were sporting activities available to World Fair visitors from 14 May to 23 November.

In February 1903, Chicago Olympic officials were informed by St Louis organisers: 'politely, but clearly, that the Olympian Games of 1904 [if held in Chicago] threatened the success of their World's Fair, and that if we [Chicago] insisted in carrying out our program they would develop their athletic department so as to eclipse our games'.[3]

Baron de Coubertin ultimately agreed to transfer the Olympic Games to St Louis, leaving Sullivan, whom he despised, as 'Director of the Olympic Games'. The British

IOC members did not attend the Games or organise a Great Britain team, and Baron de Coubertin stayed at home, rather than see Sullivan lording it in St Louis for six months. The Baron, without ever having seen St Louis, arrogantly described it as a place with 'Aucune beauté, aucune originalité'.[4]

This snobbery was deeply unfair to St Louis, and its Games organisers brought about several major and 'original' developments to the Olympic Games. These included the first purpose-built Olympic stadium at Francis Field, and the use of gold, silver and bronze medals for the first three placings in each event. St Louis was also the only city which was not a capital to host the Olympic Games before the First World War. Importantly for our story, it was the first Olympic host city to schedule an all-around championship in its programme.

KIELY'S OLYMPIC PARTICIPATION

This brings us to Tom Kiely. The AAU all-around championship had been held every year since 1894 on 4 July, the national holiday.[5] This could be a major attraction on the programme at Francis Field, and James Sullivan duly scheduled the 1904 all-around championship for 4 July in St Louis. He called it the 'All-Around Championship of the World' in order to attract greater interest. Book-ending the summer, the other senior international championships expected to comprise an 'Olympic Games' in athletics were fixed for late August. Wanting to pack the holiday months with college and school athletes, all potential Spalding customers, Sullivan duly claimed that every sporting event at St Louis was part of the Olympic Games.[6] He knew that the previous Olympic Games, attached to the Paris World Fair in 1900, had a similarly packed programme, with even less of a focus on sport. Incidentally, Sullivan later joked about how someone won an Olympic prize for fishing in the Seine in 1900.[7]

For the St Louis Games, attracting crowds of paying sports enthusiasts was all-important for Sullivan. Immediately prior to Kiely's all-around event, he packed gymnastics into his Olympic programme. Gymnastics sometimes included a triathlon of athletic events, based on long jump, shot put and the 100 yards dash, and Sullivan hoped that placing gymnastics in early July would boost interest in the all-around.[8] As already seen, the winner and runner-up in the gymnastics triathlon, Max Emmerich and John Grieb, competed in the all-around event against Kiely.

The original Chicago programme, like Paris, had also planned to pack the Olympic Games with events, including Irish Sports, as well as hurling and football competitions.[9] In that sense, St Louis merely followed the pre-defined template. At other times, Sullivan added to the ambiguity when he referred very specifically to the senior athletic championships held between 29 August and 3 September as the 'Olympic Games'. This does not mean that these games were more important, necessarily, and several of the Irish-American athletes who took part in those 'Olympic Games' left early in order to get back to New York for the GNYIAA's revival of the Irish 'Tailteann Games' on 5 September.[10] Nor did any of the victors in the later games receive the adulation back in New York that Kiely did.

Here is the nub of the problem. If Sullivan had put the all-around championship on at the same time as the athletics events of 29 August to 3 September, there would probably have never been any disagreement about Kiely's medal being an 'Olympic' medal. As things were, the official programme included the following:

> *The programme of World's championship contests, which is scheduled to take place during the Olympic year, is without question the greatest programme of its kind ever arranged ... The All-Around Championship will be held on July 4, and will be open to the athletes of the world. Three days will be devoted to International Lacrosse ... The World's Fencing Championship will occupy two days ...*[11]

It bears remembering that the Official Programme at the Paris Olympic Games in 1900 put virtually everything under the heading of *Jeux Olympiques*. However, the Official Track and Field Programme for the very same Games called them *Championnats Internationaux*, with not one reference to them being for Olympic titles at all.[12] One almost gets a sense that the term 'Olympic Games' was suggestive of festivities and activities more than serious sporting competition in 1900, and some of this 'looseness' transferred itself to St Louis.

Even the modern notion of 'winning an Olympic medal' is fraught with difficulty when you look at the early Olympics. The first Irishman to compete at the Olympics, John Boland, treasured the olive wreaths and papyrus certificates much more than he did the silver medals he won in Athens in 1896.[13] It is much more accurate, when dealing with the first three or four modern Olympic Games, to say that an athlete 'won a championship at the Olympic Games'. In Kiely's case, there is no doubt that his was a major championship, and was seen as a major part of the St Louis Olympic programme. It is almost irrelevant that his victory won him a gold medal, though it certainly did.[14]

Another important piece of contemporary evidence in support of Kiely's Olympic status is the loving cup that was presented to him by the Irish-American community of New York before he left for home. Some of those involved in the presentation, including Jim Mitchel, had even taken part in the August–September games at St Louis. Yet, etched in huge letters on the trophy, now in Clonmel museum, they were happy to have inscribed: 'Thomas F. Kiely of Ireland – All-Around Champion of the World – won at the Olympic Games, St Louis U.S.A.' This echoed the earlier wording of the US newspaper which had anticipated Kiely's win at St Louis, predicting that 'the Irish all-around athlete, stands a good chance of winning the all-around competition of the world at the Olympic games'.[15]

On the other hand, no official IOC report was ever issued and those that were issued, by Sullivan (for the Spalding company) and Charles Lucas, used the terminology of the official programme. Thus, Kiely's event was called the 'AAU All-Around Championship' and the events of August 29 to September 3 were 'Olympic Games', even though both were deemed part of the St Louis Olympiad.

Sports historian Frank Zarnowski is particularly adamant that Kiely's win was not an Olympic event: 'make no mistake about it,' he says, 'in spite of what the record books say, Tom Kiely never competed in the Olympic Games'.[16] This is a view shared by Irish historian Tom Hunt.[17]

In the opposite corner stands British AAA historian Peter Lovesey, and before him stood Irishman David Guiney.

According to Lovesey, Kiely's confirmation came (again) around 1969 as a result of a campaign 'for some fifteen years by the late David Guiney, a much-respected member of ISOH and official historian to the Irish Olympic Council, who consulted the athlete's daughter and borrowed Kiely's scrapbook and found enough evidence to campaign for the 1904 result to be recognized'.[18] Lovesey also cited many Olympic historians in support of the view that the all-around was an Olympic event.

Zarnowski's argument ignores the fact that other 'world championships' held at St Louis, including the lacrosse and fencing, have always been included as 'Olympic' titles in all known record books even though they, like the all-around, were not specifically called 'Olympic' at the time. The people responsible for commemorating St Louis' Olympic heritage, who have scrupulously examined all the competitions held there, are of the view that under the circumstances of 1904, Kiely's all-around championship constituted an Olympic event and, in practical terms, the first Olympic 'decathlon'.[19]

In reality, James E. Sullivan's naming of the all-around championship as a world championship was meant to put it above, not below or outside of, 'mere' Olympic competitions. Kiely's attendance enhanced the Olympic Games, as to most people at the time a world championship meant a lot more than the term 'Olympic'. That term in 1904 was used by Sullivan as a complementary adjective, attached to whatever sports events were happening. The concept of 'Olympic Games' did not necessarily mean world-class competition in 1896 or 1900 but calling events 'world's championships' under the 1904 Olympic umbrella was very deliberate. It would help attract quality competitors, such as Kiely, and paying spectators.

The terminology used typifies American sports culture to this day, of course, where the North American baseball championship culminates in the 'World Series' and the Superbowl is deemed the world championship in American Football. For Sullivan and the AAU at the time, the term 'Olympic' was much inferior to any of the other titles that could be put on a championship or medal in 1904. Therefore, it can be argued that the all-around was a 'world championship', awarded by the AAU at the 'Universal Exposition', as part of the 'Olympic Games'. It bears noting too that Sullivan, particularly once the Olympic Games had become more accepted as quality sports events, tended to refer to them as world championships. For instance, when he telegrammed home from the London Olympic Games in 1908, he called the Games 'the track and field championship of the world'.[20] When his Spalding company used athletes like John Flanagan and Martin Sheridan to advertise its products, they were called 'world champions', not 'Olympic champions'.[21]

For the 1904 Olympic Games, no standard medals were developed, leaving the organisers and individual sporting bodies free to put whatever inscriptions they felt appropriate on those they awarded. On Kiely's medal, one side has 'All Around Athletics Champion of the World', with 'Amateur Athletic Union of the United States 1888' on the other side. To cover all bases, the medal was hung on a red, white and blue ribbon, and attached to a bar saying '1904 Universal Exposition … Olympic Games … St Louis', with logos of victory wreaths and the Greek goddess of victory.

Among other variations of St Louis medals, athletics medals from August–September had 'Olympiad 1904' inscribed on one side, and 'Universal Exposition ... St Louis USA' on the reverse, plus the goddess of victory and several typically Greek symbols. Comparing Kiely's medal with Martin Sheridan's for the discus, there are many design similarities, but they are not at all identical.[22] Basketball medals had the inscription 'Olympic World Championship' on them, with 'Universal Exposition' and 'St Louis 1904' inscribed in much smaller text at the centre. These were totally different in design from other 1904 medals, as indeed were the golf medals, which had a logo of a golf bag on them and the bar identical to Kiely's, inscribed '1904 Universal Exposition ... Olympic Games ... St Louis'.

The variations in inscriptions on the medals came about essentially because Sullivan farmed out responsibility for much of the St Louis programme to the national bodies that oversaw specific sports in the USA. What was consistently enforced, however, was the idea that the winners got gold medals, the runners-up got silver and third place won bronze. Kiely's medal was actually purchased from D&C Jewelers of John Street, New York. Like the medals for the 29 August athletics at St Louis, the all-around was an AAU responsibility and the jewellers were literally just across downtown Manhattan from the Spalding headquarters in Warren Street. It is tempting to think that Sullivan may have bought Kiely's medal there himself, but that is pure speculation.

SETTING THE OLYMPIC RECORD STRAIGHT

In all this, one Olympic historian after another has tried to rectify the confusion and, in the opinion of many, right the wrong that the early recordists of St Louis did to Tom Kiely. Out of eight standard, well-known Olympic reference books which began to appear from the 1940s onwards, only Fritz Wasner's *Olympia-Lexicon* omitted Kiely's all-around title. Even excluding the Spalding review, which lists everything as 'Olympic', that leaves six historians who put Kiely's event as an Olympic one. Wasner's book, incidentally, refused to accept that any Olympic archery, cycling, association football or golf medals were on offer either, so its focus is particularly narrow.[23]

The late Irish journalist and sports historian David Guiney, in the 1960s, visited the Shanahan family of Portlaw, Co. Waterford, where Mrs Shanahan, Kiely's daughter, still had his 1904 medal. Guiney wrote of Kiely's medal:

This is an authentic gold medal, identical to those presented at St Louis and, in fact, is so inscribed. Yet, for some unaccountable reason, his name was not listed in the Olympic Roll of Honour for 1904. Following representations to the International Olympic Committee in 1954 by Dr Ferenc Mezö (Hungary) the mistake was, at long last, rectified.[24]

The story is even more complex than Guiney's comment might suggest, apart from the fact that Kiely's gold medal was not quite 'identical' to others presented at St Louis, as explained above. Research with the IOC Archives at the Olympic Studies Centre in Lausanne, Switzerland, indicates that there is no record of an IOC meeting to 'rectify' the position of Kiely or anyone else at that time. What did occur, however, had the same Dr Mezö as a central player in it.

In 1948, as Guiney represented Ireland at the London Olympic Games, the sports historian Bill Henry published *An Approved History of the Olympic Games*. In researching this book:

> [He] undertook an exhaustive search to collect information on Olympic background and history. A mass of letters, documents and publications were gathered from all over the world. Of particular importance was the material furnished by Baron de Coubertin, founder of the Modern Games, Count Baillet Latour, then President of the IOC, and the members of the Organizing Committee of previous Olympic Games ...
>
> Drawing upon his wealth of information, Bill Henry wrote the first draft of this book and it was submitted through Baillet Latour to de Coubertin. Later, with their encouragement, personal assistance, and constructive criticism, this history was completed. All but a small portion of the book was approved by both before their deaths.[25]

Henry's book removed a lot of the 'extra' scholastic, handicap, junior and other events like the Irish Sports from St Louis in his 'approved' Olympic records. He categorically included Kiely's win, however, and also wrote:

> Ireland had several contestants in the games, one of them Thomas F. Kiely of Carrick-on-Suir, who brought fame to the Emerald Isle by winning the all-around athletic championship.[26]

Ferenc Mezö had published several books about the Olympics, including a 1936 volume containing general results which he felt Bill Henry had used in compiling his 1948 nowledgement, not yet faultless!

That work of mine was used by F.Wasner, /see Olympia Lexi-
con,p.250/ and most probably Bill Henry must have used it
too.Booth of these books are excellently edited, ~~~~~~~~
~~~~~~~~,but at the records you will find not adequate datas. The text of Bill Henry's work is a fine piece of work,
but in the statistical part one will frequently meet with
false datas.

Will you allow me to serve herewith proofs: I can hardly
believe that the statistical part was made by him.There
are not only mistakes but contradictions too. Golonkin,
p.367. Golinkin p.225,correctly Golinken!!! E.H.Flack
Australia,p.51. Flack,/Great Britain/ p.336. Kiely/p.51/
Kiely/ p.341/The cycling results,1904 are perfectly missing,at,p.354.,so are the greater part, of rowing results
as well./p.82/ and p./362. The football winner,1904,Great
Britain,/364/ p. 80-85,is not even mentioned.

√(p. 82-3)
√ 361.-

The extract from Ferenc Mezö's letter to IOC president Avery Brundage, seeking to correct the misspelling of Kiely's name in the official Olympic records. (Courtesy of the Olympic Studies Centre, Lausanne)

publication. Mezö wrote to the IOC of his intentions of writing another definitive book of Olympic results, aided by an expert panel.[27] Mezö's correspondence with the head of the IOC, Avery Brundage, pointed out that just one correction needed to be made to Henry's recording of Kiely – the spelling! Henry had used the incorrect 'Keily' at one point and Mezö told Brundage that he was going to correct it.[28] There was no question of removing Kiely or his all-around title, and no argument from Brundage about it when he wrote back to Mezö six weeks later.[29]

This was all the endorsement that Mezö needed. Brundage had, himself, been an all-around athlete who specialised in weights events, and was a seventeen-year-old student when Kiely won in St Louis. He undoubtedly knew who Kiely was. Mezö's ongoing work was subsequently and briefly mentioned in the IOC Sessions of 1954, 1955 and 1956. During the Session in Melbourne in 1956, the IOC thanked him for the great work achieved with the publication of *60 Years of the*

Olympic Games, surely an unqualified imprimatur.[30]

Inspired by Mezö's publications and Guiney's persistence, the AAU in America conducted a detailed examination of the athletics events at St Louis and submitted their findings to the IOC, supporting Kiely's win and Olympic status.[31] According to Peter Lovesey, the 1904 all-around status was referred again to the IOC in 1969 and formally confirmed as an Olympic event.[32] Later Olympic historians have been happy to include Kiely as an Olympic champion, as do the IOC official records and website to this day.

The great Olympic historian Bill Mallon was driven to cut through the organisational chaos of the early modern Olympic Games and identify the events which should hold 'Olympic' status by any reasonable standards of today. In the 1990s he developed four tests for events held at the Paris and St Louis Games, and all four tests had to be passed before he felt comfortable in calling the titles 'Olympic'. For St Louis, he proposed the following:

> *Four criteria currently must be met for any event or sport to be considered an Olympic event in current nomenclature. One, the event should be international in scope, allowing entries from all nations. Two, no handicap events should be allowed. Three, the entries must be open to all competitors (which means mainly that limitations based on age, religion, national origin, or competency such as junior, intermediate or novice events, should not be allowed). And four, the events must be restricted to amateurs only. While amateur status is no longer a criterion for inclusion in the Olympic programme, it certainly was in 1904.*[33]

Kiely's all-around championship passed all four tests, so

Mallon, too, felt comfortable in accepting that 'world championship' as, simultaneously, an Olympic title as well.

KIELY'S NATIONALITY

Now that Tom Kiely is credited in every official record of the Olympic Games with winning an Olympic title, one more issue about the Olympic records remains to be addressed. Why is Kiely's nationality listed in most Olympic histories, including those of Henry, Mezö and today's official IOC records, as 'Great Britain'? Mallon, by contrast, lists Kiely as 'IRL', while others attempt a type of half-way house in terms of Kiely's nationality, such as:

> *Because Ireland was not yet an independent state, Kiely should be mentioned under GBR/IRE, with an explanatory footnote … Ironically, without its Irishmen (there were three), Great Britain would have been without representation at the St Louis Games.*[34]

As already seen, there was not one British athlete (from the island known as Great Britain), representing Britain at the St Louis Games. The notion that Kiely was asked to be a representative of Britain or the AAA is also an incredible one. The British Olympic Association was not formally constituted until late 1905, no British members of the International Olympic Committee attended the Games, and the English AAA sent no team to St Louis and invited no athletes to represent it either.[35] In Kiely's case, there had never been, nor would there be, an all-round championship held by the AAA until 1928. If the AAA did not 'select' athletes who were specialists in the events it actually fostered in 1904, it is preposterous to suggest that it would have selected an Irish athlete to represent it in an event that it did not promote at all.[36]

As Ireland was politically part of Great Britain and Ireland, officially Kiely, John Holloway and John Daly were 'British', but the Olympic Games has never classified athletes by where they were born, but rather by the 'nation' they represent or declare for. That is why Mo Farah's medals are for Great Britain, not Somalia. It is why John Flanagan's hammer medal in 1900 was won for the USA even though he was still an Irish (British) citizen. It is why Zola Budd in 1984 was representing Britain, not her native South Africa. It is also why some boxers have won medals for 'Ireland' in modern times, even though they were born within the borders of Great Britain, i.e. the Ireland team at the Olympics is not synonymous with specific political definitions of Ireland.

Historically, Baron de Coubertin himself wrote: 'a nation is not necessarily an independent State. There is an athletic geography that may differ at times from political geography.'[37] This was de Coubertin's view in 1911, referring specifically to Bohemia's case for having its athletes classified as Bohemian as opposed to Austrian, at a time when Bohemia was even more tied to Austria–Hungary than Ireland was to Great Britain.

It is also significant that no contemporary British newspapers claimed Kiely for Britain. No newspapers who chose to report what was for Britain an obscure event in a remote place made an alteration to the basic Reuters' telegraph, beyond the spelling of 'all-around':

Athletic Championship of the World. St Louis, Monday. Thomas F. Kiely, Ireland, has won the all round [sic] championship of the world at the World's Fair, under the auspices of the American Athletic Union, scoring four firsts in nine events.[38]

Throughout this book, it has been evident that Kiely had very little interest in political agendas. Nor did he have any antipathy towards England or Scotland. That does not mean he wanted to be considered 'British' at St Louis. Athletics bodies, administrators and journalists in England and Scotland had, as we have seen, consistently recognised Kiely as Irish, as representing Ireland or an Irish association. Everyone in St Louis knew he was from Ireland, and some may well have known he was from Tipperary too.

This misunderstanding was due to a later error, presumably at IOC level, based only on the fact that Tipperary was in Ireland and Ireland was in the United Kingdom in 1904. It was not based on what nation Kiely represented, or what nation he regarded as home. Incidentally, James Sullivan not only knew where Tipperary was, but he knew where Carrick-on-Suir was, as he called to visit the Davins in 1912 on his way home from the Stockholm Olympic Games.[39]

Every shred of evidence presented thus far suggests that Kiely travelled to St Louis alone, of his own volition and not as part of any team, Irish or otherwise. Yet, it has been claimed that he and the other two Irish athletes there (John Holloway and John Daly) formed 'a three-man Irish team' and that 'In line with Ireland's status as part of the Union, this allowed later claims about Britain's unbroken record of participation [at the Summer Olympic Games] to be maintained.'[40] This is a nice claim for the British Olympic Association to be able to make, but it is time it was 'disallowed' in the interest of fairness to Kiely, and to historical accuracy.

Surely Kiely's subsequent statement must carry weight too. He was unequivocal on the issue. When he was interviewed after his return, he said:

> *[I] felt more for the honour of my native land than for any self-distinction, and this above all others helped me on the great battle I had to make against the best athletes of the world. I have now secured this championship for Ireland and we ought to be able to keep it.*[41]

The case being made here has nothing whatsoever to do with a narrow view of Irish identity or nationalism. Kiely is a victim of having been assigned an incorrect national identity, something which has befallen many athletes who competed in the early Olympics. Britain has also had its losses in this respect. It could, for instance, make a case for Norman Pritchard's two athletics medals for India in 1900 being re-assigned as British medals. Irish sports historian Tom Hunt makes a similar case about Australia's Edwin Flack being more 'British' than Australian in 1896.[42]

Two unrelated examples, which have nothing to do with Ireland or Britain, will further help to demonstrate the unfairness of Kiely's classification in modern IOC records as British.

To this day, tennis player Hedwig Rosenbaum from Prague is listed in Olympic records as representing 'Bohemia', even though Bohemia then had no independent status, home rule or Olympic committee when she competed at the 1900

Games, and Bohemia's official and actual ruler, Austria, did have a team at those Paris Olympics.[43]

Another example concerns the 1912 Stockholm Games. Finland did not get full independence from Russia until after the Bolshevik Revolution in late 1917, and its athletes in 1912 were forced to accept the Russian flag at victory ceremonies and march behind the Russian team at the opening ceremony. Yet, Finnish medals won in 1912 have always been credited to Finland in IOC records.

It is tempting to suggest that Hannes Kolehmainen, treble gold-medallist in Stockholm, felt about as 'Russian' as Tom Kiely felt 'British', yet the former has always had 'Finland' recognised in the record books, and the latter continues to have 'Great Britain' placed beside his name. The wonderful irony in all of that is that both Kolehmainen and Kiely competed under the banner of the I-AAC at Celtic Park, New York, at different times, the Finn spending several years there, more or less as a full-time athlete after 1912.[44]

Baron de Coubertin's *Memoires* suggested years later that, if he had his way, the 'athletic geography' of Bohemia, Finland, Poland and Ireland would have been recognised at the Olympic Games long before independence or self-government.[45] De Coubertin, in truth, was ambiguous about athletic geography when it suited him, or did not suit others. Historically, the stance by ruling powers against independence-seeking nations at the Olympics really began from 1906, when Ireland's Peter O'Connor famously did battle to have his Irishness recognised at the Intercalated Games in Athens.[46] Things got tighter still when London hosted the 1908 Olympic Games, and the organising committee decided that a 'country' is 'any territory having separate representation on the International Olympic Committee'.[47] The IOC did not appoint its first Member for Ireland, J. J. Keane, until 1922.

Having examined eight St Louis newspapers, and many others, Bill Mallon decided that the available evidence from 1904 should see Kiely listed with 'IRL' after his name.[48] It is historically incorrect to argue against that. The anomalous examples given above show that the IOC's practices in recording nationality, especially in the early Games, need to be reviewed, and most definitely so in the case of Kiely. He was Ireland's first gold medal winner in Olympic track and field. Period.

Kiely was always known as 'Erin's Champion'. It is high time that he is fully and properly credited by the International Olympic Committee as Erin's *Olympic* Champion too. Very few in Ireland, or Britain, would argue with that. Thinking of his county of origin, Tipperary, as well as his sense of national pride, it is not beyond the bounds of possibility that if Kiely himself had had his way, his representative status might actually have been 'TIPP / IRL'.

A wrong needs to be righted. This is not about rewriting history but correcting a historical error. Tom Kiely's status as an Olympic champion who represented nowhere but Ireland needs to be acknowledged, not least by the International Olympic Committee.

Some of Kiely's trophies displayed in the parlour at Mullagh.
(*Kiely Collection, Tipperary Museum of Hidden History*)

TOM KIELY'S RECOGNISED IRISH RECORDS, 1906

Frank Dinneen, GAA secretary and athletics administrator, produced *The Irish Athletic Record 1906*, with Tom Kiely on the cover as 'All-Round Athletic Champion of the World'. In this little book, Dinneen devoted several pages to Irish records. It remains the most complete contemporary list of Kiely's records, even though it has several known gaps. Through no fault of Dinneen's, because of the scoring system used in Irish all-round competitions, there has never been a proper points-based calculation of Kiely's scores in the period 1892–4, or 1898. Because the events in an Irish all-round differed in some instances from the American all-around, and because the Irish scoring system gave points for placings in each event, not for times or distances, direct comparisons are impossible. All that can be said with certainty is that Kiely's performances in all-round competitions were believed in Ireland and America in the 1890s to be comfortably better than anyone else on record, anywhere.

There are even bigger gaps in Dinneen's listings that I am unable to explain. For example, he does not include the 156 feet 2 inches in the hammer achieved in 1899, which the AAA classed as a world record at the time, and still retains in its records. That was done at a GAA meeting at which Dinneen officiated. Nor does the list mention the hop, step and jump of 49 feet 7 inches from 1892, which is still classed as a world record in some quarters.[1] Dinneen even seems to have forgotten some of Kiely's records, such as one at Dungarvan in 1895 in the hammer, mentioned in Chapter 3. It has also been seen that Kiely's own scrapbook and contemporary newspaper accounts contain claims for several other records not listed below and, of course, anything done after 1906, including the hammer of 1908 against Martin Sheridan in Dungarvan, cannot be included either. It is literally the case that it is impossible to compile a table which can categorically list Kiely's records, Irish or otherwise. What has been attempted, throughout this book, is to show the organic emergence of Kiely's status as a record breaker, as reported contemporaneously. Where Dinneen lists eighteen records (see below), it is quite conceivable that this understates the contemporary total significantly.

What Dinneen's list demonstrates, very clearly, is the variety of events and styles that were the norm in Irish athletics during Kiely's career. As explained elsewhere, because of standardisation of the hammer subsequently, none of these records will now be found in official databases, at Irish Athletics, UK Athletics or the IAAF.

According to Dinneen, Kiely's Irish records, i.e. records set in Ireland, were as follows:

56lb (13 inches long):
> 27 feet 2 inches, at Sligo, 31 July 1905

56lb, unlimited run and follow (16-inch weight):

36 feet 6½ inches, at Carrick-on-Suir, 1896

36 feet 7 inches, at Tipperary, 26 September 1897

37 feet, at Clonmel, 3 October 1897

38 feet 11 inches, at Cork, 14 August 1898

56lb, unlimited run and follow, one-handed (13-inch weight):

34 feet 11½ inches, at Mitchelstown, 1893

35 feet 5 inches, at Nenagh, 1894

35 feet 5¾ inches, at Kilkenny, 1894

16lb hammer, from a nine-foot circle (4 foot long handle and head i.e. total length)*:

142 feet 5 inches, at Cappoquin, 1897

143 feet 0¾ inches, at Wexford, 5 August 1897

145 feet, at Clonmel, 3 October 1897

146 feet 10 inches, at Ballsbridge, 16 July 1898

151 feet 11 inches, at Cahir, 25 July 1898

154 feet 2 inches, at Dungarvan, 17 September 1905

16lb hammer, unlimited run and follow (4 foot long handle and head)*:

152 feet 9½ inches, at Limerick, 24 July 1898

16lb hammer, from a seven-foot circle (3 foot 6 inches long wooden handle and iron head):

122 feet 9 inches, at Nenagh, 8 August 1894

123 feet 11 inches, at Kildorrery, 8 October 1894

16lb hammer, from a seven-foot circle (4 foot long wooden handle and iron head):

140 feet 2 inches, no venue given, 31 August 1896

*The classification and dates suggest these were throws done with a wire-handled hammer.

KIELY'S IRISH ATHLETIC TITLES[1]

Event	GAA titles	IAAA titles
All-Round Championship	1	3
Long Jump	2	2
Hop, Step and Jump	3	
120 Yards Hurdles	7	1
Shot Put	1	
Putting 28lb Weight	2	
Hammer (unlimited run and follow)	5	
Throwing 7lb Weight	2	
56lb Weight (unlimited run and follow)	10	
Hammer (seven-foot circle)		1
56lb Weight (no follow)		1
Hammer (nine-foot circle)	5	7
Total	**38**	**15**

APPENDIX 3

A NOTE ON MEASUREMENTS

In Tom Kiely's time, imperial measurements were universally used in Ireland, Britain and the USA, including during the St Louis all-around competition. Accordingly, almost every contemporary document or newspaper gave Kiely's results in feet and inches for jumping and throwing distances, and in pounds for weights. The following lists are provided to give readers an accurate idea of how such measurements compare to the metric ones used almost everywhere today, allowing for the fact that it is impossible to present a readable table containing all possible measurements and equivalents.

Weights
- 7lb = 3.175 kilogrammes
- 14lb = 6.35 kilogrammes
- 16lb = 7.2575 kilogrammes
- 28lb = 12.7 kilogrammes
- 56lb = 25.4 kilogrammes

Distances (jumping/throwing)
- 1 inch = 2.54 cm
- 2 inches = 5.08 cm
- 3 inches = 7.62 cm

- 6 inches = 15.24 cm
- 9 inches = 22.86 cm
- 12 inches (a foot) = 30.48 cm
- 3 feet (a yard) = 91.44 cm
- 3 feet, 3.37 inches = 1 metre
- 5 feet = 152.4 cm or 1 metre, 52.4 cm
- 10 feet = 304.8 cm or 3 metres, 4.8 cm
- 20 feet = 609.6 cm or 6 metres, 9.6 cm
- 30 feet = 914.4 cm or 9 metres, 14.4 cm
- 50 feet = 1,524 cm or 15 metres, 24 cm
- 100 feet = 3,048 cm, or 30 metres, 48 cm
- 150 feet (50 yards) = 4,572 cm, or 45 metres, 72 cm

Distances (running/walking)

- 100 yards = 91.44 metres
- 109.361 yards = 100 metres
- 120 yards = 109.728 metres
- 880 yards = 804.672 metres
- 1760 yards (one mile) = 1,609.344 metres

ENDNOTES

INTRODUCTION

1 Zarnowski, Frank, *All-Round Men: Heroes of a Forgotten Sport* (Scarecrow Press, 2005), p. 118.

2 A note on spelling: throughout the book, spelling variations will only occur when moving from Irish/British to American contexts, so that the term 'all-around' will be used only when referring to American events.

3 Hunt, Tom, *The Little Book of Irish Athletics* (The History Press, Dublin, 2017), p. 45.

4 McCarthy, Kevin, *Gold, Silver and Green: The Irish Olympic Journey 1896–1924* (Cork University Press, Cork, 2010), p. 7.

5 Athletics was essentially a male-only sport in Kiely's time. The first female athlete at an English Amateur Athletic Association (AAA) championships was in 1922, and at the Olympic Games was in 1928.

6 *The Clonmel Nationalist*, 27 September 1893. *The Clonmel Nationalist* was the main newspaper in south Tipperary throughout Kiely's career. It will hereafter be referred to and footnoted as *Nationalist*.

7 My thanks to Ian Hodge of UK Athletics for locating this for me.

8 See: www.athleticsireland.ie/competition/statistics.

9 Zarnowski (2005), p. 115.

10 See www.athleticsireland.ie/downloads/statistics/Irish_Champions.

11 'Erin' is an old Celtic term for the island of Ireland, thought to be derived from the name of the goddess Ériu.

1. GROWING UP IN BALLYNEILL

1 *Census of Ireland 1901*. Ballyneill is found under the district heading of Kilmurry in Co. Tipperary, spelled as 'Ballyneal'. See: www.census. nationalarchives.ie/pages/1901/Tipperary/Kilmurry/.

2 'Achilles', 'The Colourful Career of T.F. Kiely', *The Irish Press*, 14 January 1955.

3 Interview with Tom Kiely, grandson of Tom Kiely, at Lisheen, Co. Tipperary, 15 January 2019. Tom grew up beside Tom Kiely's last home in Shawfield, Ballyneill and was interviewed several times at his home in

Lisheen, outside Clonmel.

4   Power, Patrick C., 'Champion Kiely, a Giant among Athletes', *Nationalist*, 25 December 1982.

5   Withers, Bob, *Tom Kiely: 'For Tipperary and Ireland'* (Tipperary County Museum, Clonmel, 1997), pp. 5–6.

6   Mehigan, P.D ('Carbery'), 'Tom Kiely of Ballyneill, Wonder Athlete', Kilfeather, Seán (ed.), *Vintage Carbery* (Beaver Row Press, Dublin, 1984), pp. 83–84.

7   Interview with Tom Kiely, 15 January 2019.

8   For a good overview of the sort of father–son relationship which was typified by William and Tom Kiely, see Bell, Jonathan and Watson, Mervyn, *Irish Farming Life* (Four Courts Press, Dublin, 2014), p. 15.

9   *Nationalist*, 27 September 1893.

10 These calculations are based on the 1901 census returns, by which time William was seventy-two and Mary fifty-nine.

11 Interview with Tom Kiely, 13 March 2019.

12 The story of the mission to Iowa is recounted in several sources about Mount Melleray, particularly in Liddy, A. J., *The Story of Mount Melleray* (Gill, Dublin, 1946), pp. 164–175.

13 This list has been compiled through a combination of the memory of Tom Kiely (grandson) and analysis of the roll books at Ballyneill National School, with thanks to Michael McHale for his help with the information.

14 Interview with Tom Kiely, 15 January 2019.

15 Irish National Teachers Organisation, *Primary School Curriculum: An Evolutionary Process* (INTO, Dublin, 1996), pp. 6–7.

16 Power (1982).

17 Coolahan, John, *Irish Education: Its History and Structure* (Institute of Public Administration, Dublin, 1981), p. 29. All of the statistical data on Irish education that I use here and in subsequent paragraphs comes from John Coolahan's seminal work.

18 My thanks for this advice and for help in analysing the Ballyneill roll books to my former colleague Paddy (Patrick F.) O'Donovan, author of a number of works on Irish education, including *A History of Ireland's School Inspectorate, 1831–2008* with the late Professor John Coolahan (Four Courts Press, Dublin, 2009).

19 All of the details about Tom Kiely's school attendance come from the Ballyneill National School roll books.

20 Withers (1997), p. 6.

21 Tom Kiely vividly recalled his grandfather playing the tin whistle to entertain them as children.

22 Sutton, P. P., article in *The Irish Wheel and Athletic News*, 3 April 1894.

23   Ó Faoláin, Seán, article in *The Irish Times*, 10 May 1941.

24   Fogarty, Canon Philip, *Tipperary's GAA Story* (The Tipperary Star, Thurles, 1960), p. 74. Fogarty draws the information from an undated article by 'Celt' entitled 'Thomas F. Kiely – The Star of the Gael'.

25   Hunt (2017), p. 38.

26   The earliest suggestion of a Davin family relationship that I have found is by 'Carbery' (otherwise known as P. D. Mehigan), in *Fifty Years of Irish Athletics* (Gaelic Publicity Services, Dublin, 1943), p. 33.

27   Withers (1997), p. 6.

28   *Nationalist*, 27 September 1893.

29   *Cashel Sentinel*, 6 August 1904.

30   Rouse, Paul, *The Hurlers* (Penguin, Dublin, 2018), p. 40. The term 6d means sixpence.

2. MOULDING THE CHAMPION

1   Rouse (2018), p. 32.

2   Fogarty (1960), p. 36.

3   *Clonmel Chronicle, Tipperary and Waterford Advertiser*, 11 August 1888. Note that James Mitchel, before emigrating later in 1888, spelled his name 'Mitchell' but dropped the second 'l' when he settled in the USA.

4   *Tipperary Independent*, 1 September 1888.

5   *Ibid.*, 13 October 1888.

6   O'Donoghue, Tony, *Irish Championship Athletics* 1873–1914 (Kilkenny People Printing, Kilkenny, 2005), p. 50.

7   Tom Kiely Scrapbook, inside back cover. This scrapbook is part of the Kiely Collection at Tipperary Museum of Hidden History.

8   Hunt, Tom, *Sport and Society in Victorian Ireland: The Case of Westmeath* (Cork University Press, Cork, 2007), pp. 226–227.

9   Central Statistics Office, *Farming since the Famine: Irish Farm Statistics 1847–1996* (Central Statistics Office, Dublin, 1997), p. 268.

10   *Sport*, 14 September 1889.

11   Tom Kiely Scrapbook, p. 1.

12   *Sport*, 21 June 1890.

13   This is comprehensively discussed in Mandle, W. F., 'Parnell and Sport', *Studia Hibernica*, No. 28 (1994), pp. 103–116.

14   Puirséal, Pádraig, *The GAA in Its Time* (Ward River Press, Dublin, 1984), p. 97.

15   Fogarty (1960), p. 53.

16   Rouse, Paul, *Sport and Ireland: A History* (Oxford University Press, Oxford, 2015), pp. 184–186. The Tobin quote is from Ryan, Eoin, 'Blaming Parnell:

Accounting for the Decline of the GAA, 1889–1894' (UCD MA thesis, 2013), pp. 12–13.

17 Ó Riain, Seamus, *Maurice Davin: First President of the GAA* (Geography Publications, Dublin, 1994), p. 204.

18 Zarnowski (2005), p. 115. Zarnowski listed the events in which the Irish held world bests in a footnote on p. 123.

19 *Sport*, 15 June 1889.

20 *Ibid.*, 8 August 1891, for instance, recorded the 'rag doll records' being achieved in the USA with adapted weights. In reality, America would soon leave Ireland behind in terms of athletics development.

21 *Ibid.*, 2 August 1890.

22 See the Consumer Price Index inflation calculator at www.in2013dollars.com/1890-GBP-in-2017.

23 These details, for example, come from an undated cutting from the *Nationalist*, in the Tom Kiely Scrapbook, p. 1, column 1.

24 Tom Kiely Scrapbook, p. 1, column 3.

25 *Sport*, 12 July 1890.

26 *Ibid.*, 4 May 1889.

27 *Ibid.*, 2 August 1890.

28 *The Irish Times*, 29 August 1890.

29 *Sport*, 6 September 1890.

30 Tom Kiely Scrapbook, p. 4, column 2.

31 *Sport,* 8 August 1891.

32 O'Donoghue (2005), p. 61.

33 *Sport*, 8 August 1891.

34 Tom Kiely Scrapbook, p. 2, column 2. This was originally from the *Nationalist*, 8 August 1891.

35 *Sport*, 26 September 1891.

36 Tom Kiely Scrapbook, p. 5, column 2.

37 O'Donoghue (2005), p. 64.

38 *Nationalist*, 23 July 1892.

39 Dooley, William, *Champions of the Athletic Arena* (General Publicity Service, Dublin, 1947), p. 35.

40 Tom Kiely Scrapbook, p. 3, column 1.

41 *Sport*, 23 July 1892.

42 *Ibid.*, 30 July 1892.

43 *Irish Daily Independent*, 1 August 1892.

44 *Sport*, 6 August 1892.

45 Tom Kiely Scrapbook, p. 3, column 3. Originally from *Sport*, 2 August

1892.

46 *Nationalist*, 6 August 1892. It is notable that other Tipperary newspapers were much less impressed with the new champion, as yet. The *Cashel Sentinel* and *Cashel Gazette* carried no report whatsoever of Kiely's win, while *The Nenagh Guardian* (6 August 1892) carried just three and a half lines.

47 Puirséal (1984), p. 103.

48 O'Donoghue (2005), p. 65.

49 Tom Kiely Scrapbook, p. 6, column 2. This comes from the 'Cuchulinn' column in *Sport*, 17 September 1892.

50 Tom Kiely Scrapbook, p. 6, column 3.

51 *Ibid.*, p. 10, column 1. This comes from the *Irish Daily Independent*, 12 September 1892.

52 This table is generated from the statistics supplied in Zarnowski (2005), p. 89, and O'Donoghue (2005), p. 65.

53 These are found in several sources, including the website of the National Union of Track Statisticians at www.nuts.org.uk/Champs/AAA.

54 See the statistics at www.athleticsireland.ie/downloads/statistics/Irish_OUTDOOR_Champions-min.pdf. It should be noted that it is unclear whether Kiely's event involved two hops and a jump, or a hop, step and jump. The former was common in Kiely's day, and in America too, but the hop, step and jump had become the norm under IAAF rules from 1912.

3. GLORY YEARS OF 1893–95

1 This report came from *Sport*, which had gotten it from the *Cork Herald* (undated). It is in the Tom Kiely Scrapbook, p. 11, column 2.

2 Interview with Tom Kiely, 15 January 2019.

3 Tom Kiely Scrapbook, p. 11, column 2.

4 *Ibid.*, p. 53. The reference to 1886 here is to the Plan of Campaign movement against some Tipperary landlords.

5 Fogarty (1960), p. 51. See also O'Meara, Micheál, *South Tipperary GAA 1907–2007* (Cumann Lúthchleas Gael, Coiste Chontae Árainn Theas, 2007), p. 12.

6 Tom Kiely Scrapbook, p. 11, column 2. This is from *Sport*, 20 May 1893.

7 *Sport*, 20 May 1893.

8 Tom Kiely Scrapbook, p. 12, column 3. This letter was published in *Sport*, 3 June 1893, commenting on 'Cuchulinn's' mistake of the previous issue, 27 May 1893.

9 Tom Kiely Scrapbook, p. 11, column 3.

10 O'Donoghue (2005), p. 68.

11 Mitchel, James S., *How to Become a Weight Thrower* (Spalding Athletic

Library, New York, 1916), p. 30.

12 Zarnowski (2005), pp. 115–116. The IAAF in modern non-amateur times has kept the acronym but changed its name to the International Association of Athletic Federations. It periodically updates its *Progression of World's Best Performances and Official IAAF World Records*. The version used here was from 2015 (edited by Richard Hymans and Imre Matrahazi). My thanks again to Chris Turner, IAAF Heritage Development Director, for confirming the absence of pre-1912 records.

13 Mitchel (1916), p. 21.

14 Tom Kiely Scrapbook, inserted between pp. 17–18.

15 *Ibid.,* p. 12, column 3.

16 *Ibid.,* all recorded meticulously by the champion himself on the back cover.

17 *Sport*, 21 October 1893. An article entitled 'A Glance at the Past Season' by the columnist 'Cuchulinn'.

18 Tom Kiely Scrapbook, p. 14, column 1.

19 *Sport*, 19 August 1893.

20 McGahon, Arthur, 'The Greatest All-Rounder World Will Ever Know', *The Irish Press*, 2 March 1958.

21 *Sport*, 21 October 1893.

22 McGahon (1958).

23 Tom Kiely Scrapbook, inside back cover.

24 *The Nenagh Guardian*, 4 August 1894.

25 *Ibid.*, 11 August 1894.

26 Tom Kiely Scrapbook, inside back cover.

27 *Ibid.*, p. 1, column 2.

28 *Sport*, 11 August 1894.

29 O'Donoghue (2005), p. 76, has all six competitors' performances.

30 Tom Kiely Scrapbook, p. 8, column 1. This comes from *Sport*, 11 August 1894.

31 O'Connor, Peter, 'Long Jumping', in Mehigan, P. D. (ed.), *Fifty Years of Irish Athletics* (Gaelic Publicity Services, Dublin, 1943), p. 92.

32 Tom Kiely Scrapbook, p. 1, column 2. This was a handwritten excerpt from the *Nationalist*, 8 August 1894.

33 *Ibid.*, p. 11, column 3. From *Sport*, this article dated 2 February 1895 was written by William Roche of Kildorrery, originally for the *Police Gazette*.

34 John Menton (2000 Olympian) and Phil Conway (1972 Olympian) have given the author fascinating insights into the science behind weight throwing, and are thanked sincerely for sharing their time and expertise.

35 *Nationalist*, 21 August 1895 and 11 September 1895.

36   *Ibid.*, 28 February 1894.

37   *Sport*, 24 August 1895.

38   *Irish Independent*, 3 July 1895.

39   *Sport*, 27 July 1895.

40   *Ibid.*, 6 July 1895.

41   *Nationalist*, 7 September 1895.

42   *Sport*, 16 May 1896.

43   Tom Kiely Scrapbook, p. 23, column 2.

44   *Ibid.*, where the note of thanks is inserted between pp. 15–16.

45   *Ibid.*, p. 23, column 1 and also inside back cover.

46   *Sport*, 7 September 1895.

47   O'Donoghue (2005), p. 83.

4. THE HAMMER OF THE SCOTS

1   Rouse (2018), p. 34.

2   Mitchel (1916), p. 19.

3   *Sport*, 11 August 1895.

4   *Ibid.*, 25 September 1895.

5   *Ibid.*, 18 July 1891, for example.

6   O'Donoghue (2005), p. 81

7   *Sport*, 31 August 1895.

8   *The Scottish Referee*, 19 July 1895.

9   For example, see Zarnowski (2005), p. 117.

10   *The Scottish Referee*, 22 July 1895.

11   Fogarty (1960), p. 75.

12   Zarnowski (2005), pp. 116–117.

13   Navin, Michael, 'Tom Kiely of Ballyneill: The World's Champion All-Round Athlete', in Maher, James (ed.), *Chiefs of the Comeraghs*, (Mullinahone, Co. Tipperary, 1957).

14   O'Donoghue (2005), pp. 100–101.

15   *Sport*, 26 July 1902.

16   *Ibid.*, 6 August 1901.

17   See, for details and reference to Kraenzlein, Wallechinsky, David, *The Complete Book of the Olympics* (Penguin Books, New York, 1984), pp. 52–53.

18   Tom Kiely Scrapbook, unprovenanced newspaper account, p. 22.

19   *The Scottish Referee*, 22 July 1895, reproduced in the *Nationalist*, 24 July 1895.

20 *Ibid.*, 16 July 1897. The references here are to characters from novels by Sir Walter Scott, depicted in statue form on the monument to Scott, i.e. several miles from the athletics stadium.

21 *The Scotsman*, 19 July 1897.

22 O'Donoghue (2005), pp. 100–101.

23 *Edinburgh Evening News*, 17 July 1899.

24 *Sport*, 6 July 1901.

25 *The Scottish Referee*, 1 July 1901.

26 *Ibid.*, 20 July 1903.

27 O'Donoghue (2005), p. 128.

28 There is a suggestion in one highly reputable source that Kiely competed in the hammer against Scotland in Belfast on 14 July 1906, but this has been checked and the Irish competitor was definitely Larry Kiely, not Tom. See *Belfast Newsletter*, 16 July 1906.

29 Interview with Tom Kiely, 15 January 2019.

30 'Achilles', 'The Champion with Whom None Could Compare', [Dublin] *Evening Herald*, 26 January 1955.

31 If one takes a look at the table, there may not appear to be too much of the spectacular about Kiely's performances in the annual match against Scotland. He lost as many events as he won, for instance, achieving nine victories in eighteen events. What the table cannot show is that Kiely represented Ireland in events that were not in his top three specialisms on at least five occasions in this annual contest, and that he, an all-rounder, was competing against event specialists in many of these. Nor can the table show the degree to which Kiely performed heroics that had a huge impact on the eventual outcome of several contests, quite often in his weaker events, and almost always in his favourite hammer event.

5. ADVENTURES IN ENGLAND

1 *Sport*, 20 April 1895.

2 Interview with Tom Kiely, 10 October 2019.

3 The website of the British Amateur Athletic Association at www. gbrathletics.com/bc/bc1.htm provides the full list of AAA champions and times/measurements from 1880.

4 Interview with Tom Kiely, 15 January 2019.

5 [Dublin] *Evening Herald*, 8 July 1895.

6 *London Evening Standard*, 8 July 1895.

7 For example, the *London Evening Standard* and *Sheffield Independent*, 8 July 1895, listed both men as IAAA, whereas the linkage of Horgan to Belfast comes from the *London Athletic News* of the same date.

8 *Sport*, 17 July 1895.

9   *Ibid.*, 31 August 1895.

10   The first three placings in each event can be found at www.nuts.org.uk/
      Champs/AAA/AAAHT.htm.

11   *Irish Daily Independent*, 7 April 1896.

12   Davin, Pat, *Recollections of a Veteran Irish Athlete* (Juverna Press, Dublin,
      1938), p. 70.

13   *Sport*, 25 May 1896.

14   McCarthy (2010), p. 17.

15   *Ibid.*, p 22, quoting *Sport*, 14 December 1895.

16   Mallon, Bill and Widlund, Ture, *The 1896 Olympic Games* (McFarland,
      London, 1998), pp. 70–73.

17   *Sport*, 8 August 1896.

18   *Manchester Evening News*, 5 July 1897.

19   *The Morning Post*, 5 July 1897.

20   *Irish Independent*, 5 July 1897.

21   *Sporting Life*, 4 July 1898.

22   *The Irish Times*, 4 July 1898.

23   *The Pall Mall Gazette*, 4 July 1898.

24   *Lloyd's List*, 4 July 1898.

25   *London Evening Standard*, 4 July 1898.

26   *The Freeman's Journal*, 3 July 1899.

27   *Sporting Life*, 9 July 1900.

28   *Sport*, 7 July 1900.

29   *Ibid.*, 13 July 1901.

30   See the British Film Institute's DVD, *Mitchell and Kenyon: Edwardian
      Sport*, segment entitled 'Amateur Athletics'.

31   *Sporting Life*, 6 July 1903.

32   These results are adjusted to imperial figures (consistent with recording
      practice in Kiely's day) from the metric form they are currently held in, at
      www.nuts.org.uk/Champs/AAA/AAAHT.htm.

6. FACING CHALLENGES AND CHANGE, 1896–99

1   Fogarty (1960), p. 63.

2   *Nationalist*, 18 January 1896.

3   Tom Kiely Scrapbook, p. 39, column 1. The poem's position towards
      the end of the scrapbook suggests it dates from the mid-1890s, but its
      provenance has not otherwise been traced.

4   Fogarty (1960), p. 67.

5   Ó Riain (1994), p. 206.

6   Puirséal (1984), p. 118.

7   *Nationalist*, 30 April 1898.

8   *Sport*, 6 February 1897.

9   Fogarty (1960), p. 76.

10 O'Meara (2007), p. 12.

11 *Sport*, 20 February 1897.

12 *Nationalist*, 14 July 1897.

13 *Ibid.*, 7 July 1897.

14 Tipperary SR Valuations Lists: Electoral Division of Kilmurry, Rural District of Carrick-on-Suir (1858–1933), Book 8, 1893–1907, p. 38.

15 Cutting from the *Nationalist* in 1896, edition unsourced.

16 *Irish Independent*, 26 May 1896.

17 I have failed to find Larry's school records, but this supposition that he continued beyond primary education is based on the later offer of a scholarship to Notre Dame University in 1904.

18 *Sport*, 1 August 1896.

19 O'Donoghue (2005), p. 87.

20 *Ibid.*, p. 88.

21 Unprovenanced article, possibly from *Ireland's Own*, entitled 'The Sporting Irish'. Some of this author's uncertainty relates to the circle diameter. This article is contained within the Kiely Collection.

22 Dinneen, Frank B., *Irish Athletic Records* (Cahill & Co., Dublin, 1906), Appendix (Irish records).

23 O'Donoghue (2005), p. 90.

24 *Ibid.*, p. 93. See also *Nationalist*, 9 June 1897.

25 *Sport*, 13 June 1897.

26 *Nationalist*, 3 July 1897.

27 See the list in Appendix 1 of this book, derived from Dinneen (1906).

28 *Nationalist*, 4 August 1897. Note that Dinneen (1906) attributes a 56lb record to Kiely at Clonmel in 1897, but contemporary newspaper accounts that have been located do not verify this.

29 *Ibid.*, 7 August 1897.

30 *Ibid.*, 18 August 1897.

31 Zarnowski (2005), p. 124 (note).

32 *Nationalist*, 8 September 1897.

33 Dinneen (1906) records the Clonmel distance in his records table.

34 O'Donoghue (2005), pp. 93–94.

35 *Mitchell and Kenyon: Edwardian Sport* (British Film Institute DVD), location 591.

36 *Sport*, 13 August 1898.

37 *Nationalist*, 25 May 1898.

38 *Ibid.*, 27 July 1898.

39 *Ibid.*, 24 May 1899 and 19 July 1899.

40 The difficulties during the 1899 season are dealt with in some detail in *Sport*, 7 April 1900.

41 *Ibid.*, 24 August 1898.

42 *Ibid.*, 17 September 1898.

43 The suggestion is found in the records tables compiled by Dinneen (1906).

44 *Ibid.*

45 *Nationalist*, 27 July 1898.

46 My thanks to Ian Hodge of UK Athletics for locating this in the AAA records, given as 46.30 metres.

47 *Sport*, 3 September 1898.

48 *Nationalist*, 31 August 1898.

49 *Ibid.*, 19 October 1898.

50 O'Donoghue (2005), p. 102.

51 *Nationalist*, 19 October 1898.

52 Zarnowski (2005), see table, p. 125. *Nationalist*, 20 September 1899, records the distance as 156 feet even, saying the distance was 4 feet 1 inch better than Kiely's British record, but this is not recorded in the AAA archives. Neither are the throws at Youghal or Carrick-on-Suir in 1899, presumably as they were not ratifiable.

53 O'Donoghue (2005), pp. 104–106. Wind speed can to this day be a factor in nullifying athletic records in sprint or long jump events, but not normally in weight throwing.

54 *The Nenagh Guardian*, 1 July 1899.

55 *Nationalist*, 30 August 1899.

56 *Ibid.*, 27 September 1899.

7. ON TOP, BUT NO FURTHER, 1900–03

1 Hunt, Tom, 'Tom Kiely: Ireland's First Track and Field Olympic Gold Medallist?', *Journal of Olympic History*, Vol. 27, No. 3 (November 2019).

2 Interview with Tom Kiely, 15 January 2019. The date of Katie's departure for Belgium is uncertain.

3 1901 and 1911 census returns for Tipperary SR, Parliamentary Division of East Tipperary, Electoral District of Kilmurry, Townland of Ballyneill

and also of Curraghdobbin.

4   Interviews with Tom Kiely, 15 January and 12 July 2019.

5   Tipperary SR Valuations Lists: Electoral Division of Kilmurry, Rural District of Carrick-on-Suir (1858–1933), Book 8, 1893–1907, p. 40.

6   *Nationalist*, 21 April 1900.

7   Unprovenanced article from Tom Kiely Scrapbook, p. 41. Withers (1997), p. 17 believes it took place in 1898.

8   *Nationalist*, 19 May 1900.

9   *Sport*, 12 May 1900.

10   *Ibid.*, 14 July 1900.

11   McCarthy (2010), pp. 62–63. This is fleshed out further in O'Riordan, Ted, 'The Unsurpassable Leahys of Charleville', *Charleville and District Historical Journal*, Vol. 3 (1988), p. 8.

12   *Sport,* 21 July 1900.

13   *Nationalist*, 22 August, 29 August and 1 September 1900.

14   *Sport*, 25 August 1900.

15   *Nationalist*, 15 September 1900.

16   *Ibid.*, 26 September 1900.

17   Dinneen (1906).

18   *Sport*, 24 August 1901.

19   *Ibid.*, 8 June 1901.

20   *Nationalist*, 3 July 1901.

21   O'Donoghue (2005), pp. 113–114.

22   *Ibid.*

23   *Ibid.*, p. 115.

24   *Sport*, 5 July 1902.

25   *Ibid.*, 5 October 1901.

26   *Ibid.*, 28 June 1902.

27   *Irish Independent*, 16 September 1902.

28   My thanks to one of my former students at CBS Dungarvan, Michael O'Brien, for his explanation of the roll of ball-bearings in hammer design, and for his help overall.

29   O'Dwyer, Michael, 'Tom Phelan', one of many short biographies on the website, www.tipperaryathletics.com.

30   *Sport*, 20 September 1902.

31   *Nationalist*, 10 and 17 September 1902.

32   *Limerick Leader*, 15 September 1902.

33   Brady, Joseph, *The Big Sycamore* (M. H. Gill, Dublin, 1951), p. 132. The

story is also found in a subsequent edition of *Ireland's Own*.

34 O'Meara (2007), p. 14.

35 Fogarty (1960), p. 94.

36 *Nationalist*, 1 July 1903 and 18 July 1903, respectively.

37 O'Donoghue (2005), p. 124.

38 *Ibid.*, p. 126.

39 Dinneen (1906), pp. 37–38.

8. ONE REMARKABLE DAY IN ST LOUIS

1 Tom Kiely Scrapbook, unidentified newspaper cutting from 1892, p. 4, column 1.

2 As passenger 100742010299, Prendergast gave this information when his ship, the *Celtic*, docked in New York on 12 September 1913. See full details under 'William F. Prendergast' at the Ellis Island Foundation website: www.libertyellisfoundation.org/passenger-details.

3 Redmond, Patrick C., *The Irish-American Athletic Club of New York* (McFarland & Co., 2018), Kindle edition, location 1020. This statement is grounded in evidence from several New York newspapers.

4 Ellis Island records for Thomas F. Kiely in 1904, at www.libertyellisfoundation.org.

5 *The Gaelic American*, 3 October 1903.

6 *Ibid.*, 11 June 1904.

7 *The New York Tribune*, 6 June 1904.

8 *The Gaelic American*, 25 June 1904.

9 *Ibid.*, 2 July 1904.

10 As mentioned earlier, I am using the American spelling 'all-around' where referring to the American championship, and the term 'all-round' when referring to the Irish context.

11 Wallechinsky (1984), p. 107.

12 Redmond (2018), location 1470. This is based on reports from *The New York Sun*, 8 April 1904; [New York] *Evening World*, 26 April 1904 and *The New York Times*, 26 July and 7 August 1904.

13 *Ibid.*, location 1493.

14 *The Gaelic American*, 18 June 1904.

15 *The Freeman's Journal*, 8 October 1904. I am indebted to Tom Hunt for alerting me to this article, which includes an interview with Kiely upon his return from the USA.

16 Zarnowski (2005), p. 117.

17 Mallon, Bill, *The 1904 Olympic Games* (McFarland, London, 1999), p. 156.

18 McGahon (1958).

19 *St. Louis Republic*, 5 July 1904.

20 Mallon, *The 1904 Olympic Games* (1999), p. 64. Mallon also points out that the seventh entrant in the all-around championship, Max Emmerich of the USA, started the 100 yards (heat 2), failed to finish and immediately withdrew from the competition.

21 *The Freeman's Journal*, 8 October 1904.

22 *Ibid.*

23 *Nationalist*, 27 September 1893.

24 *The Freeman's Journal*, 8 October 1904.

25 *St. Louis Republic*, 5 July 1904.

26 *The Gaelic American*, 11 June 1904.

27 *The Freeman's Journal*, 8 October 1904.

28 *St. Louis Republic*, 5 July 1904.

29 *Ibid.* Zarnowski (2005) offers other examples of Clark's tendency to drop out of competitions when he felt he could not win.

30 Zarnowski (2005) has a table showing this and Kiely's other all-time best performances.

31 [New York] *Evening World*, 5 July 1904.

32 See, for instance, *The Salt Lake Herald*, 5 July 1904 and *The St. Paul Globe*, 5 July 1904.

33 This table is based on data from Mallon, *The 1904 Olympic Games* (1999), pp. 63–66.

9. THE AFTERMATH OF ST LOUIS

1   *The Gaelic American*, 9 July 1904.

2   *Ibid.*, 16 July 1904.

3   Letter from Tom Kiely to Sister Camillus, 29 July 1904 (Tipperary Museum of Hidden History, Kiely Collection, document 1995.4.34).

4   *The Freeman's Journal*, 8 October 1904.

5   McCarthy (2010), pp. 77–79.

6   All results here are taken from Mallon, *The 1904 Olympic Games* (1999), pp. 95–97.

7   *St. Louis Globe Democrat*, 25 July 1904.

8   *McCarthy* (2010), p. 237.

9   *Topeka State Journal*, 4 June 1904.

10 McCarthy (2010), p. 237.

11 *Ibid.*

12 *The Gaelic American*, 30 July 1904, referring to an interview Kiely gave to

the *St. Louis Globe-Democrat*.

13 Letter from Kiely to Sister Camillus (1904).

14 The Halpins' grandniece, Helen, later married Tom Kiely, grandson of T. F. The couple lived in Ballyneill and later at Lisheen near Clonmel.

15 *Buffalo Express*, 3 August 1904.

16 *The Washington Times*, 7 August 1904.

17 *The Gaelic American*, 24 September 1904.

18 Taken from the letter itself, part of the collection of Tom Kiely (Lisheen).

19 *The New York Tribune*, 25 September 1904.

20 *The Gaelic American*, 1 October 1904.

21 *New York Daily News*, 22 October 1904.

10. WHAT SWANSONG? KIELY'S LAST YEARS IN COMPETITION

1 GAA Central Council Minutes Book, held at the GAA Library and Archive, Croke Park, Dublin, 10 July 1904.

2 *Cashel Sentinel*, 14 October 1904.

3 *Ibid.*

4 Hunt (2017), p. 48.

5 *Nationalist*, 6 July 1904.

6 GAA Central Council Minutes Book, 10 December 1904.

7 *Irish Independent*, 30 January 1905.

8 De Burca, Marcus, *The GAA: A History* (Cumann Lúthchleas Gael, Dublin, 1980), p. 65.

9 *Nationalist*, 27 July 1904.

10 *Sport*, 5 August 1905.

11 Dinneen (1906) notes this throw, from a nine-foot circle, in his records table.

12 *The Irish Times*, 26 June 1905.

13 The address given by Prendergast when he returned from a visit to Ireland in 1921. See full details under 'William F. Prendergast' at: www.libertyellisfoundation.org/passenger-details.

14 Redmond (2018), location 3778.

15 *Ibid.*, but also referenced in *The New York Times*, 7, 13, 14, 27 and 28 May 1906.

16 [New York] *Evening World*, 4 June 1906.

17 Mallon, Bill, *The 1906 Olympic Games* (McFarland, London, 1999), p. 58.

18 *The New York Times*, 4 June 1906.

19 See Zarnowski (2005), pp. 128–129, and footnotes 7 and 8 in that chapter.

20 *Sport*, 7 July 1906, citing the *New York Daily News*, 25 June 1906.

21 [New York] *Evening World*, 25 June 1906.

22 *Ibid.*

23 Zarnowski (2005), p. 119. A footnote cites this story from James B. Connolly's files, courtesy of the Boston Athletic Association archives.

24 *Sport*, 7 July 1906.

25 *The New York Tribune*, 24 June 1906.

26 *The Minneapolis Journal*, 30 December 1906.

27 *The Gaelic American*, 30 June 1906.

28 *Ibid.*, 7 July 1906.

29 [New York] *Evening World*, 9 August 1906.

30 *The Gaelic American*, 21 July 1906.

31 *The Minneapolis Journal*, 9 August 1906.

32 *Kentucky Irish American*, 11 August 1906.

33 *The Evening Statesman* [Walla Walla], 31 July 1906; *The Omaha Sunday Bee*, 7 October 1906.

34 *The Minneapolis Journal*, 9 August 1906.

35 *Nationalist*, 27 October 1906.

36 *Ibid.*, 3 November 1906.

37 Letter from Mère Lydia to Sister Camillus, Tipperary Museum of Hidden History, Kiely Collection, document 1995.4.38 (dated October 1906).

38 Letter from Mère Lydia to Sister Camillus, Tipperary Museum of Hidden History, Kiely Collection, document 1995.4.40 (dated late in 1906, probably December).

39 *Waterford News*, 17 August 1908.

40 *Sport*, 9 August 1908.

41 Sheridan Memorial Committee, *The Martin Sheridan Story* (Bohola, 1998), pp. 51–53.

42 O'Donoghue (2005), p. 88.

43 Unprovenanced and undated article, taken from *Ireland's Own*.

44 Sheridan Memorial Committee (1998), p. 53.

45 *Ibid.*

46 Molloy, Margaret, *Martin Sheridan, Mayo's Famous Son* (Bohola, 2018) has wonderful detail on the Sheridan–Kiely events of 1908, and the full text of this address, pp. 550–551.

11. FROM 1908 ONWARDS

1   Interview with Tom Kiely, 3 March 2019.

2   *Ibid.*, 15 January 2019.

3   1911 census, showing occupants at 82 and 83 Marlborough Street, Dublin, who are also named on the register of Tom Kiely's marriage to Mary O'Donnell.

4   My thanks to the staff at the Civil Registration Services at Joyce House, Lombard Street East, Dublin 2 for locating a copy of the marriage registration for me.

5   Interview with Tom Kiely, 15 January 2019.

6   *Western Australian Record* (undated, in possession of Tom Kiely), 1909. This may derive originally from a Waterford or Tipperary newspaper, though there were also relatives of Kiely's living in Australia, including the children of another William Kiely who came originally from near Curraghdobbin.

7   Interviews with Tom Kiely, 15 January and 12 February 2019.

8   Extracted from: *They Had no Choice: The Irish Horse at War* (Grey Heron Media/RTÉ Radio), 9 August 2015.

9   Interview with Jimmy Shanahan, by pupils of Kilrossanty National School (2014), for their award-winning project, 'How World War I Impacted on Our Local Area'. This can be viewed on the Scoilnet education portal at www.scoilnet.ie/uploads/resources/12152/11788.pdf.

10 Tipperary SR Valuations Lists: Electoral Division of Kilmurry, Rural District of Carrick on Suir (1858–1933), Book 9, 1908–1933, p. 14.

11 Interview with Tom Kiely, 16 July 2019.

12 Tipperary SR Valuations Lists: Electoral Division of Kilmurry, Book 9, p. 33.

13 Interview with Tom Kiely, 11 September 2019.

14 *Ibid.*, 15 January 2019.

15 Minutes of the Tailteann Games Committee, 18 April 1922, held in the GAA Library and Archives, Dublin.

16 Interview with Con Casey, Tramore, Co. Waterford, 12 July 2019.

17 Interview with Tom Kiely, 12 February 2019.

18 Interview with Con Casey, 12 July 2019.

19 Interview with Tom Kiely, 15 January 2019.

20 Interview with Anthony Kiely, Clonmel, Co. Tipperary, 16 July 2019.

21 Tipperary SR Valuations Lists: Electoral District of Carrick-on-Suir (Rural), Vol. 2, Book 5, 1908–1933, p. 25.

22 Land Registry, Tipperary, Folio 2167.

23 Interview with Anthony Kiely, 16 July 2019.

24 Recalled in interviews with both Tom Kiely, 15 January 2019, and Con Casey, 12 July 2019.

25 Central Statistics Office (1997), p. 24.

26 Interview with Con Casey, 12 July 2019.

27 Interview with Tom Kiely, 12 July 2019.

28 Interview with Anthony Kiely, 16 July 2019.

29 *Ibid.*

30 Land Registry, Tipperary, Folio 2167.

31 Interview with Tom Kiely, 11 September 2019.

32 Hunt (2017), p. 45.

33 Zarnowski (2005), p. 113.

34 'Moondharrig', *The Irish Press*, 30 March 1951.

35 Dooley, William: 'God Be with You, Tom!', in *The Gaelic Sportsman*, 24 November 1951.

36 Quoted in McCarthy (2010), p. 129.

37 *Nationalist*, 10 November 1951.

38 Interview with Tom Kiely, 1 October 2019.

12. TOM KIELY'S OLYMPIC LEGACY

1 Mallon, *The 1904 Olympic Games* (1999), pp. 10–11, offers the clearest explanation of Sullivan's appointment.

2 Barney, Robert K., 'Born from Dilemma: America Awakens to the Modern Olympic Games, 1901–1903', *Olympika*, Vol. 1 (1992), p. 95. The Sullivan quote comes from *The New York Sun*, 13 November 1900.

3 A letter from Henry Furber of the Chicago Olympic Committee to Baron Pierre de Coubertin, 26 November 1902, Archives of the International Olympic Committee, held at the Olympic Studies Centre, Lausanne.

4 De Coubertin, Baron Pierre, *Mémoires Olympiques* (Bureau International de Pédagogie Sportive, Lausanne 1931), Kindle edition, location 865.

5 Zarnowski (2005), p. 253.

6 Sullivan, James E., *Spalding's Official Athletic Almanac: Special Olympic Number* (American Sports Publishing Co., New York, 1905), p. 157.

7 Sullivan, James E., *The Olympic Games at Athens* (American Sports Publishing Co., New York, 1906), Kindle edition, location 145.

8 Mallon, *The 1904 Olympic Games* (1999), p. 150.

9 McCarthy (2010), p. 78, quoting File CIO JO 1904S at the Olympic Studies Centre, Lausanne and the *St. Louis Republic*, 12 August 1903.

10 *The Gaelic American*, 10 September 1904.

11 Universal Exposition Saint Louis, 'Preliminary Programme of Physical

Culture: Olympic Games and World's Championship Contests' (St Louis, 1904), p 4.

12   Mallon, Bill, *The 1900 Olympic Games* (McFarland, London, 1998), pp. 257–258.

13   McCarthy (2010), p. 30, quoting Boland's then unpublished diary, p. 124. This original document is held at the Olympic Studies Centre in Lausanne and was examined in 2006. The diary has since been published, edited by Heiner Gillmeister, as *From Bonn to Athens, Single and Return* (Academia Verlag, St Augustin, 2008).

14   Kiely's medal of forty-four grammes was assayed by Ryan Thomas Jewellers of Clonmel, on behalf of Tipperary Museum of Hidden History. It was made by D&C Jewelers of John Street, New York. This company, more fully known as Dièges & Clust, also made the AAU's 'Olympic' medals for the 29 August to 3 September individual events, though Kiely's medal is larger, with a diameter half a centimetre greater.

15   [New York] *Evening World*, 4 June 1904.

16   Zarnowski (2005), p. 123.

17   Hunt (2019), p. 53.

18   Lovesey, Peter, Letter to the Editor, *Journal of Olympic History,* Vol. 15, No. 3 (November 2007), p. 85.

19   My thanks to Michael Loynd, chairperson of the St Louis Olympic Legacy Committee, for his detailed response on 26 January 2019 to my queries on this matter.

20   [New York] *Evening World*, 25 July 1908.

21   The relevant Spalding advert from 1910 was published in Larry McCarthy's 'Irish Americans in Sports: The Twentieth Century', Lee, J. J. and Casey, Marion (eds), *Making the Irish American: History and Heritage of the Irish in the United States* (NYU, Glucksman Ireland House Archives, 2007). The image in question was located on the website www.wingedfist. org, which commemorates the Irish-American Athletic Club of New York.

22   Sheridan's 1904 medal is pictured in Molloy (2018), p. 558.

23   Mallon, *The 1904 Olympic Games* (1999), pp. 223–227, contains a table of each book's recognised Olympic titles.

24   Guiney, David, *The Dunlop Book of the Olympics* (Eastland Press, Lavenham, 1972), p. 24.

25   Henry Yeomans, Patricia, introduction to the revised edition of Bill Henry, *An Approved History of the Olympic Games* (Southern California Committee for the Olympic Games, Los Angeles, 1984), dust jacket.

26   *Ibid.*, pp. 53–54. Note that Daly's win in a one-mile handicap event is (correctly) not included in the lists of Olympic winners on pp. 58–59.

27   Letter from Dr Mezö to the IOC, 18 November 1948, in files at IOC

Historical Archives/IOC Members – Dr Ferenc Mezö (Hungary) – Correspondence and Written Works 1948–1978.

28 Letter from Dr Mezö to the IOC President, Avery Brundage, 27 June 1953, in files at IOC Historical Archives/IOC Members – Dr Ferenc Mezö (Hungary) – Correspondence and Written Works 1948–1978.

29 Letter from Avery Brundage to Dr Mezö, 4 August 1953 in files at IOC Historical Archives/IOC Members – Dr Ferenc Mezö (Hungary) – Correspondence and Written Works 1948–1978.

30 Checked and confirmed to the author by Estel Hegglin, Research Coordinator, by email on 24 January 2019.

31 Hunt (2017), p. 48.

32 Lovesey (2007).

33 Mallon, *The 1904 Olympic Games* (1999), p. 13. A similar rationale for the Paris Games is found in Mallon (1998), pp. 12–13.

34 Iowerth, Hywel, Jones, Carwyn and Hardman, Alun: 'Nationalism and Olympism: Towards a Normative Theory of International Sporting Representation', *Journal of Olympic History*, Vol. 18, No. 1 (April 2010), pp. 46–47.

35 Sincere thanks to Ian Hodge at British Athletics for his confirmation and assistance with this query.

36 See the AAA decathlon championship results at www.nuts.org.uk/Champs/AAA/AAADec.

37 De Coubertin, Baron Pierre, Letter to the Editor, *Allgemeine Sportzeitung*, Vienna, and published in *Revue Olympique*, April 1911, pp. 51–52.

38 *Leeds Mercury, East Anglian Daily Times, The Northern Whig, The Shields Daily Gazette*, all 5 July 1904.

39 Ó Riain (1994), p. 213.

40 Jeffreys, Kevin, *The British Olympic Association: A History* (Palgrave Macmillan, Basingstoke, 2014), p. 13.

41 *The Freeman's Journal*, 8 October 1904.

42 Hunt (2019), p. 54.

43 Pelc, Martin, 'Mistaken Identities – Hedwig Rosenbaum the First Olympic Medallist from Bohemia', *Journal of Olympic History*, Vol. 27, No. 2 (2019), pp. 54–59.

44 Redmond (2018), location 889.

45 De Coubertin, *Mémoires Olympiques*, location 1517.

46 McCarthy (2010), pp. 144–159. Quinn, Mark, *The King of Spring* (Liffey Press, Dublin, 2004) is easily the most comprehensive account of O'Connor's career.

47 Senn, Alfred E., *Power, Politics and the Olympic Games* (Human Kinetics, 1999), p. 29.

48   Mallon, *The 1904 Olympic Games* (1999), p. 64.

APPENDIX 1: TOM KIELY'S RECOGNISED IRISH RECORDS, 1906

1   Zarnowski (2005) uses this to inform his belief that Kiely was the last man ever to hold world best marks in a jumping and a throwing event at the same time.

APPENDIX 2: KIELY'S IRISH ATHLETIC TITLES

1   Based on the compilation by Hunt (November 2019), p. 45.

BIBLIOGRAPHY

BOOKS

Bell, Jonathan and Watson, Mervyn, *Irish Farming Life* (Four Courts Press, Dublin, 2014)

Bracken, Pat, *The Growth and Development of Sport in County Tipperary 1840–1880* (Cork University Press, Cork, 2018)

Brady, Joseph, *The Big Sycamore* (M. H. Gill, Dublin, 1951)

Central Statistics Office, *Farming since the Famine: Irish Farm Statistics 1847–1996* (Central Statistics Office, Dublin, 1997)

Coolahan, John, *Irish Education: Its History and Structure* (Institute of Public Administration, Dublin, 1981)

Coolahan, John and O'Donovan, Patrick F., *A History of Ireland's School Inspectorate, 1831–2008* (Four Courts Press, Dublin, 2009)

Cronin, Mike, Duncan, Mark and Rouse, Paul, *The GAA: A People's History* (The Collins Press, Cork, 2009)

Davin, Pat, *Recollections of a Veteran Irish Athlete* (Juverna Press, Dublin, 1938)

De Burca, Marcus, *The GAA: A History* (Cumann Lúthchleas Gael, Dublin, 1980)

De Coubertin, Baron Pierre, *Mémoires Olympiques* (Bureau International de Pédagogie Sportive, Lausanne, 1931)

Dinneen, Frank B., *Irish Athletic Records* (Cahill & Co., Dublin, 1906)

Dooley, William, *Champions of the Athletic Arena* (General Publicity Service, Dublin, 1947)

Dunne, Katie (ed.), *Grangemockler Church and People, 1897–1997* (Grangemockler Centenary Committee, Co. Tipperary, 1997)

Fogarty, Canon Philip, *Tipperary's GAA Story* (The Tipperary Star, Thurles, 1960)

Guiney, David, *The Dunlop Book of the Olympics* (Eastland Press, Lavenham, 1972)

Guttmann, Alan, *The Olympics* (University of Illinois Press, Chicago, 2002)

Henry, Bill and Henry Yeomans, Patricia, *An Approved History of the Olympic Games* (Southern California Committee for the Olympic Games, Los Angeles, 1984)

Hunt, Tom, *Sport and Society in Victorian Ireland: The Case of Westmeath* (Cork University Press, Cork, 2007)

Hunt, Tom, *The Little Book of Irish Athletics* (The History Press, Dublin, 2017)

Hymans, Richard and Matrahazi, Imre (ed.), *Progression of IAAF World Records* (IAAF, Monaco, 2015)

Irish National Teachers Organisation, *Primary School Curriculum: An Evolutionary Process* (INTO, Dublin, 1996)

Jeffreys, Kevin, *The British Olympic Association: A History* (Palgrave Macmillan, Basingstoke, 2014)

Kamper, Eric and Mallon, Bill, *The Golden Book of the Olympic Games* (Vallardi & Associati, Milan, 1992)

Liddy, A. J., *The Story of Mount Melleray* (Gill, Dublin, 1946)

Lyons, F. S. L., *Ireland since the Famine* (Fontana Press, London, 1985)

Mac Fhinn, Padraig Eric, *An tAthair Micheal P. O hIceadha* (Sairseal agus Dill, Dublin, 1974)

Mallon, Bill, *The 1900 Olympic Games* (McFarland, London, 1998)

Mallon, Bill, *The 1904 Olympic Games* (McFarland, London, 1999)

Mallon, Bill, *The 1906 Olympic Games* (McFarland, London, 1999)

Mallon, Bill and Widlund, Ture, *The 1896 Olympic Games* (McFarland, London, 1998)

Matthews, George R., *America's First Olympics* (University of Missouri, Columbia, 2005)

McCarthy, Kevin, *Gold, Silver and Green: The Irish Olympic Journey 1896–1924* (Cork University Press, Cork, 2010)

Mehigan, P. D., *Fifty Years of Irish Athletics* (Gaelic Publicity Services, Dublin, 1943)

Mitchel, James S., *How to Become a Weight Thrower* (Spalding Athletic Library, New York, 1916)

Molloy, Margaret, *Martin Sheridan, Mayo's Famous Son* (self-published, Bohola, 2018)

O'Donoghue, Tony, *Irish Championship Athletics 1873-1914* (Kilkenny People Printing, Kilkenny, 2005)

O'Meara, Micheál, *South Tipperary GAA 1907–2007* (Cumann Lúthchleas Gael, Coiste Chontae Árainn Theas, 2007)

Ó Riain, Seamus, *Maurice Davin: First President of the GAA* (Geography Publications, Dublin, 1994)

Puirséal, Pádraig, *The GAA in Its Time* (Ward River Press, Dublin, 1984)

Quinn, Mark, *The King of Spring* (Liffey Press, Dublin, 2004)

Redmond, Patrick C., *The Irish-American Athletic Club of New York* (McFarland & Co., New York, 2018)

Rouse, Paul, *Sport and Ireland: A History* (Oxford University Press, Oxford, 2015)

Rouse, Paul, *The Hurlers* (Penguin, Dublin, 2018)

Ryan, Eoin, 'Blaming Parnell: Accounting for the Decline of the GAA, 1889–1894' (unpublished, UCD MA thesis, 2013)

Senn, Alfred E., *Power, Politics and the Olympic Games* (Human Kinetics, Illinois, 1999)

Sheridan Memorial Committee, *The Martin Sheridan Story* (self-published, Bohola, 1998)

Sullivan, James E., *Spalding's Official Athletic Almanac: Special Olympic Number* (American Sports Publishing Co., New York, 1905)

Sullivan, James E., *The Olympic Games at Athens* (American Sports Publishing Co., New York, 1906)

Universal Exposition Saint Louis, 'Preliminary Programme of Physical Culture: Olympic Games and World's Championship Contests' (St Louis, 1904)

Wallechinsky, David, *The Complete Book of the Olympics* (Penguin Books, New York, 1984)

Watman, Mel, *The Official History of the AAA: The Story of the World's Oldest Athletic Organisation* (SportsBooks, London, 2011)

Withers, Bob, *Tom Kiely: 'For Tipperary and Ireland'* (Tipperary County Museum, Clonmel, 1997)

Zarnowski, Frank, *All-Round Men: Heroes of a Forgotten Sport* (Scarecrow Press, Lanhan, 2005)

ARTICLES

'Achilles', 'The Champion with Whom None Could Compare', [Dublin] *Evening Herald*, 26 January 1955

'Achilles', 'The Colourful Career of T. F. Kiely', *The Irish Press*, 14 January 1955

'Celt', 'Thomas F. Kiely – The Star of the Gael' (source unknown)

Barney, Robert K., 'Born from Dilemma: America Awakens to the Modern Olympic Games, 1901–1903', *Olympika*, Vol. 1 (1992)

de Coubertin, Baron Pierre, Letter to the Editor, *Allgemeine Sportzeitung*, Vienna, and published in *Revue Olympique*, April 1911

Dooley, William, 'God Be with You, Tom!', *The Gaelic Sportsman*, 24 November 1951

Hunt, Tom, 'Tipperary Hurlers, 1895–1900, a Socio-economic Profile' *Tipperary Historical Journal* (2009)

Hunt, Tom, 'Tom Kiely: Greatest Athlete of Ireland's Greatest Athletic Period' (unpublished)

Hunt, Tom, 'Tom Kiely: Ireland's First Track and Field Olympic Gold Medallist?', *Journal of Olympic History*, Vol. 27, No. 3 (November 2019)

Iowerth, Hywel, Jones, Carwyn and Hardman, Alun, 'Nationalism and Olympism: Towards a Normative Theory of International Sporting Representation', *Journal of Olympic History*, Vol. 18, No. 1 (April 2010)

Lovesey, Peter, Letter to the Editor, *Journal of Olympic History*, Vol. 15, No. 3 (November 2007)

Mandle, W. F., 'Parnell and Sport', *Studia Hibernica*, No. 28 (1994)

McCarthy, Larry, 'Irish Americans in Sports: The Twentieth Century', Lee, J. J. and Casey, Marion R. (eds.), *Making the Irish American: History and Heritage of the Irish in the United States* (Glucksman Ireland House Archives, New York, 2007)

McGahon, Arthur, 'The Greatest All-Rounder World Will Ever Know', *The Irish Press*, 2 March 1958

Mehigan, P. D. ('Carbery'), 'Tom Kiely of Ballyneill, Wonder Athlete', Kilfeather, Seán (ed.), *Vintage Carbery* (Beaver Row Press, Dublin, 1984)

Navin, Michael, 'Tom Kiely of Ballyneill: The World's Champion All-Round Athlete', Maher, James (ed.), *Chiefs of the Comeraghs*, (Mullinahone, Co. Tipperary, 1957)

O'Connor, Peter, 'Long Jumping', Mehigan, P. D. ('Carbery'), *Fifty Years of Irish Athletics* (Gaelic Publicity Services, Dublin, 1943)

Ó Faoláin, Seán, article in *The Irish Times*, 10 May 1941

O'Riordan, Ted, 'The Unsurpassable Leahys of Charleville', *Charleville and District Historical Journal*, Vol. 3 (1988)

Pelc, Martin, 'Mistaken Identities – Hedwig Rosenbaum the First Olympic Medallist from Bohemia', *Journal of Olympic History*, Vol. 27, No. 2 (2019)

Power, Patrick C., 'Champion Kiely, a Giant among Athletes', *Nationalist*, 25 December 1982

Sutton, P. P., untitled article in *The Irish Wheel and Athletic News*, 3 April 1894

Unprovenanced article, possibly from *Ireland's Own*, entitled 'The Sporting Irish'

DOCUMENTARY SOURCES

File CIO JO 1904S, Olympic Studies Centre, Lausanne

GAA Central Council Minutes Book, GAA Library and Archives, Croke Park, Dublin

Interview with Jimmy Shanahan by pupils of Kilrossanty National School (2014), for their award-winning project, 'How World War I Impacted on Our Local Area'

Land Registry, Tipperary, Folio 2167

Letter from Avery Brundage to Dr Mezö, 4 August 1953, files at IOC Historical Archives/IOC Members – Dr Ferenc Mezö (Hungary) – Correspondence and Written Works 1948–1978, held at the Olympic Studies Centre, Lausanne

Letter from Dr Mezö to the IOC President, Avery Brundage, 27 June 1953, Files at IOC Historical Archives/IOC Members – Dr Ferenc Mezö (Hungary) – Correspondence and Written Works 1948–1978, held at the Olympic Studies Centre, Lausanne

Letter from Dr Mezö to the IOC, 18 November 1948, files at IOC Historical Archives/IOC Members – Dr Ferenc Mezö (Hungary) – Correspondence and Written Works 1948–1978, held at the Olympic Studies Centre, Lausanne

Letter from Henry Furber of the Chicago Olympic Committee to Baron Pierre de Coubertin, 26 November 1902, Archives of the International Olympic Committee, held at the Olympic Studies

Centre, Lausanne

Letter from Mère Lydia to Sister Camillus, Tipperary Museum of Hidden History, Kiely Collection, document 1995.4.38 (dated October 1906)

Letter from Mère Lydia to Sister Camillus, Tipperary Museum of Hidden History, Kiely Collection, document 1995.4.40 (dated late in 1906, probably December)

Letter from Tom Kiely to Sister Camillus, 29 July 1904, Tipperary Museum of Hidden History, Kiely Collection, document 1995.4.34

Minutes of the Tailteann Games Committee, 18 April 1922, GAA Library and Archives, Croke Park, Dublin

Roll Books for Ballyneill National School

Tipperary SR Valuations Lists: Electoral District of Carrick-on-Suir (Rural), Vol. 2, Book 5, 1908–1933

Tipperary SR Valuations Lists: Electoral Division of Kilmurry, Rural District of Carrick-on-Suir (1858–1933), Book 8, 1893–1907 and Book 9, 1908–1933

Tom Kiely Scrapbook, Tipperary Museum of Hidden History, Kiely Collection

INTERVIEWS

Con Casey, Tramore, Co. Waterford, 12 July 2019
Anthony Kiely, Clonmel, Co. Tipperary, 16 July 2019
Tom Kiely, Lisheen, Co. Tipperary, multiple dates throughout 2019

NEWSPAPERS

Irish

Belfast Newsletter
Cashel Sentinel
Clonmel Chronicle, Tipperary and Waterford Advertiser
Cork Herald
Evening Herald [Dublin]
Irish Daily Independent
Irish Independent
Limerick Leader
Nationalist [The Clonmel]
Sport
The Cork Examiner

The Freeman's Journal
The Irish Press
The Irish Times
The Nenagh Guardian
Tipperary Independent
Waterford News

British

East Anglian Daily Times
Edinburgh Evening News
Leeds Mercury
Lloyd's List
London Athletic News
London Evening Standard
Manchester Evening News
Sheffield Independent
Sporting Life
The Morning Post
The Northern Whig
The Pall Mall Gazette
The Scotsman
The Scottish Referee
The Shields Daily Gazette

American

Buffalo Express
Evening World [New York]
Kentucky Irish American
New York Daily News
St. Louis Globe–Democrat
St. Louis Republic
The Brooklyn Daily Eagle
The Evening Statesman [Walla Walla]
The Gaelic American
The Minneapolis Journal
The New York Sun
The New York Times
The New York Tribune
The Omaha Sunday Bee
The Salt Lake Herald
The St. Paul Globe
The Washington Times
Topeka State Journal

Other

Western Australian Record

WEBSITES
Athletics Ireland:
www.athleticsireland.ie/downloads/statistics/NR_Progression_2019.
  pdf
www.athleticsireland.ie/downloads/statistics/Irish_Athletics_
  Olympians_1896-2016
www.athleticsireland.ie/downloads/statistics/Irish_Champions
www.athleticsireland.ie/downloads/statistics/Irish_OUTDOOR_
  Champions-min.pdf

British Amateur Athletic Association:
www.gbrathletics.com/bc/bc1.htm

Census of Ireland:
www.census.nationalarchives.ie/pages/1901/Tipperary/Kilmurry/
  Ballyneill/
www.census.nationalarchives.ie/pages/1911/Tipperary/Kilmurry/
  Ballyneill/

Ellis Island Foundation:
www.libertyellisfoundation.org/passenger-details

National Union of Track Statisticians:
www.nuts.org.uk/Champs/AAA
www.nuts.org.uk/Champs/AAA/AAADec
www.nuts.org.uk/Champs/AAA/AAAHT.htm

Tipperary Athletics:
www.tipperaryathletics.com

AUDIO-VISUAL MATERIAL
They Had no Choice: The Irish Horse at War (Grey Heron Media/RTÉ
  Radio), 9 August 2015
Mitchell and Kenyon: Edwardian Sport (British Film Institute), broad-
cast by the BBC in 2004

ACKNOWLEDGEMENTS

There are many, many people to thank for their help over the past two years of my work on Tom Kiely's career. First and foremost, I wish to thank the curator at Tipperary Museum of Hidden History (formerly the County Museum), Marie McMahon, for her own and the museum's unswerving support, and for the ongoing access I was afforded to Kiely archival material and to museum personnel, including Michael Fanning and Jayne Sutcliffe who dealt directly with my archival searches. I was a frequent visitor to Tipperary Local Studies room at *The Source*, Thurles too, where Jane Bulfin and my old acquaintance Mary Guinan Darmody could not have done more to assist my research. It was useful to be able to 'bounce' some Tipperary-focused questions off other *Source* regulars occasionally, among whom I number Des Marnane and Joe Tobin specifically. Joanne Clarke at the Croke Park archives was also incredibly helpful when I visited there, as was my friend Steve O'Shea on land registry issues.

The many staff I had dealings with at the National Library, National Photographic Archives, Civil Registration Service and the Valuations Office in Dublin were always courteous and helpful. As a former civil servant myself, it was wonderful to deal with so many obliging and 'civil' people in those research centres. Still in the civil service vein, a special thanks to Paddy O'Donovan, my former colleague in the Department of Education and Skills, for his considerable assistance on nineteenth-century educational matters.

It was also a real pleasure to be able to discuss issues with experts when I needed them. These ranged from local historians like Mick Ahearne of Clonmel, Michael Cody of Carrick-on-Suir and Willie Fraher of Dungarvan, chairperson of Waterford County Museum, to weight-throwing experts like Michael O'Brien (Wexford), John Menton (Kilkenny) and Phil Conway (Dublin). The latter three were very helpful on the technical side of athletics, and Phil in particular has a wealth of archival material as well, which he happily shared. My sincere thanks too go to Michael McCabe of Ballyneill National School and Noel Looby of Cappoquin, for their assistance with educational and farming matters, respectively. I should also remember the many people in and around Ballyneill who have worked so hard to preserve and commemorate the memory of Tom Kiely, Even though I have met only a handful in my visits there, their efforts have certainly done Kiely proud over the years.

Sports history is a bit of a niche market, but one which is now populated with many fine historians, some of whom I was able to talk with, 'borrow' research from or just rely on unashamedly for advice. Paul Rouse was very encouraging when I spoke with him and very clear on the need to place Kiely in his historical context. Pat Bracken was able to advise on both Tipperary sport and on proofreading issues whenever asked. Tom Hunt, my fellow Waterford man, was a huge support, with advice, locating material that I was unaware of, and making his own research and photographic material available without hesitation whenever he felt he had something of value to offer, as was often the case. Pat and Tom were particularly useful sounding boards and editors for me all through, and also I'd like to thank my former teaching colleague and sports enthusiast Jim Ryan for his editing work and advice on the section about Kiely's legacy particularly.

As always, when researching sports history with an international dimension, I sought and received invaluable assistance from people whom I have never met. These included Michael Loynd of the St Louis Olympic Legacy Committee; Ian Hodge at UK Athletics; Sue Gyford, Arnold Black and Alex Wilson at Scottish Athletics; Estel Hegglin at the Olympic Studies Centre in Lausanne; and Chris Turner at the International Association of Athletic Federations (IAAF).

My family, as always, have endured my research interests, occasional distractedness and the usual 'mess' of books and paper with great patience. My love and thanks, as ever, to Tricia, Elaine and Carole.

I was honoured to work with Mary Feehan, Deirdre Roberts and other members of the Mercier Press team for a number of years before I became an author of one of the company's books. On this 'Kiely project', Pa O'Donoghue was a very positive and helpful commissioning editor from day one. In the work of turning the manuscript into this book, I must say that Noel O'Regan, Wendy Logue, Sarah O'Flaherty, Deirdre Roberts and Jennifer Armstrong have been superb to deal with all through.

It has been one of the great pleasures of working on this book that I was able to get to know some members of the Kiely family much better. It was not possible to meet with some branches, including the Crottys and Shanahans and the Kielys abroad, but their added contribution to the work of preserving medals, photographs and documents pertaining to Tom Kiely has been important to his story, without doubt. Those Kiely descendants that I have met are hugely proud of 'the Champion' and very honest in their stories of him. All have inherited some of Tom Kiely's physical, commercial and leadership qualities. Among them, Tom's grandsons, Anthony Kiely (a multiple *Rás Tailteann* cyclist) and Con Casey (former chairperson of Waterford County Council) were most gracious with their time and in making their collections of pictures, newspaper clippings etc. available to me.

I know that Anthony and Con will be fully understanding of the special thanks I owe to 'young' Tom Kiely. Tom, another grandson of the 'original' Tom, is now happily retired from business, though not from gardening, and living at Lisheen near Clonmel. For my purposes, Tom was a goldmine of memories, information and insights, and incredibly generous with his time and with permissions to use the photographs, medals, etc. from the Kiely Collection at Tipperary Museum of Hidden History for this book. We had some great chats, and I'd like to think I learned a lot about life from Tom too. My sincere thanks to Helen Kiely, naturally, and their three dogs, for tolerating my many visits to their home so readily. This book could never have happened without those visits.

INDEX